Religious Life
in the 21st Century

More Orbis Books by Diarmuid O'Murchu

Adult Faith

Ancestral Grace

Consecrated Religious Life

Evolutionary Faith

God in the Midst of Change

In the Beginning Was the Spirit

The Meaning and Practice of Faith

Transformation of Desire

Inclusivity: A Gospel Mandate

Religious Life
in the 21st Century

The Prospect of Refounding

Diarmuid O'Murchu, MSC

ORBIS BOOKS
Maryknoll, New York 10545

ORBIS BOOKS
Maryknoll, New York 10545

Fathers and Brothers
MARYKNOLL™
TOGETHER IN GOD'S MISSION OF MERCY

Third Printing, August 2017

Founded in 1970, Orbis Books endeavors to publish works that enlighten the mind, nourish the spirit, and challenge the conscience. The publishing arm of the Maryknoll Fathers and Brothers, Orbis seeks to explore the global dimensions of the Christian faith and mission, to invite dialogue with diverse cultures and religious traditions, and to serve the cause of reconciliation and peace. The books published reflect the views of their authors and do not represent the official position of the Maryknoll Society. To learn more about Maryknoll and Orbis Books, please visit our website at www.maryknollsociety.org.

Manufactured in the United States of America.

Copy editing and typesetting by Joan Weber Laflamme.

Library of Congress Cataloging-in-Publication Data

Names: O'Murchu, Diarmuid, author.
Title: Religious life in the 21st century : the prospect of refounding /
    Diarmuid O'Murchu.
Description: Maryknoll : Orbis Books, 2016. | Includes bibliographical references
    and index.
Identifiers: LCCN 2016001749 (print) | LCCN 2016005769 (ebook) | ISBN
    9781626982079 (pbk.) | ISBN 9781608336562 (ebook)
Subjects: LCSH: Monastic and religious life.
Classification: LCC BX2435 .O165 2016 (print) | LCC BX2435 (ebook) | DDC
    248.8/94—dc23
LC record available at http://lccn.loc.gov/2016001749

Contents

In Grateful Appreciation

In my writing career this is a landmark book and an opportune moment to acknowledge a landmark editor and publisher, Mike Leach, who over many years has cajoled, encouraged, challenged, and affirmed some of my finest writing endeavors. Many thanks, Mike! And several publications were done also through Orbis Books with Mike and his successor as publisher, Robert Ellsberg, and his enthusiastic staff, offering consistently generous service and support.

The present work has been reviewed and improved by the following gifted people:

- Elizabeth Smyth, from the University of Toronto, whose historical wisdom proved an invaluable resource.
- Sr. Brenda Peddigrew, RSM, whose intuitive wisdom is much appreciated; Brenda also generously provided the framework for the study questions that conclude each chapter.
- Sr. Bernadette Flanagan, PBVM, whose sharp eye for contemplative wisdom led to some important additional insights.
- Sr. Barbara Fiand, SNDdeN, who offered alternative suggestions for key sections.
- Fr. Gerry Arbuckle, SM, an anthropological genius, who initially inspired in me the need to explore the concept of refounding in the vowed life.

Much of this book is inspired by the great foundresses of Religious Life, twelve of whose stories are narrated in Chapter 6. All of these stories have been checked and verified by respective members of the Congregations in question. Too many people to list individually, but all are held in deep gratitude.

Despite my frequent disagreement with clerical Religious Life, I owe a debt of gratitude to my colleagues in the MSC Congregation whose friendship and brotherly care have long sustained and reassured me.

Beyond all those listed above are the thousands of sisters, brothers, and priests I have encountered on every continent over a span of forty years. It is conversations with so many kindred spirits that awaken and sustain in me the zeal for Religious Life that has inspired the present work. In some small way I hope this book serves as a token of my love and appreciation for such mutual enrichment.

Introduction

My writing career began with a book on Religious Life, *The Seed Must Die: Religious Life, Survival or Extinction*, first published in 1981. I have now arrived at my twenty-fifth book, and it seems all too right to return once more to the vowed life. During the intervening years much has changed in Religious Life with declining numbers, an aging profile, a diminished pastoral presence, and an identity crisis amid a vastly changing cultural context.

The decline continues, and as I indicate in this book, is likely to influence the wider Christian Church as we move further into the twenty-first century. The paschal journey still engages us, and as we enter more deeply into the Calvary experience of diminishment and decline, we also face the challenge of discerning and embracing the first seedlings of resurrection hope. This is the promised *refounding* analyzed in detail in the present work.

Over the years, in my reflections and workshops on the vowed life, I have been greatly inspired by the words of Vaclav Havel, one time president of the Czech Republic: "Hope is not the conviction that something will turn out well but the certainty that something makes sense, regardless of how it turns out." Too often we try to camouflage the paschal journey with false utopias. They blind us to the true nature of Christian hope, which consistently seeks to ground us afresh in the incarnational truth of daily existence. There, the challenge is about "trying to make sense," thus leading to a more realistic sense of hope, more refreshing and empowering than any set of illusive promises.

For me, it is the history of Religious Life, more than any other aspect, that grounds my hope and enables me to make sense of what has been transpiring over the past several decades. Within the historical overview I detect an unfolding pattern that helps to make sense of the rise and fall of Religious Orders and Congregations over time. The present work is a further attempt to read history more imaginatively and to embrace its outcomes in more discerning ways.

Undoubtedly, we'd all like to be living at those historical moments when Religious Life was growing and flourishing. But ours is a different kind of moment, not of triumph and glory but of decline and disintegration. While many Religious talk and write about this downward phase, few embrace its unfolding with hope-filled resignation. Denial is quite widespread, amid a subdued complacency that is resistant to any kind of disturbance of the morbid status quo. Let's die in peace seems to be the unspoken undercurrent.

Ours, too, is a moment of grace, indeed of a type far more unsettling and prophetically disturbing than that of our triumphant moments. And, undoubtedly, our God is calling us to live with integrity—and even with fresh vision—in the midst of the fragmentation all around us. In these Calvary times, as in every dark night, seeds are fermenting, maybe even beginning to sprout. It takes discerning hearts to see where the enduring hope is arising.

For me, the history of Religious Life has long served as a beacon of light amid the confusion and painful letting go that characterize every era of decline and diminution. Sometimes we are so wrapped up in the story of an individual Order/Congregation that we miss the empowering richness of the larger landscape of the vowed life. It illuminates our collective past, grounds our present-day transitions, and provides a liberating hope for possibilities beyond our ultimate demise, described in the present work as the grace of refounding.

The refounding of a Religious Order/Congregation is a paradoxical undertaking that none of us can engineer for ourselves. Refounding is a divine initiative, but one we can anticipate and open ourselves to receive, if it is God's will for us. It is a creative endeavor in which we can become co-creators, a participative challenge of social dislocation, huge risk, and enormous creativity. And history reassures us that it can, and does, happen.

My hope is that the present work "makes sense," that it will help us to see the bigger picture and the deeper prospects that will empower women and men Religious to walk the paschal journey of these challenging times and to persevere with a realistic and resilient hope.

Part One

Revisioning the Foundations

The foundations upon which we reconstruct the vowed life in the twenty-first century are radically different from previous epochs. While I hold on to—and endorse—the *Sequela Christi* (the following of Christ) as the basic rationale for the vowed life, I propose a substantial redefinition arising from contemporary biblical scholarship and a rapidly changing Christian consciousness among a growing body of contemporary Christians.

Many features of the vowed life in the past, specifically the static and unchanging nature of our key values, do not stand up to discerning scrutiny in the evolutionary culture of the twenty-first century. The spirituality of the *fuga mundi* (flee the world)—escaping from this vale of tears to guarantee individual salvation in a life hereafter—gives way to the urgent spiritual and cultural challenge to engage more responsibly with God's world (the earth) entrusted to our care.

Perhaps the most substantial shift of all is that of transcending the metaphor of the *hero* that has underpinned so much of our patriarchal domination and the religiosity of empire building. Classically, we portray the early Christian monastics as ascetical heroes, battling the forces of evil in the lonely isolation of the desert wilderness, a kind of white martyrdom sought out to complement blood martyrdom, the ultimate mark of Christian heroism.

The ideology of the hero has given way to the archetype of the lover. The concept of the monastic archetype, explored in Chapter 2, may seem very new to contemporary readers, but as indicated, we are, in fact, seeking to reclaim a deep, ancient wisdom inscribed in both monastic and apostolic forms of the vowed life—but largely subverted by the ideology of the patriarchal hero. The true heroism of this age, and every other, is creative discipleship of the incarnational Christ, striving to realize a deep love for God, in and through the compassionate empowerment of people and planet alike.

The christological foundations for this "asceticism of love" are outlined in Chapter 3. It is no longer a case of imitating a sacrificial, suffering hero but of embracing the daring empowering mission of the gospel imperative of the new reign of God on earth. When we seek *first* this gospel prerogative, we are invited to a following of Christ *(Sequela Christi)* that is much more about the transformation of this world and all the inhabitants of planet earth than a privileged escape to salvation hereafter.

Evolutionary transitions throughout the ages—whether understood in cultural, social, or religious terms—require us to let go of past securities, so that we are more open and receptive to the new things God is co-creating, as the emerging future lures us forth. And nothing can escape such evolutionary emergence (as I explain in the opening chapter). Perhaps the reader also needs to be reassured that in the evolutionary process nothing sacred is ever lost entirely but can be so transformed that it requires discerning wisdom to see the rich interweaving of the old and the new in all that unfolds.

For many people these are daunting times full of disturbing challenges. So were the parables of Jesus as initially experienced. Christian discipleship was born out of a massive paradigmatic shift, despite the continuities with Judaism that modern scripture scholars like to highlight. We are co-disciples in the endeavor of making all things new (Rev 21:5). Let's embrace the task with vision and hope!

Co-disciples also strikes a collaborative note I wish to honor throughout this book. Although written largely from a Catholic perspective, I definitely want to include Religious women and men from other Christian denominations, specifically members of Anglican communities who have been significant in my own life story. And I want this book to be also a resource that might open avenues for dialogue with vowed people in the other great faith traditions, particularly Hinduism and Buddhism. Finally, I support and endorse the growing awareness in the Christian world today that lay people in "secular" life are integral to the core meaning of the vowed life, as many Congregations with associates, or partners in mission, are beginning to realize. This book has been written not merely for a Religious Life readership, but also for the millions who journey with us, and, as is becoming abundantly clear, without whom our life witness remains seriously deficient.

Chapter 1

The Evolutionary Context
of Religious Life

Evolution is a general condition to which all theories, all hypotheses, all systems must bow and which they must satisfy henceforward if they are to be thinkable and true. Evolution is a light which illuminates all facts, a curve that all lines must follow.
—Teilhard de Chardin

With this new sense of moving forward, from simple to complex life forms, from bacteria to humans, science shows that evolution is more than a method of collecting and classifying the facts of life; rather it is the means by which humanity can move forward into the future.
—Ilia Delio

John and Maria Mitchell had much to celebrate on the twenty-fifth anniversary of their wedding day. Proud of their three children, all now in their twenties, and their joint achievements—she as a nurse and he as a sheep farmer—this was a special day for cherished memories. All had agreed to a quiet family luncheon gathering with close relatives from both sides of the family.

But the "children" also had plans for the afternoon, a surprise trip to the beach, nearly one hundred miles away. "Fine by me," said John, "except for one hitch: the veterinary surgeon is scheduled to come early tomorrow morning to inoculate my sheep; so I guess I had better gather them in from the lower paddock (almost a mile away) to the paddock here beside the house. Let's finish lunch and I will gather in the sheep and then we can head for the beach."

Lunch complete, the women set about tidying up, other family members packed the picnic box for the beach, while John changed into working clothes and headed out to fetch the sheep. He whistled for his sheepdog, who surprisingly did not respond. He jumped on to his farm tractor and headed for the lower paddock. As he drove out of the farmyard, there, to his shock, were all his sheep in the home paddock. His sheepdog was lying across the gateway to ensure they did not go out!

"What in the name of God is going on?" John muttered to himself. Calling Philip, his oldest son, they both stared in disbelief as it dawned on them that it was the sheepdog had fetched the sheep without any human assistance and had brought them to the paddock where John needed them for the vet the following morning. With tears in his eyes, John approached his beloved and faithful dog and gave him one of the warmest hugs man and beast could ever exchange. And as he stared lovingly into the dog's eyes, subliminal echoes of fidelity and gratitude reverberated: "This is the least I would do for you on your wedding anniversary; enjoy the day!"

It was John's brother, a Catholic priest in Australia, who shared this amazing story with me, having witnessed it at first hand. If Jesus was around today, I guess this would be one of his parables. This is not just the fable of a brilliantly intelligent animal. Much more is going on here. This is soul stuff, defying all the criteria of scientific fact and of rational discourse. This is the truth of parable, "the surplus of meaning" described by French philosopher Paul Ricoeur.

And it also marks a paradigm shift! It opens up not just one but several new worlds of meaning. It stretches horizons of possibility to the point of human incredulity. It evokes the discerning mind and heart to see alternatives to our conventional modes of understanding and to acknowledge, however tentatively, that other worlds are possible, and that none of us, nor any of our philosophies, embodies the whole truth.

Why an Evolutionary Perspective?

Why begin a book on Religious Life[1] with a story that on the surface has nothing at all to do with the vowed life? Because I want to invite the reader into a disposition of receptivity, very different from our usual mode of comprehension. To see our way through the crisis of Religious Life today requires enormous vision characterized by deep

---

[1] Throughout the book I use the term *Religious Life* (with capitals) to denote the vowed life as lived in both the monastic and apostolic contexts. The word *Religious,* with a capital R, refers to members of Orders and Congregations, while the non-capitalized word refers to adherents to one or another faith system.

perception, creative imagination, and a great deal of Christian discernment. The obvious facts on the surface are often too complex to look at directly; they will not yield their deeper truth to rational analysis or ecclesiastical theorizing.

All over the Catholic world Religious Life is changing rapidly. Even in the Southern Hemisphere, where substantial numbers are still entering and initial formation continues to be quite "monastic," questions of credibility frequently surface, and internal tensions arise universally. The declining pattern, reaching a terminal stage in the West, is also affecting several southern countries, albeit at a slower pace. Within the vowed life today, death and decline are taking place among us on a universal scale, and the Spirit is inviting us all to an unfolding future, often confusing and chaotic. We are asked to embrace a parabolic endeavor, a paradigm shift, with radical new horizons inviting our graced discernment.

And that undertaking makes a great deal more sense within the *evolutionary consciousness* of our time. Sadly, the major institutions of today's world (including religions and churches), as well as academic scholars in general, pay scant attention to this way of viewing reality. The patriarchal, metaphysical certainties block and inhibit this alternative mode of discernment, one that exerts an expanding and deepening resonance with the sensitivities of our time. This relatively new awakening is surreptitiously and crudely dismissed as postmodern relativism and sometimes demonized as New Age speculation. Clearly, the powers that be feel extremely threatened by this new emergence.

I am not going to outline a defense for this way of seeing things and for the ensuing methodology adopted in this book. A vast literature exists on the subject, referenced throughout this book.[2] Instead, I invite readers to do their own homework on the subject, trusting their adult faith-intuition, while I proceed to indicate its application to the evolving nature of the vowed life in the twenty-first century.

---

[2] Currently, Ilia Delio, OSF, the Josephine C. Connelly chair in theology at Villanova University in Philadelphia, is the most widely known proponent of this evolutionary perspective. Largely inspired by the vision and writings of the Jesuit priest and paleontologist Teilhard de Chardin, she integrates a range of different insights from both science and theology (see Delio 2013; 2014). Another inspiring and well-informed source is John Haught, distinguished research professor at Georgetown University (see Haught 2010; 2015). How the Darwinian understanding of evolution can be integrated with mainline Christian theology is compellingly illustrated by theologian Elizabeth Johnson in *Ask the Beasts* (2013). A fine overview of both the Teilhardian and Darwinian perspectives, infused with deep spiritual wisdom, is provided by American journalist Carter Phipps in *Evolutionaries* (2012), while Barbara Marx Hubbard's *Conscious Evolution* (1998) provides a popular introduction for those coming fresh to the topic.

These are the characteristics of the evolutionary perspective that will have a direct bearing on the reflections of this book:

1. *Aliveness.* Over the past twenty years our understanding of aliveness has changed substantially. The propensity for aliveness is no longer a reserve of the human, deemed to be superior to all other life-forms. On the contrary, we know that everything that constitutes our embodiment as earthlings is given to us from the earth itself, as a living organism, itself energized from the larger cosmic web of life. In theological terms it is the Holy Spirit who enlivens all that exists (cf. Boff 2015; Haughey 2015), not merely humans. For us Religious, this expanded, more pervasive sense of being alive requires us to revision the historical unfolding of our existence, adopting more organic models rather than those based on cold, historical fact. This new reframing of aliveness alters significantly the meaning of the vows, as we shall indicate in later chapters.

2. *Emergence.* The all-embracing sense of aliveness unfolds along an evolutionary trajectory that transcends simple cause and effect, with a sense of direction that is open and unpredictable, always evolving into greater complexity. The culture of patriarchal certainty and hierarchical ordering is increasingly understood as an anthropocentric projection that alienates humans themselves precisely by separating us from the womb of our becoming and attributing to us an elevated status increasingly viewed as exploitative and dangerous. Earlier notions of perfectionism and heroic asceticism belong to this perverted anthropology. While in the past *stasis* defined our value and integrity (the essentials never change), Religious Life in the twenty-first century needs to adapt to more organic modes of growth and development, requiring us to redefine our sense of mission for the world and church of our time.

3. *Paradox.* Creation's evolutionary unfolding is endowed with the paradoxical interplay of creation-*cum*-destruction, an unceasing cyclic rhythm of birth-death-rebirth. Major religions tend to dismiss this paradox as a fundamental flaw requiring divine salvific intervention. The future credibility of the vowed life largely depends on our graced ability to befriend the paradox (within and without), discern its God-given significance, and become active in the redemptive tasks of justice, liberation, and gospel empowerment for the troubled and confused world of the twenty-first century. A deeper appreciation of this enduring paradox alters significantly our understanding of suffering in the world. Whereas in the past Religious often adopted a spirituality of suffering for the sake of holiness, in the future our option must

be that of getting rid of all meaningless suffering, facilitated through a more forthright commitment to peace, justice, and the integrity of God's creation.

4. *Lateral Thinking.* Much of Christian theology and its ensuing spirituality are defined and described in terms of classical Greek metaphysics, rational thought, and logical process. It is a linear, sequential process favored by dominant males seeking control and mastery. It is a strategy alien to evolutionary unfolding, lacking in the creativity, imagination, and intuition necessary to apprehend the complexities of this age and every other. If women and men Religious want to serve creation as prophetic catalysts, adopting lateral rather than linear perspectives, they will need a scriptural and theological grounding embracing the ecumenical, multi-faith, and inter-spiritual wisdom of our age (cf. Johnson and Ord 2012). Conventional academic, ecclesiastical (seminary) training falls well short of this ideal.

5. *Consciousness.* The metaphysical worldview also favored the philosophy of divide and conquer, thus segmenting wisdom and knowledge into binary opposites (dualisms) and uniform categories, alien to the multidisciplinary and trans-disciplinary philosophy of our age. According to this view, a multidisciplinary perspective is necessary to comprehend the complex mysterious nature of all living reality. For Religious in the twenty-first century this will require a radical new approach to formation and skills for ministry, transcending the ecclesiastically determined learning of the past in favor of a wisdom that will equip us for a more engaging service to the new reign of God at the heart of creation.

6. *Spirituality.* All over the contemporary world mainline religion is in recession (with the possible exception of Islam), yielding pride of place either to more amorphous spiritual offshoots or to violent ideologies that will eventually destroy the very religion they seek to safeguard and promote. The age-long tension between Religious and the institutional church belongs to this frame of reference. In our finest hours Religious have espoused a spiritual empowering vision that has stretched conventional religious allegiance to new heights. And such spiritual empowerment tends to veer into active justice-making to a degree that often evokes negative and defensive reaction from mainline Christianity. At the refounding thresholds of the twenty-first century the gap between new spiritual horizons and inherited conventional religion is likely to grow, not decrease.

7. *Discernment.* Christian discernment describes the human effort to discover, appropriate, and integrate God's desires for our growth and development as people of faith. In its popular (Ignatian) sense it

is very much an individual process between the person and God, with the spiritual director acting as a kind of facilitator. Group discernment is a more loosely defined process often invoked at chapter meetings and in areas of pastoral accountability. In the ecclesiastical context, discernment is understood to be the divinely bestowed prerogative of the teaching authority of the church—to which all other forms of discernment need to be accountable. In a world and church becoming increasingly suspicious of the integrity and truth of institutional guidance, the task of discernment for the future will become much more localized, dialogically mediated, and informed by the skills and wisdom of systems theory. Increasingly, personal and group discernment will interweave with wisdom from the ground up, commanding much stronger credibility than that which comes from the top down. Religious across the world talk about *discernment,* frequently using the term in an ill-defined manner; for the future, it requires substantial, focused attention.

Our evolutionary propensities mark a seismic shift from a worldview in which we have been

> captivated by the spell of solidity, the fallacy of fixity, the illusion of immobility, the semblance of stasis, but [in which] the evolution revolution is starting to break that spell. We are realizing that we are, in fact, not standing on solid ground. But neither are we adrift in a meaningless universe. . . . We are part and parcel of a vast process of becoming." (Phipps 2012, 26)

Phipps goes on to identify three characteristics common to evolutionary thinkers in the twenty-first century:

- Evolutionaries are cross-disciplinary generalists;
- They develop the capacity to cognize the vast timescales of our evolutionary history;
- They embody a new spirit of optimism. (Phipps 2012, 32)

Religious Life as an Evolutionary Process

Throughout this book I embrace and affirm the view that *evolution is central to our understanding of life at every level* and that we stand a better chance of a more authentic reading of our reality—past, present, and future—when we adopt an evolutionary imperative. Without such a perspective we are condemned to offer a false picture, one that very likely will be stuck in the static paralysis that clings to a rigid past, immobilizing us, keeping us from being able to opt for a more creative, open-ended, and hope-filled future.

Volumes have been written on evolution, and much of it is narrowly and ideologically defined in neo-Darwinian terms. For the present work I wish to transcend much of the sophisticated rhetoric and get straight to the core elements of *growth-change-development*. These three words captivate the deep truth of what we mean by *evolution*:

1. Everything within and around us *grows*; that seems an indisputable fact of the natural and human world.

2. We perceive *change* all around us, and this involves decline and death. Such disintegration is not an evil or the consequence of sin (cf. Rom 6:23) but a God-given dimension of all creation.

3. There is an arrow of direction to all evolutionary unfolding that Teilhard de Chardin described as *growth into greater complexity*. As things become more complex, we need to adopt new knowledge and wisdom to make sense of the ever-emerging context. Clinging to time-honored concepts or absolutizing metaphysical claims (as in many religions) leads to stagnation and stillbirth.

I also adopt a key insight of philosopher Karl Popper, articulated anew by contemporary theologian John F. Haught (2010; 2015), that the direction of evolution takes shape primarily in response to *the lure of the future*, not merely solidifying what has served us well in the past. Theologically, I understand that the central attraction of the lure of the future is a fruit and wisdom of the Holy Spirit.

A leading proponent for evolutionary consciousness in our time—herself a Religious Sister—Ilia Delio (2013), advocates that our graced discernment for this time requires of all of us a new openness to what is unfolding around and within us. Contrary to the mechanistic, closed, systemic thinking of the past, we perceive all around us new expanding horizons awaiting our response and engagement. We are acutely aware of a decline and dying of so much we have long cherished, leaving us often in thrall to confusion and chaos—largely because we don't know how to grieve our losses in an appropriate way. Some spiritual writers describe this disintegration as a new paschal journey, and in our eagerness to arrive at a place of resurrection we miss the painful, grieving grace of our Calvary experience, a paradox elaborated at length in many of the writings of scripture scholar Walter Brueggemann (1978; 1986; 2014).

Throughout this book I seek to honor the evolutionary process characterizing Religious Life today. Clearly, former models (or paradigms) are disintegrating, and some (perhaps, many) Orders and Congregations will die out completely; it will not be the first time in the history of Christian Religious Life that we have had to deal with this demise. As priest-anthropologist Gerald A. Arbuckle (2015) chronicles, we are not handling the crisis very well. Our entire culture is addicted to a false sense of immortality, so alien to the natural world where everything evolves through the organic process of birth-death-new life. We dread chaos, and we can't stomach the thought of extinction, the need to let go when we have done our work. We need to grieve and mourn our losses, thus freeing ourselves to welcome the new breakthrough of resurrection possibility.

We are further paralyzed by a linear, rational sense of history whereby we frequently miss the empowering complexity of history's rhythms and creative breakthroughs. Our patriarchal addiction to mastery and control has severely impoverished our creative imaginations. As Brueggemann illustrates with typical prophetic wit:

Our known world is under judgment and is ending, the known world of moral certitudes, technological superiority, political dominance and economic monopoly. All of the energy used to keep that old imperial world intact is not helpful, is wasted, and is in fact a way of disobedience. . . . There is a kind of conspiracy of deception that keeps the dominant values in our culture credible. . . . We cover over the realities of human hurt and human hope with slogans of mastery, control, and security. . . . To some extent we have all become apostles of continuity, extrapolation, and derivation. Such a view of newness that is not real newness makes us grudging and fearful. It urges us to keep the wagons tightly in a circle. Such a view of the future robs us of vitality because we believe that what we have is the only source of anything in the future. (Brueggemann 1986, 17, 28, 29; for more, see Brueggemann 2014, 92, 101, 120)

How then do we hope to be open to the new future our God forever co-creates for us? How can we be surprised by the Spirit who blows where she wills? As decline and diminution have an impact upon us, seeds of resurrection are beginning to come alive all around us. Can we even see them? Are we so conditioned and blinkered by our allegiance to the past that we cannot discern the evolving face of a new future? This is the challenge for refounding explored throughout the pages of this book.

Like everything in God's creation, Religious Orders and Congregations are also destined to go through the process of birth-death-rebirth. Otherwise, they are likely to mutate into some type of frozen life-form devoid of all the God-given propensities to grow and flourish. We must not project onto our Orders and Congregations our false anthropocentric addiction to immortality. Even Jesus had to go through the process of death to the life he knew in order to be reborn into a higher level of evolutionary becoming.

Faith in the paschal journey is not just for funerals; neither is it a wisdom reserved for painful life transitions. The process is organic to all life-forms and to all structures imbued with the vitality of God's creative spirit. As I shall indicate in later chapters, the decline and death of Religious Life today has historical precedents and in all probability is God's will for us. It is a time for profound discernment, more likely to be embraced when accompanied by the graced ability to let go, grieve, and mourn our losses. As Arbuckle (2015) amply describes, such grieving is necessary to liberate us from our morbid fears and make us transparent to the possibilities of transformation that await us in God's providential wisdom.

Theological Foundations Reconsidered

We stand a better chance of being transparent and disposed to such transformation if we can review with greater honesty what has sustained us in the past and how these ancient guidelines need to be revisioned for the evolutionary context of the twenty-first century. Foremost is our time-honored definition of the vowed life itself as the *Sequela Christi*. Such following of Christ is the goal of all Christian life, which Christian monastics and other Religious have stretched to deeper limits. How to make sense of that stretching within the new evolutionary horizon of our time is the primary task of this opening chapter.

Theologically, the fundamental issue confronting us is our allegiance to the new reign of God, named in the Gospels as *the kingdom of God* and described afresh in the present work as the *Companionship of Empowerment* (explained in Chapter 3). I wish to honor the gospel imperative to "seek *first* the kingdom of God" (Matt 6:33). For much of Christian history that has not been our priority. Arguably, at many times in the past two thousand years, the Orders and Congregations sought to reclaim the primacy of the kingdom despite the monarchical approach favored by the both the church and the secular culture. That primary fidelity to the new companionship becomes a more forthright challenge for the sustainability of the vowed life in the twenty-first century.

For too long the Christ we have sought to follow has been a projection of our patriarchal compulsion for domination and control. It has been the imperial Christ of the fourth-century Constantine rather than the subversive empowering Jesus of the Christian gospel. We have been living out of a *Sequela Christi* tainted and distorted by both Greek metaphysics and Roman imperialism. The heroic, ascetical warrior we were invited (sometime compelled) to follow in a sacrificial battle for salvation frequently had little or no resemblance to the liberating, empowering Jesus of the Christian gospel.

While we liberally talk and write about being fashioned in the image and likeness of Jesus, in truth we have expended enormous energy throughout the two thousand years of Christendom molding God (and Jesus) in our image and likeness. Our prayers, hymnologies, and devotions insinuate a co-dependent allegiance to an all-powerful deity, a king-like hero above the sky, who alone can rescue us from our depraved plight "down here." This is a long way from the Jesus who invites us to be friends and not servants (Jn 15:15), the Jesus who pointed the finger away from himself toward the new companionship (kingdom), inviting us to co-discipleship in co-creating a better world characterized by gospel liberation.

For too long we have lived out of a dysfunctional, co-dependent Christology, historically and theologically designed to uphold and perpetuate imperial power while deviously disempowering any attempt to challenge and dislodge such hegemony. Thus, the Jesus who gave all—in life and death—to bring about God's new reign on earth is reduced to a submissive, obedient martyr to pacify an angry patriarchal deity threatened by human creative ingenuity. And the outstanding Christian is subsequently portrayed as the one who is willing to endure prolonged suffering and humiliation in allegiance to this demanding patriarchal deity. As I indicate in previous works (O'Murchu 2011; 2014), the devotion of consolation dislodges the gospel imperative of the spirituality of liberation.

Empowering discipleship for the future—both within and outside Religious Life—needs to outgrow the individualistic, heroic projections inherited from past patriarchal conditioning, so that we relearn to be co-disciples with Jesus in bringing about God's new reign on earth. The Jesus of the Gospels is consistently accountable to a reality greater than himself (described as "the Father" in John's

Gospel), rather than drawing attention to his individual self. This requires us to outgrow our inherited Hellenistic anthropology that favors the autonomous, separate, rational hero as the only authentic embodiment of what it means to be human. This is not the incarnational humanity that Jesus embraced, and neither should we. It is a Hellenistic imposition that has generated centuries of disempowering co-dependency and, sadly, continues to dominate the cultural hegemony of our time with some devastating effects for humans and planet alike.

Instead, we need to appropriate a more evolutionary understanding of our God-given humanity, often captured in the statement: "I am at all times the sum of my relationships" (O'Murchu 2002, 133). That is what confers my identity. Each one of us—including the historical Jesus—is born out of a web of relationships both divine and earthly, and it is from within this relational matrix that we all grow and flourish. This is the understanding we have embodied and embraced for much of our evolutionary time on earth (O'Murchu 2008), the sense of self that is still upheld by many of our indigenous peoples (at least in theory) and the understanding of our humanity embraced by the historical Jesus (O'Murchu 2011, 42–55).

Here I suggest a number of theological correctives that belong to the prophetic task of speaking truth to power. Another description of the prophetic adopted later in this book invites us to name reality in a way that liberates a deeper truth. Religious Life has long been considered to hold special responsibility for guarding and promoting the primacy of the prophetic over imperial institutionalization, an attribution the official church has consistently viewed with suspicion and negative regard, one that Religious themselves have often neglected to foster and promote.

Spirituality and the Vowed Life

Despite several shifts in both theology and spirituality throughout the latter half of the twentieth century, the spiritual dimension of the vowed life is strangely suspended between a church that still endorses the *fuga mundi* (flee the world) ideal (albeit in a modified fashion), and Religious themselves, whose spiritual values vary enormously. The integration of Religious Sisters into the pastoral life of the church in the years after Vatican II was a move of mixed blessings, with Religious Sisters adopting a kind of pseudo-clerical role that often undermined their prophetic identity.

In our evolutionary context both Religious and believers in general face a spiritual shift of focus articulated by Benedictine Sister Joan Chittister in the opening words of her book *Heart of Flesh* (1998, 1): "There is a new question in the spiritual life; it is the spirituality of the spiritual life itself. Life here, and how we relate to it, rather than life to come and how we guarantee it for ourselves, has become the spiritual conundrum of our age."

Despite the overt endorsement of the ministerial nature of the vowed life, the Roman document *Vita Consecrata* (nos. 32, 33, 59) endorses the spirituality of escape from this vale of tears, as does Pope John Paul's desire to rename Religious Life the "consecrated life," suggesting a holier way of being more conducive for salvation in a life hereafter. Joan Chittister is inviting us to acknowledge the evolutionary shift from a spirituality of *escapism* to a spirituality of *engagement*, from salvation only obtainable in an afterlife to one more readily realized in our gospel engagement with the whole of God's creation.

Because several Religious have failed to acknowledge this significant shift, some have veered into a life of activism often deprived of nourishing spiritual vitality, while others seek to redraw a sense of balance by frequent allusions to deficiency in prayer life and mediocrity in our fidelity to Christ. The problem is more one of confused spiritual horizons rather than anything to do with how we live our lives. When we fail to acknowledge the evolutionary shift (noted by Joan Chittister), we are unlikely to engage the transition from a spiritual focus (of escape), which served us well in earlier understandings for both the Christian and the vowed life but is no longer adequate for our evolving context. We need to make a conscious choice to embrace the spirituality of engagement, with the substantial implications involved for spiritual formation, prayer life, praxis, and lifestyle.

Whereas, in the past, spirituality was the primary frame of reference for all aspects of our lives, we now realize that our spirituality must be informed by, and integrated with, our theology. As suggested above, we must be unrelenting in our prioritizing of the new reign of God, and this requires us to redefine several aspects of our spirituality. For one thing, we must abandon all semblance of dichotomizing spiritual allegiance; we must transcend all the dualisms that separate the sacred from the secular, body from soul, and matter from spirit. And we must come to terms with the ubiquity of the Holy One, who does not reside in some distant heaven but inhabits the whole creation.

Instead of escapism we must espouse engagement. Instead of embracing suffering to do penance, we embrace the sufferings involved in the works of love and justice as we seek to bring about heaven on earth. Our spirituality must not be based on endless recitation of approved prayers, sometimes addressing a violent God in patriarchal language (some of the psalms), but on a transparency to the Spirit, who prays in us (Rom 8:26–27), inviting us to levels of discernment largely unknown in previous times. And like Jesus, we will often need the solitude of the mountain, not to build tents for our comfort (like Peter on the Mount of the transfiguration), but to ready ourselves to embrace afresh the tormented epileptic in the valley and the city (Matt 17:14ff.).

Religious Life still lacks an integrated theology, without which we cannot hope to negotiate authentically the evolutionary challenges of the twenty-first century. We need not an ascetical spirituality encouraging us to escape, but an empowering one admonishing us to engage. Without such a theologically informed spirituality we cannot hope to negotiate creatively the refounding challenges coming our way in the latter half of the twenty-first century.

The Consecrated Life

Despite the attempts at Vatican II to overcome the two-tier division of Christian holiness and promote instead the fundamental equality of all the baptized, Pope John Paul II reintroduced the superior status of the vowed life, designating it with a special quality of consecration above and beyond our shared baptism. This was a regressive step that has damaged rather than enhanced the unique meaning of the vowed life.

As I indicate in the next chapter, all forms of the vowed life—monastic and apostolic—articulate a cultural yearning that I and others describe as the monastic archetype. It is an archetypal yearning for a spiritual integration of the human and the transhuman, not through an escape to a harmonious life hereafter (the popular misguided interpretation), but through a deep desire for incarnational union with God, who permeates all creation. The ancient and indigenous belief in the Great Spirit is immensely helpful in comprehending what is at stake in this aspiration (see O'Murchu 2012).

The traditional spirituality, therefore, inviting Religious to flee from and abandon the world, needs to give way to a fresh sense of integration, described later in this book as the *call to liminality*. As

Religious, we are called into a deep cultural solidarity with all God's people—*even deeper than baptismal identity*. And our uniqueness is in the call and challenge to make more transparent the inculturation[3] of those values that have enduring worth for a meaningful life as divinely missioned earthlings. We are not better than everyone else; rather, we are called to deepen and make more transparent the deep values to which all humans aspire as creatures of God.

We all serve a primary sense of consecration, divinely "commissioned" to radiate on earth the enduring values of divine empowering and to wrestle with the challenge of how these values need to be inculturated in each new evolving time and place. As Religious, we cannot serve this liminal mission without a deep sense of solidarity with all our fellow humans (irrespective of religion or culture) and a graced sense of being at home in the heart of God's creation.

Evolutionary Becoming

Religious Life is an ancient phenomenon that has surfaced in all the great religions of humanity and is likely to endure into the open-ended future. As a species we have not yet discerned how best to inculturate its contribution to our evolving growth and development. In its current public expressions it tends to be couched within formal religious institutions, encased in legal and canonical structures that have enhanced its growth and development but occasionally have suffocated it. Amid the new evolutionary impetus of the twenty-first century a cultural container, above and beyond formal religion, seems to be desirable. As I indicate in later chapters, the nature and purpose of that container may become the greatest challenge for the refounding, likely to emerge in the latter half of the twenty-first century.

---

[3] Throughout this book I use the term *inculturation* to indicate the cross-fertilization of an inherited Christian value with the cultural aspirations of our time. This is broadly in keeping with the definition employed by Pope John Paul II in *Redemptoris Missio* "the intimate transformation of authentic cultural values through their integration in Christianity" (no. 52). Occasionally, I adopt the notion of *acculturation*, which denotes the merging of cultures as a result of prolonged contact resulting in the assimilation of behaviors of the adopted culture. Neither of these terms should be confused with *enculturation*, which describes the process through which people (particularly children) are socialized into the values and practices of a particular culture. For further clarification on the use and misuse of the three terms, see Andrew Byrne, "Some Ins and Outs of Inculturation," *Annales Theologici* 4 (1990): 109–49.

For mainstream Christianity the vowed life has always been something of an enigma. As long as Religious proved to be useful functionaries—as teachers, nurses, social workers, or serving diocesan structures such as parish communities—they were acceptable, and the church was happy to have them. And as long as monks and enclosed women were devoted to prayer and penance behind big walls, it was assumed that such holiness would benefit the entire church. But as for those frontline people who claimed to be champions of the poor or seekers after justice, those who disturbed the equilibrium between the sacred and the secular, the female Religious who tried to dismantle the male-imposed restrictions of enclosure or supported controversial healthcare programs to benefit the poor and marginalized, those people often became the target of church suspicion and sometimes of its censure and open disapproval. And to suggest that the vowed life had a flair for the prophetic above and beyond the institutional church was definitely anathema, not tolerated.

To suggest that a tension has always existed between Religious and the formal church strikes me as a trite, superficial statement. It sounds much like sibling rivalry. Suggesting that such tension is undesirable trivializes a creative force that deserves a far more serious discernment, a focused attention on the outrageous freedom with which the Spirit dispenses giftedness—not merely for the church, but for the whole of God's creation. Instead, the tension requires a quality of discernment—reading what the Spirit is up to—embracing imagination, intuition, and mystical attunement. It is the kind of wisdom that underpins the gospel parables, a complex, disturbing set of truths that, two thousand years later, we are still trying to fathom. With such parabolic construct and its inherent prophetic wisdom, we stand a better chance to reclaim the subliminal truth of Religious Life, too long masked and distorted by legalism, historical distortion, and over-institutionalization.

❧

In the spirit of empowered companionship, you are invited to gather or join with another person or group to consider the vision of this book through the study questions at the end of each chapter. At first, the length and breadth of history might seem daunting, but if you ride it through, it will take you into an arc of history—of Religious Life—seldom revealed in one place. Taken together, these study questions provide a way to navigate the arc of time in which this book is laid out. The questions and suggestions are offered as a guide to conversation, but please follow wherever else some of these considerations might lead you.

Study Questions: Revisioning the Foundations

1. What surprised you in the Introduction and Chapter 1?
2. What stirred your heart?
3. What challenged your accustomed thinking?
4. What is your experience of the tension that has always existed between Religious and the formal church, and how might it actually be a creative force with which the Spirit dispenses giftedness?

Chapter 2

The Parable and the Paradigm

A talent for speaking differently, rather than arguing well, is the chief instrument of cultural change.
—RICHARD RORTY

The work of the cell requires a capacity to inhabit a space of fluidity and paradox, always seeking a place to dwell and never ceasing to take upon oneself the mind of an exile.
—DOUGLAS E. CHRISTIE

Two words create the title and focus for this chapter: *parable* and *paradigm.* In fact, they become the connecting threads throughout this book. They will also be the anchors keeping us grounded in gospel wisdom. To reclaim that wisdom for our twenty-first-century context, I return momentarily to the parabolic story at the beginning of Chapter 1: the remarkable sheepdog that apparently gathered in the sheep, acting on its own intuitive wisdom. Several years ago scripture scholar C. H. Dodd suggested that each parable unfolds through a triune process of *orientation, disorientation,* and *reorientation.* In the story of the sheepdog, one can readily see all three dimensions at work, the reorientation being the most daunting of all.

The story defies rational explanation. How did the dog "know" what to do? And why on such a unique occasion? Did the dog "hear" or overhear the conversation at the lunch table, or was the dog the recipient of a quality of wisdom beyond all possibility of human analysis? As I raise these questions, I can feel in my inner being that I am actually doing something inappropriate, even distasteful. The questions are too rational, too anthropocentric, to yield up the wisdom I am seeking. What I need to do is to sit with John (the sheep farmer) in a kind of contemplative stillness while he narrates his experience of what happened on that memorable occasion. And the more I can listen deeply to his story, the more I am likely to discern what the creative Spirit was up to in that inspiring, parabolic experience.

The truth of parable—and my primary influence is that of gospel parable—shifts the focus from the rational to the trans-rational, from reason to intuition and imagination, from the useful convention to creative possibility. The shift of focus is well stated by business consultant Margaret J. Wheatley:

> My growing sensibility of a quantum universe has affected my organizational life in several ways. First, I try hard to discipline myself to remain aware of the whole and to resist my well-trained desire to analyze the parts to death. I look now for patterns of movement over time and focus on qualities like rhythm, flow, direction, and shape. Second, I know I am wasting time whenever I draw straight arrows between two variables in a cause and effect diagram, or position things as polarities, or create elaborate plans and time lines. Third, I no longer argue with anyone about what is real. Fourth, the time I formerly spent on detailed planning and analysis I now use to look at the structures that might facilitate relationships. I have come to expect that something useful occurs if I link up people, units, or tasks, even though I cannot determine precise outcomes. And last, I realize more and more that the universe will not cooperate with my desires for determinism. (Wheatley 1992, 43–44)

Much of this book is based on a historical overview of the vowed life, adopting a narrative reconstruction that views history not so much as a sequence of events or a repertoire of outstanding achievements, but rather as an *unfolding, evolving story*, ever open to new surprises, yet strangely predictable in its cyclic unfolding patterns. And I want to give special attention to the neglected subverted wisdom of those who were either callously made invisible, namely, the great foundresses of female Religious Life, or those whose truth was too subversive to be embraced, namely, the prophetic rebellious characters too controversial to be included in our historical narratives.

In a word, my historical overview is intertwined through and through with the *disturbing wisdom of parable* as I seek to uncover and unravel subverted wisdom that I suggest will be immensely useful for the rediscovery (refounding) of Religious Life. I believe that this refounding is likely to transpire in the latter half of the twenty-first century. This futuristic claim is itself based on my parabolic understanding of history.

Shifting the Paradigm

The second concept I frequently adopt throughout the text is that of *paradigm shifts,* a mode of understanding that has been much invoked since the seminal work of Thomas Kuhn in the early 1970s. Kuhn's research is largely confined to paradigm shifts in the developments of mainline science, such as the transition from Newtonian physics to Einstein's relativity theories. Many others have taken these valuable insights and transferred them to other social and historical contexts, highlighting the following as the key processes involved in contemporary paradigm shifts:

From	Toward
Isolated parts operating autonomously	The whole is greater than the sum of the parts
Emphasis on separation/differences	Emphasis on integration/commonalities
Objectivity and the rational	Subjectivity, imagination, and intuition
Focus on external expertise	Focus on inner wisdom and resilience
Clarity on power and control	Emphasis on trust and empowerment
Desire to standardize	Appreciation of diversity
Judge by the quality of product	Discern deeper meaning in process
Top down	Bottom up

These two sets of characteristics should not be viewed in opposing dualistic terms. I am not describing a choice between one and the other, with the latter being desirable above and beyond the former. I am outlining an *evolutionary* movement from one set of namings, largely endorsed by the dominant culture, toward an emerging set of values often viewed suspiciously as posing a threat to what many consider to be the one and only enduring truth.

Paradigms represent a strong background force for the way human cultures work; they can be thought of as the unwritten rules of society. They enable us to understand the background context for many of the social trends and cultural forces we take for granted. In moving from one paradigm to another, many people don't recognize that change has occurred until much later. Those who can "anticipate" these shifts in paradigms are at an advantage and are likely to contribute in anticipation rather than in reaction to the newly emerging wisdom.

Theologian Hans Küng (1989) applies Kuhn's theory of paradigm change to the entire history of Christian thought and theology. He identifies six historical "macromodels": (1) the apocalyptic paradigm of primitive Christianity, (2) the Hellenistic paradigm of the patristic period, (3) the medieval Roman Catholic paradigm, (4) the Protestant (Reformation) paradigm, (5) the modern Enlightenment paradigm, and (6) the emerging ecumenical paradigm of more recent times. Contrary to the widespread—and largely unexamined—assumption that religious truths remain fixed and unchanged, Küng highlights cultural influences that consistently affect Christian faith, requiring a religious and intellectual flexibility if theology is to develop in a wholesome, organic, and evolutionary way.

Additionally, in the present work, I wish to highlight the fact that the changes involved in paradigm shifts require a *different kind of language and narrative* to explain and explore what is transpiring. Our rational, logical, and deductive strategies will not be adequate. A more creative, intuitive, and paradoxical process is required. Hence the notion of the parable, which I borrow from the Christian Gospels, denoting a wisdom that belongs to a much wider cultural context.

Paradigm movement is also characterized by an evolutionary sense of direction very different from the dominant linear approach adopted in Western rational thought. *Paradigms are more circular and spiral in their unfolding.* They launch us toward new possibilities with an almost frightening sense of urgency. But on closer examination they are actually reclaiming an underlying wisdom of great depth and age. It takes a great deal of discerning wisdom to see and honor the ancient enduring wisdom (which, later in this chapter, I explore through the notion of archetypes).

While Western culture is addicted to rational discourse, logical process, and linear progression (see the valuable critique of Val Plumwood 2002), the paradigm approach chronicles a different set of research options, invoking imagination and intuition, systemic complexity (including its often chaotic features), lateral vision, and the subtlety of mysticism rather than the overt analysis often used to describe religious praxis. Paradigmatic visioning favors relational webs over isolated parts (or facts), connections over distinctions, collaboration over competition; it celebrates commonalities rather than differences. In scientific terms its more natural home is quantum theory rather than the classical Newtonian approach, the systems worldview rather than monotheistic imperialism.

The Notion of Refounding

In the closing decades of the twentieth century Religious Life entered a period of decline characterized by a drop in the number of entrants (vocations), an increasing age profile, and a diminished presence in several traditional apostolates. While numbers rose significantly in Latin America, Africa, and Asia, the overall pattern was, and continues to be, a downward one. Some analysts have described it as an old paradigm dying while a new one waits to be born, but few have attempted a compelling narrative of the new paradigm with the parabolic flavor suggested in the present work.

One attempt at a fresh narrative arose in the closing decades of the twentieth century, pioneered by priest-anthropologist Gerald A. Arbuckle, SM (1988; 1996; 2015). It aroused an enthusiastic response, particularly from leaders of Religious Orders and Congregations in the West, and several tried to implement the preconditions that would make refounding possible. For a range of reasons (reviewed in Chapter 12 below), the euphoria dissipated rather quickly, and the refounding appears not to have taken off.

Arbuckle himself, particularly in his more recent writings, elaborates on the complexities involved in the refounding process:

- the need for a coherent founding vision in the first place and how best to retrieve it in our contemporary situation;
- our human reluctance to engage with chaos, disintegration, and grieving;
- our inability (or unwillingness) to discern what is authentically new (reading the signs of the times); and
- the lack of courageous risk-taking to accommodate the new in a novel way.

For Arbuckle, the choice is urgent: *refound or die out!* It is that graphic choice I am picking up in the present work, but with a significantly different context. Whereas Arbuckle is dealing primarily with individual Orders and Congregations, *my purview is Religious Life as a global spiritual movement with a distinctive historical narrative*. I cherish many of Arbuckle's rich insights (which I synthesize in Chapter 12), and I integrate them into my historical analysis. Our respective insights are undoubtedly mutually enriching, but the reader needs to keep in mind the focus of research is different for each of us. While Arbuckle seeks to challenge individual Congregations toward the possibility of refounding, I am striving to discern how the Holy Spirit is reweaving the story of the vowed life amid the global decline and disintegration of the late twentieth century and early twenty-first century, along with the historical likelihood of a large-scale revitalization in the second half of the twenty-first century.

Words such as *relaunching* or *revitalization* may describe more accurately what I am about. I adopt the notion of *refounding,* sensing that it carries a deeper resonance for many contemporary Religious seeking a more coherent and meaningful future. My attraction to the larger picture arises from the inspiration of quantum physics, with its underlying principle that the whole is greater than the sum of the parts. Many Religious, while identifying strongly with their specific Order or Congregation, seem to have little or no awareness of the fact that all our groups belong to a global movement of great age and with an enduring cultural and spiritual impact (the greater whole). It is that larger, informative, and empowering context that I am seeking to reclaim.

In terms of the history of Religious Life I am in search of a *grand narrative*, despite the unpopularity of the idea among several postmodernists. While Arbuckle's strategy for refounding can challenge and inspire individual groups, my hunch is that individual refounding needs the reinforcement of the larger context if it is to be truly sustainable. Just as individual organizations of our time are becoming increasingly aware of their globalized context and its necessity for their relevance and survival, so increasingly Religious Orders and Congregations will need to reincarnate their global agenda, rooted in what I presently describe as the monastic archetype.

Discerning the Archetype

In subsequent chapters I outline an abbreviated history of the vowed life, with particular attention to the shift in focus arising within each new historical cycle. I view the Religious Life as a powerful, enduring, cultural phenomenon, consistently morphing into novel expression in response to the ever-new needs of our changing and evolving world. Traditionally, Christian scholars, and Religious themselves, cherish continuity over discontinuity, values and cultural expressions characterized by enduring unchanging features. There may be cultural adjustments, but the underlying values, the ecclesial sense of mission, and the standard behaviors (for example, the three vows) remain essentially the same. This is how the church down through the ages has also viewed the vowed life.

I wish to suggest that the true picture is vastly different, characterized by an extensive range of expressions and diverse cultural articulations—and each new wave of refounding makes this abundantly clear. In fact, the more the institutional church sought to control Religious Life, the more it seemed to morph into diverse growth and movement in response to the novel needs of various times and places. However, despite this complexity and diversity, there is, and continues to be, an enduring underlying vision, which, I suggest, is subtle, mystical, alluring, and transformative for person and culture alike. In ancient monasticism it was often referred to as *conversatio morum*.[1] In more recent times it has been named *the monastic archetype*.

We cannot hope to engage the refounding process in a discerning and enlightened way without internalizing—consciously or otherwise—this enduring archetypal wisdom. This, I believe, is what set the great founders and foundresses on fire with the innovative Spirit. This is also the sustaining inspiration that nourishes, affirms, and challenges every Religious in our prophetic calling (further described as our liminal identity in Chapter 7 below). It needs to be highlighted as the launching pad for every attempt at recapturing the meaning of Religious Life, including the refounding vision being reviewed in the present work.

First, I offer a brief overview of the meaning of *archetypes*, a term derived from two Greek words: *arche,* "first," and *tupos,* "type or form." Archetypes have been adopted by both anthropology and psychology to name and explain those sublime energetic forces that transcend our rational and commonsense modes of understanding. All archetypal truth is spiritual in nature, often transcending the doctrines and structures of the formal religions. In Christian language we consider the Holy Spirit of God to be the energizing source

---

[1] The Benedictine *conversatio morum* denotes the shift from one set of values to another as the devotee enters more deeply into the monastic life. Undertaking *conversatio* is a recognition of God's unpredictability, facing up to the demands of growth and change as the devotee is confronted with his or her own love of comfort or safety. Monastic commentator Michael Casey captures the crucial change in this terse sentence: "Monastic life is the diametric opposite of aimless living" (2005, 5).

and sustaining power of all creativity, embodied foundationally in archetypal values.[2]

For the purposes of the present work I offer two descriptions of what *archetypes* mean. The first is from William J. Bausch, who describes archetypal values as follows:

> That is why certain basic myths called archetypal keep popping up. Some are the sharing of food, denoting the sharing of the very substance that keeps one alive; hence the supreme hospitality, brotherhood, fellowship; the shedding of blood as a loss of vitality, and drinking it as drinking the source of life. There are Gods who died and rose again to explain the seasons. Miracles were used as proof of divine power. Virgin births were spoken of. The point is that these symbols are not unique to Christianity nor should they be. They are basic myths that explain humanity's eternal hopes, answers to the meaning of life, birth, death, tragedy and suffering. (Bausch 1975, 70–71)

The second is from theologian Paul F. Knitter, who describes archetypes as

> predispositions toward the formation of images, a-priori powers of representation, inbuilt stirrings or lures that, if we can feel and follow them, will lead us into the depths of what we are and where we are going. They might be called messages-in-code, which we must decode and bring to our conscious awareness. It is difficult to speak about what these messages contain. Their general contents, Jung tells us, have to do with light and darkness, death and rebirth, wholeness, sacrifice, and redemption. He saw such archetypes as the common seedbed of all religions. (Knitter 1985, 57)

The vowed life, therefore, embodies an archetypal orientation, serving to highlight *values* that are crucial for the growth and evolution not merely of human life but of planetary well-being. As I shall

---

[2] This understanding of the Holy Spirit as the foundational, empowering energy of everything in God's creation takes on a new impetus in the recent publications of two contemporary theologians: Leonardo Boff, *Come Holy Spirit* (Maryknoll, NY: Orbis Books, 2015); and John C. Haughey, *A Biography of the Spirit* (Maryknoll, NY: Orbis Books, 2015). A similar understanding is reviewed in my own research on the notion of the Great Spirit among contemporary indigenous peoples (see O'Murchu 2012).

indicate in later chapters, it is not the case of Religious possessing values unknown to the rest of humanity; rather, we are called to acculturate afresh the deep values that all humans—across time and culture—yearn for. Hence, the liminal meaning of the vowed life that I explore in Chapter 7 below.

Drawing on the seminal insights of Indian priest and scholar of multi-faith dialogue Raimundo Panikkar, Sandra Schneiders describes the monastic impulse as "the aspiration toward simplicity and the integration of complexity" (2000, 7). In 1980, in the United States, Panikkar was the keynote speaker for a conference entitled "The Monk as Universal Archetype." For Panikkar, the monk archetype represents the polarity between being something difficult and strange while also being a vocation for every human being. Being a monk, therefore, is not an isolated human experience but rather *an intensification of the human wholeness to which every person aspires*:

> By monk, *monachos,* I understand that person who aspires to reach the ultimate goal of life with all his being by renouncing all that is not necessary to it, i.e., by concentrating on this one single and unique goal. Precisely this single-mindedness *(ekagrata)*, or rather the exclusivity of the goal that shuns all subordinate though legitimate goals, distinguishes the monastic way from other spiritual endeavors toward perfection or salvation. . . . The thesis I am defending is that the monk is the expression of an archetype which is *a constitutive dimension of human life*. This archetype is a unique quality of each person, which at once needs and shuns institutionalization. (Panikkar 1982, 25–26)[3]

According to this description, the monk embodies a set of values that all humans—not just religious believers—desire and aspire toward. The monk makes more real and explicit what in conventional human life is an orientation toward integrity that tends to remain more illusive and ambiguous. Of course, the archetype is never complete;

---

[3] In Part II, entitled "The Canon of the Disciple" (26–100), Panikkar addresses the monastic vocation as it prevails today and forms the fundamental core of the book, elaborating "Nine Sutras on the Canon of the Disciple" through which he develops the basic principle of simplicity: (1) opening up to the primordial aspiration; (2) the primacy of being over doing and having; (3) silence; (4) Mother Earth; (5) overcoming spacio-temporal parameters; (6) transhistoric consciousness; (7) fullness of the person; (8) primacy of the sacred; and (9) memory of the absolute.

it is always evolving and yearning for a fullness not realizable in this life.

Echoes of this archetypal wholeness are detectable in the interpretation of the rule of Benedict suggested by Australian monastic scholar Michael Casey when he writes:

> It seems to me that the first and foremost call that comes to us today from Benedict's Rule is to become what we're meant to be. . . . Those who faithfully follow Benedict's Rule are not usually fiercely world-rejecting, body-denying, self-hating people. They are not fanatics. Those formed by monastic tradition more often than not come out the other end as prudent, gentle, and tolerant, both toward themselves and toward others. (Casey 2005, 1, 23).

There is a further nuance to what we are exploring, implicit in Panikkar's exploration but largely unexplained, namely, that humans can only live out their God-given potentialities in the context of God's creation. Our long history of dualistic splitting—for example, sacred vs. secular, soul vs. body, spirit vs. matter—leaves us in a deeply alienated state when it comes to the challenge of archetypal integration, an undertaking addressed more forthrightly by monastic researcher Douglas E. Christie, who describes the monastic archetype in these words:

> The image of the monk, standing in the midst of a broken community, helping by his very presence to heal all that has been torn asunder, suggests the kind of spiritual power contemplative practice could yield in the life of one who embarked on this path. It also suggests the integral relationship between solitude and community, contemplation and action. Monastic anachoresis (withdrawal), which has often been construed as simple refusal or abandonment of the world, should instead be seen as a strategy aimed at freeing the monk from the compulsions and anxieties that prevent him from seeing and engaging the world with simple awareness and compassion. The monks came to believe that it was only by acquiring consciousness transformed through a long process of purification that they could hope to participate in healing the deeper wounds of the world. (2013, 51)

Christie broadens our understanding of the monastic archetype, grounding it afresh in the web of universal life, not a fleeing from the world in any sense *(fuga mundi)*, but, on the contrary, a reconstituted relationship with all creation. Thus daily discernment of the monastic person involves

> the practice of apprehending the Divine through the created world. If the practice of paying attention to the created world in this way was sometimes ambiguous or fraught with tension, there was nevertheless a clear sense in this tradition that authentic contemplative practice could and often did involve learning to see deeply into the created world. (Christie 2013, 158)

In effect Christie opens up a largely unexplored dimension of the monastic archetype, namely, the fascination with place (for which he uses the Greek word *topos*), typically described as desert or wilderness. Our tendency to depict the ordeals of the ancient monks as an ascetical battle with the forces of evil seriously distorts parabolic affiliation with place, environment, ecology, and our grounding in the sacredness of earth. The dualistic spirituality displaces the serious ethical options, which several contemporary eco-spiritual writers rename as a recovery of the aesthetic (see Heise 2008), requiring us to broaden our understandings of ethics, which in Catholic terms are often reduced to the realm of sexual behavior. Thus we are invited to reimagine the subliminal monastic yearning to reclaim our sacred earth, our embodied earthiness in an incarnational aesthetic that carries grave environmental and ecological responsibilities. As we shall see (in Chapters 8 and 9), these ideas require a radical new understanding of the vows—particularly that of poverty—for our time.

While Panikkar and Christie address the archetype primarily in monastic terms, they each envisage a wider application, relating not merely to humans in isolation but to how we engage God's creation as earthlings, beings whose very existence is derived from the earth, which is necessary at all times for our growth and flourishing. The archetype, therefore, is not merely a pursuit of union with God in a life hereafter, but also one with substantial ethical and aesthetical consequences for how we live on God's earth. In the present work I extend this notion of the underlying archetype to include all Religious, and, in the context of the twenty-first century, to an awakening consciousness that also impinges upon humanity at large.

Now, we must face what might well be the single biggest challenge of the archetype under consideration: *it does not belong exclusively to vowed members!* We are dealing with an enduring foundational value system that touches the deep truth of every human being, and as already indicated, one that cannot be integrated apart from a meaningful relationship with the surrounding web of life. This new integrated spiritual horizon was revisioned afresh in the closing decades of the twentieth century and continues to flourish in the twenty-first century under the rubric of the *new monasticism* (see Bucko and McEntee 2015; Ponzetti 2014). It constitutes a diverse group of people—single, married, and lay—all yearning for the deeper integration referred to above, all, in one way or another, lured by the power of the archetype I am describing.

Endorsing this evolving archetypal understanding, Irish scholar of the new monasticism Sr. Bernadette Flanagan often cites the catchy phrase of the Camaldose monk Emanuela Bargelini, "Monasticism isn't a container, it is an energy" (quoted in Flanagan 2014, 12). All expressions of the vowed life arise as a response to the creative Spirit energizing anew everything in God's creation. As we move deeper into the twenty-first century that response will not regress to some idealistic eremitical enclosure but is likely to morph into a range of communally based, earth-centered, intentional groups composed of a diverse range of people all united, consciously or otherwise, by an archetypal awakening that seems to be gathering fresh momentum in our time.

The Communal Dimension

Thus far my explanation carries connotations of the old eremitical heroism, with the focus on the ascetical achievements of the individual spiritual warrior. This is a patriarchal slant that has been much exaggerated—as Candida Moss (2013) points out in the case of early Christian martyrdom—to the detriment of a more grounded communal endeavor, which, as we shall see in Chapter 4, was probably the determining feature of early monastic praxis. Religious Life, from its ancient origins, embodied a strong communal set of values. The monks in the Egyptian desert were not just isolated heroes in some kind of Lone Ranger struggle with the temptations of Satan. They often gathered in small groups—currently described as the apotactic movement—for fellowship, prayer, support, and discernment. Our popular patriarchal rendition of history scarcely does justice to this less heroic, but deeply incarnational, way of being.

We get a glimpse of this more communal approach in these words of Panikkar, in his further elaboration of the monastic archetype. The archetype being described by Panikkar is none other than the radiant face of God made incarnationally visible on earth (sometimes referred to as the *Sequela Christi*). What is most revolutionary in his insights is the move away from the heroic individualism so cherished in patriarchal history to the communally sustained personhood so central to incarnational Christianity. Panikkar writes:

> The principal of simplicity is at work here in a peculiar way. It entails getting rid of the complexity of the individual in favour of the simplicity of the person. An individual is a closed system. Its boundaries are clear-cut. The mine and the thine cannot be mixed. A person is an open system. Its limits depend only on the power of the center. Each person is an expanding universe. You need not keep anything for yourself because the real self is not a private substance of your own. (Panikkar 1982, 71)

Here we reach depths of understanding almost incomprehensible to the prevailing anthropology of the contemporary world, which views each person is a self-contained, self-sufficient, individualized organism. This is an Aristotelian legacy that is extensively taken for granted and is adopted right across the sciences from anthropology to religion, from politics to educational theory. For Aristotle, a person is defined by the ability to be self-sufficient as an autonomous, separate, rational individual, superior to all other creatures on earth. This was the view of human personhood adopted at the church councils of Nicea and Chalcedon, and it underpins contemporary educational programs in virtually every nation on earth.

We assume this to be an understanding of great age, indeed divinely bestowed on the human race. And we also assume that Jesus appropriated and endorsed this view of human personhood. In fact it is little more than twenty-five-hundred years old (bearing in mind that humanity has inhabited the earth for an estimated seven million years). For most of our time as earthlings we espoused a very different self-understanding, reappropriated in recent decades with the catchy phrase: *I am at all times the sum of my relationships, and that is what defines (or confers) my identity.* In a word, I take my identity not from my individual inflated status but from the web of relationships in which I am always embedded.

Panikkar's distinction between the individual (as closed) and the person (as an open system) is not mere semantics. It is of paramount importance for his understanding of the monastic archetype and its application to the vowed life down through the centuries. Controversially, what is being described is our interdependence with the entire web of cosmic and planetary life and not merely relationships among humans themselves. Our parents are merely the co-creative channels through which we are formed from the stuff of the universe. Our survival and growth are determined throughout our lifespan by how we appropriate and negotiate the web of relationships to which we intimately belong. Moreover, this new anthropological understanding claims that each one of us is not so much an entity as *an unfolding process* (a wave rather than a particle, in terms of quantum physics). And that is the foundational meaning of human existence that Panik-kar seeks to integrate into the monastic archetype.

Lest the reader feel that I have drifted into the realm of anthro-pological fantasy, I now want to introduce the Christian story and its central myth on the notion of *incarnation*. For Christians, the historical Jesus exemplifies and models anew how we are called to ground our humanity. Jesus embodied our human nature not along the lines of Aristotelian individualism (a long-held but erroneous view of the Christian churches), but according to the relational values in-dicated earlier. I have explained this in greater detail in another work (O'Murchu 2011, 42–55) and will not repeat the argument here.

The monastic archetype now takes on global and transpersonal significance (in fact, all archetypes do). It is not merely about humans and their mutual interactions. It relates to all the other creatures who share the web of life with us in our unfolding as planetary beings and cosmic creatures. This is the complex mystery being held and embodied in all attempts at monastic/vowed living. It predates the institutional expressions of the vowed life by many thousands of years and is further illuminated in subsequent chapters of this book. In the next chapter I elucidate the Christian articulation of this ideal, encapsulated in what the Gospels describe as the kingdom of God.

A Critique of the Prevailing Paradigm

My central contention in this chapter is that we tend to judge the vowed life by its institutional structures and the various legalities required to keep the institution functioning. We adopt a spiritualized gloss, extensively assumed to be of authentic divine origin. Central to that spirituality is the patriarchal hero, the divine warrior, expected to sacrifice all to build divine imperialism on earth.

This is not an authentic Christian paradigm, although it is widely assumed to be so. It carries many patriarchal projections that need to be reexamined and in several cases discarded. These include:

- an excessive preoccupation with rational and logical clarity, adopting hierarchical ordering protected by the force of law
- a God image, heavily infiltrated with imperial divine power, a God to be passively obeyed, even to the point of death

- Jesus, imaged as the sacrificial victim to take away human sin, requiring the ardent Christian to embrace suffering and sacrifice as primary means to obtain salvation
- a dualistic worldview of a corrupt sinful earth from which all must seek escape to redemption in a life beyond; monks and nuns are the ones who have mastered the escape routes
- because the world is so corrupt, we need within it sacred enclaves where people can work out the best means to obtain salvation, the monastery being a perennial example
- a Jansenistic type of spirituality, heavily based on atonement theory, requiring the ardent Christian (read *monk* or *nun*) to be willing to embrace suffering, even to the point of death, to procure salvation. From this arises the conviction that suffering for the sake of suffering is good and holy
- since the church alone has a monopoly on salvation (outside the church there is no salvation), then women and men Religious must be unambiguously affiliated with the church, having a special allegiance to the clergy and hierarchy
- a confusing ambiguity around the sacredness of God's creation, rationalized through the ambivalent language of *eschatology*, so preoccupied with the next life that mature adult responsibility for our earthly status was often neglected

Embracing a New Paradigm with Parabolic Creativity

It is the shift from excessive rationality and undue reliance on law that marks the new paradigm, which relies a great deal more on intuition, creative imagination, prophetic narrative, and mystical expansiveness. Moreover, a marked shift in worldview underpins many other novel features outlined above. No longer is it deemed responsible or even ethical to espouse the language of fleeing or abandoning the earth. It is becoming increasingly clear that it is this kind of thinking has led to many of the major ecological and environmental problems that bedevil humanity today. The monastic archetype, in its ancient depth and in its revamped twenty-first-century articulation, encounters God's creation with warmth and trust, not with denial or abandonment.

Consequently, both the spirituality and theology undergirding this new paradigm belong to a genre that seeks to transcend all dualistic splitting and to embrace a more integrated vision congenial to gospel evangelization in the context of the twenty-first century. That wisdom will not belong exclusively to the spiritual or theological realms. It will be a multidisciplinary mode of discernment that embraces the new skills and learnings necessary to engage the complex social and political landscape of our time. Those skills will be reviewed in Chapter 12.

In addition, the enveloping spirituality will be integral rather than dualistic. It will focus on the celebration of commonalities rather than the juxtaposition of differences. It will seek to transcend the long-establish distinction between the monastic and the apostolic and to undo the dualistic split between contemplation and action. The monastic archetype seeks to outgrow all that divides, challenging us to recreate anew the oneness—the at-one-ness—that heals what for too long has divided humans among themselves and alienated us from the living earth.

The refounding of Religious Life, being explored in this book, is not, therefore, a renewal process or task of revitalization exclusive to Religious. In a world of growing interconnectedness we cannot deal with any one phenomenon in isolation. Religious Life is not some divinely bestowed gift for the select few (the "consecrated" life); that understanding belongs to the old paradigm. In the new understanding—reawakening the archetype—the vowed life must be revisioned so that we see it unfolding, interdependently interwoven with all the other spiritual callings of our age. And that new spiritual horizon includes the whole creation in its planetary and cosmic dimensions.

Confronted with this enlarged vision, Christians fear a loss of true identity, a relativism that dilutes its unique core. It seems to me that it is not uniqueness that is under threat but the allurement of patriarchal power. As I have indicated in previous works (O'Murchu 2010; 2011), Christians were rarely as clear about their uniqueness as they are today. Reclaiming the monastic archetype—"Monasticism isn't a container, it is an energy" (Emanuela Bargelini)—invites us to a fresh reappropriation of the role of God's Spirit energizing every movement of the creation we inhabit. It also leads us to new christological horizons, casting in fresh relief the ancient monastic ideal of the *Sequela Christi*.

This following of Christ has been the inspiring light for every new Religious foundation in history. And it remains foundational to all our future endeavors. However, its meaning has shifted significantly in the closing decades of the twentieth century as a fresh paradigm gives shape to a new face for our faith in Christ. How we interweave the monastic archetype with Christian discipleship for the twenty-first century is the subject of our next chapter.

૭

Study Questions

1. How have you experienced Religious Life as being in the triune process of orientation-disorientation-reorientation?

2. Are you seeing Religious Life today as shifting from rational, logical, and linear to imaginative, intuitive and systematically complex?

3. What new horizons does this chapter open up for the meaning of Religious Life today?

Chapter 3

Parable and Paradigm: The Christian Context

Jesus' strategy was based on an egalitarian shar-
ing of spiritual and material power at the most
grassroots level. . . . Here, I think, is the heart of
the original Jesus movement.
—JOHN DOMINIC CROSSAN

It is no longer a case of converting old build-
ings into a new kind of work. It is a case now
of knowing what part of the reign of God we
are in the process of creating, with or without
buildings. And then each of us must be about
creating it wherever we are.
—JOAN D. CHITTISTER

For much of Christian history Religious Life has been described as
the *Sequela Christi* (the following of Christ). As indicated in the
opening chapter, the Christ we have been trying to follow has often
been a projection of a narrow anthropocentrism (as if only humans
mattered), adorned with many of the accolades of imperial power.
Consequently, the underlying archetype was that of the *individualized hero*, preoccupied with conquering the power of sin and evil to
procure personal salvation in a world beyond.

This is a very different set of aspirations from the archetypal
horizon described in Chapter 2 above. In fact, it is the distortion
or corruption of an archetype rather than its alternative. It isolates
humans, particularly the individual, in a way that seriously jeopar-
dizes incarnational wholeness. It juxtaposes humans with our organic
earthly foundation in a dualistic split that leaves both humanity and
the earth impoverished. More serious still, it displaces our rootedness
in Christian faith, adopting as a primary focus the colonial residue

of Constantine rather than the authentic parabolic vision of gospel liberation.

From the Gospels we inherit a paradigm that Christendom has not fully honored and rarely has embraced authentically. The new paradigm I seek to unveil in the present work is in many ways quite ancient. It is the disturbing prophetic vision to which Jesus committed his entire life, culminating in his untimely death on a cross. To the ground of that radical vision we now turn our attention.

The Monastic Archetype and the New Reign of God

The foundational paradigm of our faith, with its distinctive parabolic flavor, was subverted and compromised even before the Gospels themselves came to be written. The Synoptic Gospels of Mark, Matthew, and Luke point to a central feature of Christian faith, named in the Gospels as the *kingdom of God*. Certainly from the mid-twentieth century onward, scripture scholars considered the vision of the kingdom to be the central focus for the life witness and ministry of the historical Jesus. "Seek first the kingdom of God and its justice" (Matt 6:33) has been reclaimed as possibly the single most important assertion of gospel wisdom. For those seeking authentic Christian discipleship in our time, it must remain our perennial guide.

Many volumes have been written on the notion of the kingdom of God, and while scholars exhibit a strong consensus on its primary significance for the historical Jesus, and its iconic importance for authentic Christian faith, there is still quite a degree of disparity on what precisely it means. In fact, it is becoming increasingly clear that we will never reach a uniform understanding and that the challenge facing Christians today—as people *with* the book—is to learn the discerning skills for the unceasing task of engaging the kingdom anew in every age and culture.

As for the teaching authority of the church, the kingdom continues to be an issue that engenders fear and apprehension in the face of which the official teaching tends to spiritualize the kingdom as

- an inner personal disposition (the kingdom *within*),
- fulfillment to be realized in a life hereafter (sometimes described as the *eschatological*), or
- recreating God's reign on earth in and through the *church*.

On this latter understanding more progressive scripture scholars and theologians consider the church to be the primary but not exclusive

embodiment of the kingdom, whereas more traditional and funda-
mentalist Christians claim that the kingdom can be established only in
and through the church. In the case of Religious Life, it seems to me,
allegiance to the church has camouflaged, diminished, and confused
our fidelity to the new reign of God; this problematic relationship has
been particularly deleterious for the countercultural witness of male
clerical Religious.

Although *Gaudium et Spes (The Pastoral Constitution on the
Church in the Modern World)* of Vatican II asserts that the kingdom
is greater than the church and that the church must always render
accountability to the kingdom (nos. 39, 45), certainly the Catholic
Church still retains ambiguity and a confused set of understandings
on this matter of central importance. As Hans Küng and others have
pointed out, this is the paradigm shift characterized in the vision of
Vatican II, one that has been poorly appropriated and discerned by
church authorities throughout the intervening years.

There is an added complexity in our time, but also a parabolic horizon with enormous significance for the prophetic vision of the vowed
life, namely, the fresh postcolonial understanding of what the Gospels
name as the *kingdom of God*, translated from the Greek *basileia tou
theou*. Various attempts have been made to recapture what the vision
of the kingdom would be like through the medium of the original
Aramaic. One version, which I adopt in previous works (O'Murchu
2011; 2014) and wish to employ throughout this book, is that of the
Companionship of Empowerment.

This term seems to provide a more reliable aperture for how the
original hearers heard Jesus promoting a radically new empowering
vision, not aimed merely to reform patriarchal structures, whether
understood in Jewish or Roman terms, but to awaken anew a *communal sense of empowerment* from the ground up, exemplified in
the parabolic wisdom of the subversive and healing stories of the
Gospels. Many of the parables were narrated in the rural context of
first-century Galilee, and many describe the dysfunctional relationship to the land, usurped and exploited by Roman invasion. Here we
glean something of the earthly dimension of the monastic archetype
described in Chapter 2 above.

What the Gospels do not exemplify well is the earthy, embodied
affiliation to land that Jesus would have inherited from his Jewish context. In the covenant of the Hebrew scriptures the land is God's great
gift to the people. And the Jubilee regulations (Lev 25:1–13; Exod
23:10–11; Deut 15:1–6), whereby major debts were wiped out every
seventh year (at least in theory), were not just about the alleviation of

poverty, but a requirement that the people could retain a meaningful relationship with the land.

The point I wish to highlight here is that the vision of the new dispensation, renamed the *Companionship of Empowerment*, is not just a novel paradigm for human liberation and empowerment. It also carries substantial earthly, planetary, and cosmic implications. This is vividly illustrated in the parable of the late-night visitor seeking food for an unexpected guest (Lk 11:5–8).

Unfortunately, Luke allegorizes this parable, using it as a rationale for persistent prayer. In its foundational meaning the parable is about hospitality, with a strong ecological undercurrent. In the Palestine of Jesus's time people often preferred to travel after dark in order to avoid the heat, and it was not uncommon for visitors to arrive unannounced. No matter what time of day or night a visitor arrives, the Jewish norms of hospitality require that the host attends to the person's needs (Gen 18:1–8; Heb 13:2). There is no question of refusing. For a host to be unable to offer hospitality to a guest would be shameful; more important, it would bring shame not only on the host but on *the entire village*. A guest is guest of the community, not just of the individual host, and to comply with the cultural (and religious) expectations, a guest must leave the village with a good feeling about the hospitality offered not only by individuals but by the village-as-community.

Here we encounter a prototype of the global interconnectedness invoked in our time. The person in isolation is a kind of aberration; everybody belongs to a family, and each family belongs to a village (in contemporary ecology, a *bioregion*), and each bioregion is sustained and advances through the interconnectedness of the planet, which is itself held in the embrace of the universe or cosmos. Walter Brueggemann claims that for the Jewish Torah, the "neighborhood" is the most elemental unit of social meaning, the nexus of liberating and empowering relationships (Brueggemann 2014, 142; see also 129, 146, 162).

Hidden within the Gospels is a cosmic/planetary spirituality, which, it seems to me, is best rediscovered and reclaimed through a fresh appropriation of the kingdom of God as the Companionship of Empowerment. The new companionship is the global worldview of the historical Jesus. Jesus serves as the first disciple for a universal, cosmic, planetary truth that is greater than the individual Jesus, embracing an enduring context out of which the historical Jesus developed and appropriated a particular historical identity. The Companionship of Empowerment is primarily about God's reign in creation; that is,

God's radical, grace-filled presence in the whole universe. In the life and ministry of the historical Jesus it assumes a more definitive expression, which is itself an articulation of the divine incarnational radiance in each and every human who has ever lived on earth.

This, I suggest, is the more authentic foundation for how we are called to understand and appropriate afresh the *Sequela Christi* in the context of the twenty-first century. It marks a radical departure from the personal call to follow a heroic, individual Jesus in order to procure individual salvation in a world beyond. It embraces an understanding of discipleship largely unknown for much of Christendom, when the archetype was that of heroic individual purification rather than transpersonal transformation[1]—in a deeper engagement with God's creation and not by escaping from it. In archetypal terms the spiritual, theological, psychological, and anthropological growth of the human person is only possible within an ethical and aesthetical value system deeply interconnected with the planetary and cosmic web of life. This, I also believe, is the often unarticulated aspiration of the monastic archetype in both its ancient expressions and in its contemporary aspirations.

Shifting Allegiance

From earliest times Christian Religious Life was associated with the church, and for much of its history was assumed to be an integral dimension of the church. As indicated in subsequent chapters, this is a kind of utopian vision, with several misleading elements. The bedrock tradition of Religious Life (reviewed in Chapter 4) highlights a countercultural dimension to the vowed life, posing several challenges not merely of an ecclesiastical nature but to Christian faith as a whole, as well as to the secular culture of each and every age.

As we move into the refounding challenges of the twenty-first century, perhaps the most formidable task facing us is a Christian one rather than anything to do with the Catholic Church. What is it that

---

[1] The critical issue here is our understanding of human personhood, long influenced by the Aristotelian emphasis on the robust, ascetical individual separated from the natural world and perched over against it with rational superiority. The alternative view of personhood embraced by modern anthropology is often captured in this statement: "I am at all times the sum of my relationships, and that is what defines my identity." I believe that it is this latter statement that represents the humanity embraced by Jesus in his day, by many of the great mystics, by ancient and contemporary First Nations' peoples, and the only authentic mode of being human that can be considered congruent for Religious in the twenty-first century. Once again, paradigm and parable come into play.

we seek first? What is our archetypal inspiration? And what quality of discernment do we need to embrace if we are to prioritize what is central to our life witness and mission? As I indicate frequently throughout this book, history seems to indicate that Religious Life is potentially a powerful cultural prophetic movement, with all God's people—Religious or otherwise—as the subjects of our engagement. The gospel blueprint of the Companionship of Empowerment stretches horizons far beyond creed, denomination, or ethnicity. It incorporates an inclusivity that is difficult to honor while we remain hidebound by patriarchal, ecclesiastical canonicity. There is much to suggest that Religious Life should never have been reduced to that narrow denominational enclave.

Nor should we have reduced the vowed life to the ascetical type of spirituality highlighting *fuga mundi* (flee the world) as a prerequisite for attaining eschatological salvation for our individual souls in a world beyond. Throughout the post–Vatican II period all church documents and several devotional commentaries have continued to highlight the eschatological significance of Religious Life (see *Vita Consecrata*, nos. 23–28). What precisely is being stated is far from clear, while both the biblical and theological complexities of Christian eschatology are rarely if ever evoked.

Frequently, the *eschatological dimension* carries a yearning for the old idea of the *fuga mundi,* suggesting that the true home for all humans is in a heaven beyond this transitory earthly abode, and that Religious are meant to embody the paradoxical identity of being in the world but not of it. This often leads to overly spiritualizing the notion of the kingdom of God, identifying the kingdom primarily with the afterlife in a distant heaven (precisely the rendering in *Vita Consecrata*, no. 27). Some commentators, adopting a more incarnational, earth-centered spirituality, describe the eschatological as bearing witness to those values that transcend false attachments and espouse the values that endure eternally. Because of the inherited anti-creation and unincarnational baggage associated with the term, I doubt if *the eschatological* is a helpful concept to hold on to. I suggest its meaning—if it still has some—is better subsumed in the notions of *liminality* and the *prophetic,* as developed subsequently in this book.

In archetypal terms the *Sequela Christi* is not, and was never meant to be, an abandonment of God's creation in exclusive loyalty to a patriarchal divine hero. Rather it is about *being seized by a mystical allurement to co-create with our creative God in the incarnational renewal of God's creation.* Christian discipleship is no longer understood (if indeed it ever should have been) as an individual pursuit of salvation beyond, apart from, and irrespective of every other human being. Nor is such discipleship about humans first and foremost. Authentic incarnational human becoming cannot be realized apart from a growth-inducing environment—social, ecological, political, economic—in which we are all called to be co-creators with our co-creative God. It is to this truth that Religious should be bearing exemplary witness.

Central to this new understanding of discipleship—as already indi-cated—is a fresh reappropriation of the kingdom of God, renamed the Companionship of Empowerment. Two words capture the challenge before us: *empowerment* and *companionship*. The former denotes sharing power with rather than exerting power over. It articulates a desire to transcend all hierarchical structures in favor of a new egali-tarian mutuality, denoted by the word *companionship*. Equality and respect for diversity are central to this aspiration.

The shift is best assessed in two simple but radically different images, namely, the *triangle* and the *circle*. The triangle signifies the power descending downward in a linear line from those with the power to those deprived of it. No matter how well intended, this strategy inevi-tably breeds an unhealthy co-dependency. In the circle image, power is mediate from the center outward, a process best described as one of animation or empowerment. Mutuality—embracing the diversity of gifts and talents, skills and strategies—is the goal of this endeavor.

Once again, I need to highlight the communal consciousness being invoked here. It is not merely about human beings and some new way of relating more intimately among ourselves. It includes all the other creatures who share with us the organic web of life, with planet earth and the universe at large viewed not as material objects but subjec-tive organisms with which we relate interdependently. In theological terms the God inviting us to this new relationality is none other than the trinitarian God of Christian faith—understood, however, not in the metaphysical categories of the fourth and fifth centuries of the Christian era but as a foundational assertion of God's own nature as the ultimate source and energy for all forms of interrelating, personal and planetary alike.[2]

Therefore, when we describe the Religious Life vocation as a mys-tical type of allurement—what Sandra Schneiders (2013) calls the "God quest"—we are describing something vastly different from the

---

[2] Catherine La Cugna (1991) is often regarded as a pioneering advocate for this new relational understanding of the Trinity. Other notable advocates include John D. Zizioulas (2004) and Patricia A. Fox (2001).

traditional notion of an ascetical, individual pursuit. The foundational
orientation, in terms of the archetype, is a communal endeavor committed to recreating heaven on earth. In that process person and planet
weave into one another in a type of mystical symbiosis that matures
into the Companionship of Empowerment, for which the historical
Jesus serves as an eminent disciple. All the rest of us—whether vowed
or not—are called into incarnational co-discipleship for the sake of
that same new reign of God that awaits not our ascetical purification
for a life beyond but our wholehearted creative collaboration in recreating heaven on earth.

The challenge of this endeavor, in its widest possible application, is
captured by Beverly Lanzetta in these inspiring words:

> I am certain that the monastic call is intrinsic to all people and
> is not confined to religious organizations or orders. It is a free
> call within the self, one that is born with us into the world
> and to which we owe allegiance. The years I spent avoiding
> the monk within, too busy with family and work, and perhaps
> afraid that it would make me more different or too pious, were
> full of empty concerns. Because there is nothing more natural
> than to affirm one's monastic nature, living in God's time, seek-
> ing transformation into the heart of reality, and loving creation
> with one's whole soul.
>
> The monastic archetype will take new forms during this cen-
> tury and those to come. The Great Vocation will evolve, as the
> human heart grows closer to the divine heart. (Lanzetta 2014,
> 136)

Monastic researcher Douglas Christie captures a similar sense of
the need to relocate the Religious Life vocation (which he calls "the
contemplative call") in the heart of God's creation when he writes:

> The aim of contemplative living, in its wider application, is to
> address the fragmentation and alienation that haunts existence
> at the deepest possible level and, through sustained practice,
> come to realize a different, more integrated way of being in the
> world. . . . The contemplative's daily attentiveness, alertness, and
> eagerness of the senses turned outwards, help rescue the world
> from oblivion, even as the contemplative is saved by the simple
> beauty of the world, by recognition that the fabric is whole and
> we are woven deeply into it. (Christie 2013, 36, 56)

This is the paradigmatic parable of the vowed life, ever old and ever new. Today, Religious Life is undergoing a period of decline and disintegration, most obvious in the West but likely to become universal in the next few decades. History assures us beyond all semblance of doubt that it is not the end of the vowed life. Already amid the dying embers new sparks are igniting. And perhaps most important of all, new wisdom illuminates our horizon.

It is that new wisdom that I seek to share in the present work. Undoubtedly, some readers will feel uneasy about my historical presuppositions and the attention I give to features often ignored by conventional historians (for example, the virgins in the early church). Others are likely to dismiss my pursuit of archetypes as a misguided New Age meandering. Of course, there is security in what we have known and cherished for so long and in explanations that have stood the test of time. But ours is a new time. Ours is a Calvary experience pointing us toward resurrection.

All the Gospels inform us that the original experience of resurrection took place in a dark dawn amid great fear and trembling. The official guardians of truth—the Twelve—all had fled in fear. Remaining was a petrified group of liminal women who remembered his words (Lk 24:8). Despite the devastating despair of the moment, these women stood their ground and made the breakthrough possible. Far beyond the empty tomb they followed him to Galilee to encounter the Risen One (Matt 28:7).

Why Galilee? Because that is where Jesus first proclaimed the Companionship of Empowerment. That is where the archetypal foundations were laid, and that is where we too will rediscover them in the twenty-first century. The pathway becomes clearer from there on.

Enter the Prophetic

Parabolic speech broaches an alternative consciousness, often a whole new way of perceiving and understanding. And to one degree or another, it is always a subversive kind of speech, sometimes publicly declaring the former ways of understanding to be archaic and irrelevant, proffering instead new models, threatening and usually unacceptable to the conventional culture. All the parable stories in the Gospels invoke the power of imagination. In seeking to recreate hope and empowerment, Jesus calls on all disciples to use imagination and adopt a creative spirit in conjuring alternative ways of being to the time-honored but staid institutions of the dominant culture.

In scriptural terms this alternative consciousness is often termed the *prophetic*. It has been noted that there is no obvious parallel in the New Testament to the prophetic vision in the Hebrew scriptures. The usual explanation suggests that we no longer need the prophetic witness since its vision is now fulfilled in the historical Jesus. Alternatively, we can view the gospel parables as the continuation of Old Testament prophecy. Here I am following scholars such as Abraham Heschel (1969), Walter Brueggemann (1978; 1986; 2014), and Michael Crosby (2004). All three highlight the change in language itself, away from rational discourse toward poetic, subversive speech. In the prophetic wisdom a different awakening of the creative imagination is being called forth, as conventional patriarchal wisdom is subjected to a penetrating critique.

For Walter Brueggemann (1978; 1986; 2014) the perennial challenge of prophetic witness is to *criticize in order to energize*. Brueggemann claims that the leading prophets of the Hebrew scriptures articulate a damning critique of the prevailing patriarchal ideology, epitomized in the king and delegated thereafter through a linear line of hierarchical structures. The voice of the prophet is that of an alternative consciousness seeking to replace the linear with the lateral, for the liberation and empowerment of the millions of people disempowered and disenfranchised. The prophets become the voice for the voiceless, the champions for new freedom and fresh hope.[3]

---

[3] Much of the literature on Religious Life throughout the post–Vatican II era advocates a prophetic vision, with the outstanding prophets of the Hebrew scriptures as models. Much of this literature tends to glamorize the notion of the prophetic, failing to point out the complexities of Old Testament prophecy outlined by scholars such as Michael Walzer. Walzer claims that the challenging rhetoric of the prophets is not targeted on empowering the marginalized of society or of promoting political and social reform; rather, it invests heavily in the hope of God's sovereign intervention to bring about real change: "The prophets became the representatives of God in the world, with no practical tasks except criticism. . . . No prophet, once prophecy had emerged from the court into the streets, showed any interest in the actual politics of reform" (Walzer 2012, 87–88). Certainly, the Old Testament prophets desired justice and liberation, but it seems that they will be delivered more as a divine prerogative than anything the people can do—individually or communally—to bring them about. In the present work, and in earlier writings (O'Murchu 1991, 52ff.), I adopt the research of Abraham Heschel (1969) and that of Walter Brueggemann (1978; 1986; 2014), who highlight a quality of prophetic vision that engenders subversive hope, evoking not merely a divinely delivered better future, but a wake-up call to embrace the work of justice in a co-creative partnership with the God who seeks to make all things new. Here the emphasis is much more on incarnational involvement with God ("I call you friends, not merely servants"—Jn 15:15), rather than passive reliance on divine initiative.

And there is another subtle but significant shift noted by former Anglican Bishop John Davies (1983), who writes that with the coming of Christ, the prophetic focus shifts from the *individual* to the *community*. Apart from John the Baptist we have no outstanding prophetic voice in the Gospels, but we have the penetrating criticism seeking to energize anew. It is articulated primarily in the parables, through the newly framed community-based empowerment that is being evoked in the new gospel companionship.

I often invoke the notion of the prophetic in the pages of this book to denote the creative alternative consciousness seeking to transform

- divinely mandated imperialism toward incarnational egalitarianism (see also O'Murchu 2014);
- patriarchal, top-down power in the direction of bottom-up communal empowerment, and rigid institutions in the direction of fluid, flexible networks;
- the use of creative imagination above and beyond the monopoly of rational discourse;
- human need, read primarily from the base of the voiceless and powerless rather than from the perspective of those who dictate and control power;
- empowering justice above and beyond patronizing charity;
- discerning truth not merely through wisdom from on high but through dialogue involving a wide range of voices, human and non-human alike, aptly named by Brueggemann (2014, 157ff.) as the movement from despair to realism.

The true boldness of the prophetic endeavor is expressed in this courageous statement of the Cistercian monk Thomas Merton:

> One of the central issues in the prophetic life is that a person rocks the boat, not by telling slaves to be free, but by telling people who *think* they are free that they're slaves. That's an unacceptable message. There's nothing new about telling the blacks that they're having a rough time. The prophetic thing is to tell white people that they need the blacks to be free so *they'll be liberated themselves*. Few people say this. (Merton 1992, 133)

The dominant culture, whether in politics, economics, social policy, or religion, not merely resists the prophetic voice but frequently seeks to eradicate and suppress it. In formal religions the prophetic often morphs into the mystical wing, where unfortunately it tends to lose its more overt political and social potential for transformation. We note in passing that the prophetic is unlikely to plumb the depths of liberation and empowerment without the contemplative nourishment of the mystic as indicated vividly in the life of the Cistercian monk Thomas Merton.

Nor must we ever forget that the call to be prophetic is a gifted grace, never given for our own sanctity or salvation but always for the benefit of mission—not merely to the church but to God's entire creation. Abraham Heschel states it quite succinctly: "In contrast, prophetic inspiration is for the sake, for the benefit, of a third party. It is not a private affair between prophet and God; its purpose is the illumination of the people rather than the illumination of the prophet" (Heschel 1969, 202).

I will return to the notion of the prophetic in Chapter 7 when I explore the concept of liminality, providing freshly empowering insight for the refounding of the vowed life in the twenty-first century. For the moment I simply want to highlight that the dynamic of prophetic witness, long associated with outstanding (male) individuals, becomes an integral dimension of the communal empowering vision of the New Testament, described in this book as the Companionship of Empowerment. *The emphasis has shifted from individual heroic holiness to empowering communal wholeness.* In turn, this requires a change of emphasis on discernment and how we strive to attend to what the Spirit of God is awakening in the transformative forces at work in our age.

Discernment: Our Primary Task

In the opening chapter I introduced the notion of *discernment,* a recurring theme throughout this book. I employ the concept in its basic biblical meaning of seeking to understand what the Holy Spirit is trying to awaken in our heart and where the Spirit wishes to lead us. Christian discernment tends to be understood in individual and personal terms, whereby one seeks to ascertain what God is asking in one or another life situation and how best to respond to God's initiative. A spirit of prayer and receptivity to divine urging are considered primary dispositions. A process of discernment related to major life changes usually involves periods of desolation and consolation—what Barbara Fiand (1996) describes as a wrestling with God—leading to a growing sense of clarity and trust in God, even though a final resolution may never be fully realized.

In the present work my primary focus is *communal/group discernment,* which involves a great deal more than a collectivity of individuals all versed in the skills and wisdom of personal discernment. As with all group processes we need to remember the principle: *the whole is greater than the sum of the parts.* Desirable though it is for the individual participants to be acquainted with the processes of discernment, and open and receptive to the surprises of the Holy Spirit of God, the communal endeavor is a great deal more complex and requires even greater trust in providence. It also needs to draw on a wider canvas of insight, experience, dialogue, and story. To that end the historical reflections in the subsequent chapters of this book can contribute significantly to a more informed outcome.

My primary focus, therefore, is communal rather than individual discernment. From a Christian perspective I wish to honor the primacy of "seek first the Companionship of Empowerment" (cf. Matt 6:33). The communal stretch in this endeavor involves a great deal more than humans. It has organic, planetary, and even cosmic dimensions to it. It is both systemic and evolutionary; the former requires at least some awareness of the complex interrelatedness of our daily interactions, not merely as individuals, but also as relational beings, always operating within, and influenced by, a range of cultural systems (see Capra and Luisi 2014). We live and relate within a dynamic evolutionary universe in which change is normative for growth and development (Delio 2013; 2014). These various complex factors need to be included in our discerning reflection and operative processes; excluding any one is likely to undermine our faith in the trinitarian God, whose relational blueprint is mediated in our Christian experience through the gospel notion of the Companionship of Empowerment.

Former Jesuit priest Louis M. Savary has attempted a reformulation of the Ignatian wisdom of discernment, adopting insights from the vision of priest-paleontologist Teilhard de Chardin. He names some of the key ingredients necessary for the communal discernment I am adopting throughout this book. Savary introduces his suggested guidelines with this observation:

> In the original spiritual exercises, Ignatius had no need to establish basic principles foundational to his own thought and spirituality, for his theological assumptions were much the same as those shared by almost everyone in Christian Europe at the time. These usually included a preoccupation with sin, temptations, the devil, death, fear of hell, doing penance, the agonies of Christ, and one's individual salvation. However, the same is

not true today. We are in a very different place, theologically, ecologically, and especially in spirituality. (Savary 2012, 14)

In a word, we are now dealing with a different paradigm, one required by the new evolutionary moment in which we find ourselves. Like many major evolutionary shifts, advancement tends to involve recapitulation. Theologian and evolutionary scholar John Haught (2010; 2015) describes the process of life being pushed from the past and lured from the future. Contrary to the conventional Darwinian approach, which sees the fixed past as the solid ground upon which we always reconstruct, Haught suggests that there is a great deal more involved. The drive from the past is merely one aspect, and probably not the major part, of the process. The *lure of the future*, the pull from beyond, is the critical dynamic, as the Holy Spirit weaves the web of new directions and novel possibilities. These may be totally new but often involve a reworking of deep ancient wisdom, as with my proposed renaming of the kingdom as the Companionship of Empowerment.

I have synthesized Louis Savary's research into nine key points, outlined below. These provide a very a useful set of guidelines for the communal discernment envisaged throughout this book, incorporating the personal and interpersonal as well as the systemic and wider global considerations.

- The discoveries of modern science must form an important foundation of any contemporary spirituality if it is to be true, relevant, and inspiring.
- Evolution is happening continually on every level of being—and it has a direction.
- The law of attraction—connection—complexity—consciousness gives evolution its direction.
- The principle of self-convergence is now operating; we all live and move and have our being in the divine milieu.
- We are all called to know, love, and serve the universe with a passion.
- Evolution is based primarily on spirit, not on matter; at present, evolution is focused on the envelope of consciousness named by Teilhard as the Noosphere.
- Any true spirituality today must be a collective, inclusive spirituality.
- Today, even an individual spirituality, that is, a private and exclusive redemptive relationship between God and the individual, must include all other human beings and the rest of creation.

- An evolutionary spirituality is focused primarily on grace, not on sin. (cf. Savary 2010, 13)

Beyond the devotional context that often governed discernment in the past we enter a new landscape that transcends the boundaries of conventional faith and religion. Mainline religion has scarcely begun to catch up with the evolutionary thrust of recent decades. Religion, more than any other field of wisdom, seems to be rigidly set on holding back the evolutionary momentum of our time. Institutionalized religion, for the greater part, clings to rational, literal fact rather than parable-like wisdom. Not surprisingly, therefore, spirituality is breaking loose from mainline religion at an ever-accelerating pace (Johnson and Ord 2012).

Religious Life that clings too closely to religion and fails to discern meaning in the evolutionary breakthroughs of our time is not likely to survive the twenty-first century. But that will not be the end of the vowed life. It has survived many previous crises. On careful examination, along lines outlined in subsequent chapters, the resulting breakthrough was not based on rigid adherence to a cherished past, nor did it always abide by the guidelines of the church at a particular time in history (see especially the story of the great foundresses in Chapter 6). The breakthrough arose from a radical new option to serve God in the heart of creation, knowingly or unknowingly embracing the vision of the Companionship of Empowerment.

Discernment for Refounding

Every new breakthrough in the history of Religious Life is characterized by a creative response—and usually one that is radically new—to the signs of times, particularly to the task of addressing the pressing cultural needs. Less obvious, but equally important, is the retrieval or reclaiming of the enduring archetype, the subliminal wisdom that evokes anew our attention at the threshold of each new breakthrough. Priest-anthropologist Gerry Arbuckle captures the novel challenge in this catchy statement: "The new is elsewhere" (Arbuckle 1988, 110). I fully endorse this fidelity to the new while also trying to safeguard that which deeply underpins the tradition I am seeking to rework. My interest is not that of rigidly holding on to or clinging fiercely to the past (the usual connotation of the word *tradition*). Instead, I want to embrace the deeper meaning of *tradition* (the Latin *traditio*) that denotes the responsible and creative *passing on* of that which we love and cherish.

How is that done in a refounding context? I respond to that question in my final chapter, while here offering a preview that will clarify for the reader what the notion of *refounding* denotes as used throughout this book:

- Refounding denotes *drastic change.* It is not something we can plan or execute in a rational way. It happens to us, rather than being something that arises from our initiative. And it involves a great deal of dying and grieving, of chaos and dislocation.

- In rational terms we are never ready for refounding. There is a *timing* to refounding that is neither linear nor rational. However, as I indicate in later chapters, there are historical precedents that enhance a more discerning engagement, with the prospect of being a surprised beneficiary rather than a fearful reactionary.

- In the case of Religious Life, it is not Religious alive today who do the refounding. Refounding is a *divine prerogative.* It is God who refounds, not us. The best we can do is strive to be open to being refounded—if that is God's will for our Orders and Congregations.

- The deeper meaning of refounding is best discerned in terms of a response to current acute needs rather than fidelity to a well-established set of inherited values. Several questions arise here about *continuity* and *tradition,* questions that require sophisticated analysis and discernment in dealing with contemporary issues such as preserving First Nations' cultures or honoring religious and ecclesiastical traditions.

- Huge *personal and social dislocation* accompanies refounding, reflected in the fact that over 70 percent of all Religious Orders/Congregations ever founded have become extinct. Allegiance to a particular charism or denomination—narrowly understood—is often a major barrier.

- How refounding is connected with an original founding (charism) will be explored in subsequent chapters. *Charism* embraces the double notions of vision and tradition. There is a distinctive original flare to every charism. Over time, it becomes institutionalized, and this needs to happen if the vision is to be translated into creative action. However, the progressive institutionalization of the tradition inevitably undermines the foundational vitality of the vision, paving the way for decline and ultimately death. Refounding in its deeper meaning is not so much about revitalization of a former vision (which sometimes does happen) but rather about a new, fresh dream with a distinctive relevance for contemporary times, imbued with an inspiring impetus for the future.

As suggested earlier, Religious in the twenty-first century find themselves on a kind of paschal journey, with decline and disintegration all too apparent and no clear guidelines on what lies ahead. However, there are landmarks that at the very least will offer some semblance of hope and can serve as encouraging pointers regarding the way ahead. Most of these landmarks are historical in nature and will occupy us in the chapters that follow.

In these opening chapters I have highlighted what might be described as the nonnegotiables. I adopt the double dynamic of parable and paradigm to illustrate the inescapable reality of evolutionary change, which has an impact on all life-forms, including women and men Religious. Evolutionary growth never regresses. It can only move forward—often through quantum leaps that defy our need for rational explanation. Amid the waves of change there are enduring truths, and these tend to be encased not in legal or institutional structures but in archetypes, which themselves will require new language and cultural containers if their enduring truth is to remain relevant. For Religious that enduring truth is what I describe as the *monastic archetype.*

This foundational archetype reconnects us with the deep yearnings of the human heart for those values upon which human becoming can thrive and flourish. In gospel terms, it is the fullness of life promised to all (Jn 15:15), mediated in gospel terms through the root metaphor of our faith, namely, the kingdom of God, which I redefine as the Companionship of Empowerment. In describing this Christian grounding I highlight the planetary and cosmic dimensions without which we cannot reclaim the reawakening of the monastic archetype described in my opening chapter.

The faith horizon engaging us, therefore, needs to transcend the narrow anthropocentrism—viewing people in an arrogantly superior fashion—that has bedeviled both faith and human civilization for far too long. Humans can only reclaim an authentic incarnational presence in God's world by learning afresh our interdependent role amid all the creatures with whom we inhabit God's creation. Something of that more organic and empowering vision is inscribed in the great founding myths of the vowed life. How to reclaim them afresh and incarnate them anew is the challenge for the rest of this book.

᪈

Study Questions

1. Read the paragraph below three times, in the reflective mode of *Lectio Divina*. Read it aloud. Notice what it evokes for you.

From the Gospels we inherit a paradigm that Christendom has not fully honored and rarely has embraced authentically. The new paradigm . . . is in many ways quite ancient. It is the disturbing prophetic vision to which Jesus committed his entire life, culminating in his untimely death on a cross.

2. Write a sentence responding to this statement:

As we move into the refounding challenges of the twenty-first century, perhaps the most formidable task facing us is a Christian one rather than anything to do with the Catholic Church. What is it that we seek first? What is our archetypal inspiration? And what quality of discernment do we need to embrace if we are to prioritize what is central to our life witness and mission?

3. What new meanings do these familiar words take on in the context of the present chapter?

> *discernment*
> *prophetic*
> *evolutionary spirituality*
> *refounding*

4. What is your gut reaction to the phrase *Companionship of Empowerment?*

Conclusion to Part One

The Discerning Process

Seeking to honor priorities is always a delicate task in Christian discernment. It seems to me that the top priority is unambiguously clear: "Seek first the new companionship" (cf. Matt 6:33). Yet we know that for much of history, and from within the church itself, that priority has not been upheld or promoted. Time and again the Spirit of truth has been derailed by the false power of imperial contagion.

Central to the new companionship is the need to ensure that empowering always transcends power and posturing. It seems to me that this is an important discerning guideline for all Religious, for both our inner structures and for our various outreaches to the people of God. When we continue to honor the priority of the new companionship and keep it as the central focus of all our attempts at discernment, we stand a much better chance of upholding and fostering the incarnational flair embodied in what I describe as the monastic archetype (Chapter 2).

Combining the two—the new companionship and the foundational archetype—we are much more likely to adopt a process of discernment that is more congruent with the evolving energy of our time. As we devote more focused attention to the paschal process of birthing and dying, we stand a better chance of being clearer on when the time has come to let go, not clinging to the old for its own sake, and being much more open and transparent to the new unfoldings to which the creative Spirit is ever inviting us.

Formation in discerning wisdom, for all our members, and discerning strategies for all our communities (whether residential or intentional) seems imperative for our evolutionary future. And it must be a quality of discernment that transcends the dualistic split between sacred and secular, soul and body, matter and spirit. If we truly want to encounter and serve God, in the midst of God's creation, we need integrated approaches, with particular urgency in the process of discernment itself.

Part Two

Reclaiming Our Subverted History

The patriarchal desire to divide and conquer has had a tremendous influence on our sense of history. What I describe below as the "underside of history" is rarely documented and across the centuries has received scant attention from historians and policymakers. The imperial story of the powerful (hero) tends to dwarf the struggles and joyful achievements of the masses. Imperial truth infiltrates and distorts the dislocating truth of parable and paradigm.

The history of Religious Life is largely an imperial narrative of ascetical heroes and founders who advanced ecclesiastical might and right. The outstanding foundresses are not even mentioned in several historical monographs. Nor do we encounter the liberation and empowerment that millions of people experienced through revolutionary breakthroughs in land reform (Bendictine monks), education, healthcare, and personal and communal empowerment on several fronts.

Historically, Religious Life has prioritized the communal over the institutional, a fact that is camouflaged due to the preoccupation with ascetical heroism and fidelity to the imperial church. In this way we often miss the communal empowerment so crucial to Christian discipleship, ancient and modern.

And, perhaps most serious of all, is the negligence of creative imagination. Our history books are full of outstanding heroes who won battles and conquered lands; who forced others into subjugation and wreaked havoc on the weak and vulnerable. There is another way of reading history, highlighted in the present work, that seeks out emerging patterns following the organic trajectory of birth-death-rebirth. This, I suggest, is a far more responsible way to read history, and from a Christian viewpoint, far more empowering.

Let's move beyond the distorted legends, which may have served us well in the past, while also seeking to integrate their enduring wisdom into a historical narrative that will liberate and empower us for a new and different future. As Religious, our history is a rich reservoir, in many ways untapped, with enormous potential to co-create a more hope-filled future.

Chapter 4

Parable and Paradigm
in the History of Religious Life

Several times in Catholicism's history, waves of religious communities have burst upon the scene and flourished, only to institutionalize, rigidify, and ultimately decline, as a result of a repeated pattern of internal and external causes.

—Patricia Wittberg

Thus the old theory that traced the monastic impulse in all corners of the Empire back to an original Egyptian inspiration has proven to be a literary fiction.

—James E. Goehring

We now move into the story of Religious Life as we have known it for almost two thousand years. This is our historical narrative, the true meaning of which cannot be deciphered merely through cold fact and dominant trends. There is a subtlety to this narrative requiring another mode of discernment. We are dealing with something more akin to a *parable* story, full of surprise, breakthrough, and creative elaboration.

The historical story of Religious Orders and Congregations tends to be ensconced in books describing the history of the church. In the past many such books were written by male scholars—often priests—with a strong interest in the triumph and success of the faith as mediated by the institutional church. Allusions to Religious Life tended to be minimalized, recording contributions that enhanced the church's progress as a powerfully influential institution, often resulting in a slanted perspective and an interpretation with many disturbing features.

Most history books highlight the achievements of the great found-ers, notably, Anthony of Egypt, Pachomius, Benedict, Francis, Dominic, Ignatius, Vincent de Paul. These texts tend to prioritize those who advanced the church's progress and defended it against heresy and attack, namely, outstanding patriarchal males. Women in general, and vowed women specifically, were not meant to be visible in the church's agenda of power and control, and therefore for most of Christian history (down to the nineteenth century) women were officially "si-lenced" by monastic enclosure. Rarely, therefore, do we hear of the outstanding witness of foundresses such as Angela Merici, Mary Ward, Nano Nagle, Elizabeth Seton, Mary McKillop, and Margaret Anna Cusack. In most church history books these names are not even cited, never mind acknowledged.

The historical texts rarely if ever acknowledge that throughout Christendom women Religious made significant, even major, contribu-tions. If records had been responsibly maintained, we would see that females frequently outnumbered male Religious. The religious and pastoral impact of vowed women has been outstanding, enhancing the growth and development of the church, frequently in a manner far more profound and effective than the witness borne by male clerics. Yet the female members are characterized by their invisibility, not to mention their historical oppression. This grave injustice needs to be addressed and rectified.

The Underside of History

Church history, along with other forms of historical documentation, follows a well-established strategy to communicate its wisdom and truth. Most ancient history was written by and for the ruling classes or the winners of military campaigns, from the Gilgamesh epic of ancient Babylon to the musings of Confucius and Plato and the histories and heroic achievements documented by Herodotus and Thucydides. A careful analysis of most textbooks used in history lessons for schools around the world today clearly shows a bias for triumphalism and victors. The discerning eye clearly sees that Chapters 4, 5, and 6 herein are largely if not totally about the winners; the loser has been virtually obliterated, condemned to utter invisibility. This is what is meant by the *underside* of history. The concept was first popularized by Quaker sociologist Elise Boulding (1920–2010) in *The Underside of History: A View of Women through Time* (1976). Here we have a panoramic view, going deep into ancient time, of how women have been con-sistently marginalized and undermined by the dominant patriarchal culture. In many ways their unique giftedness has been suppressed, even to the point of invisibility. Peruvian liberation theologian Gustavo Gutiérrez expanded the historical suppression to include all those condemned to poverty (in this case, material poverty), deprived of voice and agency to outwit colonial and patriarchal domination (1983). In their tribute to another liberation theorist, philosopher Enrique Dussel, Linda Alcoff and Eduardo Mendieta (2000) unmask the complex and sinister political dynamics that generate and sustain the underside of history. In a word, it ensures that power is maintained for those addicted to it, to the point that the maintenance of such power becomes an end in itself, to the detriment of the common good which politics—and religion—is meant to serve.

The history of Religious Life also has its underside, with the undesirable outcomes noted above. Most historians don't even allude to the rich Eastern traditions of Jainism, Hinduism, and Buddhism with their several enriching parallels with Western forms (see De Dreuille 1999). Within Christianity itself, a patriarchal approach to history takes clear precedence, with a tendency to highlight the advancement of ecclesiastical domination in a linear historical outline that leaves us with a seriously distorted view. An alternative cyclic approach has received scant attention, but despite limited research and paucity of evidence, I wish to highlight its potential value for a more empowering and inclusive view of the vowed life.

Despite the fact that the cyclic approach to history seems to be a phenomenon of great age, and adopted in several ancient civilizations, it has been largely overshadowed by the rational, linear approach that came to the fore after the Enlightenment, usually dated from 1650 to 1780, also known as the Age of Reason. History prioritized rational analysis, factual statement, linear progress, male achievement, and the exaltation of the winner irrespective of the plight of the loser.

Many ancient cultures held a mythical conception of history and time, evidenced in the Indian Vedas (leading to the concept of the wheel of life in both Hinduism and Buddhism), Chinese dynastic cycles, Egyptian mythology, ancient Greek philosophy, and also discernible in the writings of the Islamic scholar Ibn Khaldun. Cyclical conceptions were maintained in the nineteenth and twentieth centuries by authors such as Arnold Toynbee, Oswald Spengler, Pitrim Sorokim, and Nikolay Danilevsky. However, it was those favoring linear/evolutionary models—Herbert Spencer, Karl Marx, and Auguste Comte—who exerted greater influence, exhibiting strong faith in secular science and in the inevitability of human progress. Still, interest in the cyclic approach continues to our own time, exhibited in works such as Peter Turchin's mathematical modeling outlined in his book *Historical Dynamics* (2003), and G. J. Whitrow's cultural overview of cyclic patterns across several millennia (Whitrow 2004).

Toward a New Historical Paradigm

The first attempt to outline a cyclic version of the history of Religious Life was undertaken by a French Jesuit, Raymond Hostie (1972), and further refined by Lawrence Cada and co-authors (Cada et al. 1979). This version proposes a cyclic pattern of recurring timespans, approximately three hundred years each, during which a dominant model evolves, expands, stabilizes, and declines. In all, six cycles have been identified, beginning with the Egyptian model around 300 CE and culminating in the current cycle, which commenced around 1800 CE:

- 300–600: *The Egyptian Monastic Model*—consisting of communal foundations in Syria and Egypt, and a more popularized diverse set of eremitical expressions, extensively documented in the writings of John Cassian (360–435).
- 600–900: *The First Benedictine Era*—marking the launch of the Benedictines and their spread across mainland Europe of the time.
- 900–1200: *The Second Benedictine Era*—documenting the Cluny-led renewal and restructuring of the Benedictine movement, the rise of the Cistercians as a further attempt to salvage the Benedictine ideal, up to the emergence of Religious Life into the wider culture of commerce and learning.
- 1200–1500, *The Mendicant Era*—describing the rise of the Franciscans, Dominicans, and Carmelites, with a range of attempts to bring the wisdom of the vowed life into the wider ecclesial and human realms.
- 1500–1800: *The Apostolic Era*—beginning with the Jesuits and followed closely by Orders of brothers and the first groups of apostolic women (for example, the Ursulines), the new Orders/ Congregations sought to engage afresh with the spiritual and cultural challenges, initially of Europe and later of China and the Americas.
- 1800– : *The Missionary Era*—in a spirit of solidarity with the missionary thrust of the church a range of new groups came into being, many initially serving local apostolic needs but quickly embracing the international missionary outreach of the nineteenth and twentieth centuries.

According to the above schema, the present missionary cycle is likely to complete its course toward the end of the twenty-first century, thus yielding pride of place to a new thrust for women and men Religious. The veracity of this prediction is borne out in the numerical decline of Religious in the Catholic Church from 1960 to 2014. The Center for Applied Research in the Apostolate (CARA) reports that there were 1,300,000 members in 1960 and 895,600 in 2014, a decline of 31 percent. Even if the decline remains stable, which is unlikely, Religious in the Catholic world will number fewer than 200,000 by the end of the twenty-first century.

To the best of my knowledge, historians of Religious Life have given scant attention to the cyclic approach. Some point to the superficial nature of the original research by the Jesuit scholar, Raymond Hostie, based exclusively on male groups and largely from a European perspective. Since Religious Life is now a global movement, not merely a European phenomenon, Hostie's research is of limited value, but it is nonetheless worthy of serious consideration. The strongest criticism comes from those who believe the model lacks rigorous research, ensuing in an outline that is too simplistic, almost to the point of being deterministic, bypassing or ignoring the more haphazard nature of history generally and the consequent inability to discern any kind of enduring or broad set of patterns.

Although I cannot offer a logical or rational response to these critical concerns, I want to support the wisdom embedded in Hostie's cyclic thesis, adopting a more interdisciplinary set of insights.

- The cyclic approach to history carries an enduring credibility over several thousands of years and across a range of cultural and religious contexts.
- Sister Patricia Wittberg (1994) provides a valuable endorsement of Hostie's approach, incorporating additional wisdom and insight from extensive sociological research.
- Rank-and-file Religious discern within the cyclic approach an intuitive wisdom, a compelling sense of truth that rational analysis fails to deliver.
- There is a consistency within the paradigm that defies rational analysis. The first one hundred years of each cycle is characterized by numerical growth and cultural impact, despite internal strain or conflict, as in the case of the early Franciscan movement in the thirteenth century, torn and divided over the ideal way to live the call to poverty. And the last one hundred years begets a sense of stalemate leading to eventual disintegration—or in the case of a minority of Religious families, a revitalization.

- In face of the impending decline, individual groups, or the move-ment at large, can do little (it seems) to halt the ultimate disinte-gration. In the eleventh century the Cistercians set out to capture afresh the pure Benedictine charism in the hope of prolonging the Benedictine influence. As we know, the revival was short lived, despite the fact the both the Benedictines and Cistercians survived the demise of the late eleventh century. Most intriguing of all is the emergence in the late eighteenth century; according to a census taken in Europe around 1775, there were 400,000 Religious inhabiting the continent, and on the surface the mem-bers seemed to be living holy and dedicated lives. Yet, when another census was taken in 1805 in the aftermath of the French Revolution, it numbered only 40,000 Religious throughout the entire continent, a decline of 90 percent, coinciding accurately with the end of a three hundred year cycle.[1]
- The Holy Spirit is the catalytic agent within this cyclic unfolding of the vowed life. Not that the Spirit can be boxed into a three hundred year configuration, but rather that the Spirit, who for-ever draws order from chaos, is the one who befriends Religious Life through both its growth and decline, forever recreating new possibilities for renewal and refounding for those ready to em-brace this dangerously promising adventure.
- What is under review is similar to the organic trajectory that characterizes all life-forms, a dynamic movement flowing through a pattern of growth, stabilization (maturity), decline, and death. The viability of life at every level depends on this process. Why should Religious Life be an exception? Might it not be our addiction to immortality (a feature of patriarchal domination) that prevents us from seeing the deeper truth and engaging more wisely with it?

The cyclic approach offers courageous hope in the sense that it indicates that Religious Life will prevail, come what may. It seems to

---

[1] Critics are quick to point out that this example was triggered by an external event, the French Revolution. I suspect the decline would have happened anyway, since most Religious in Europe were influenced by the remnants of a Jansenistic spirituality, taking their attention away from God's world—and the building up of God's kingdom on earth—and preoccupied with their internal religious comfort (see Rapley 2011, 213ff.). Here we detect a work of divine providence difficult to explain, because it comes dangerously close to determinism.

be a divine gift to humanity that has always flourished (in one way or another) and apparently always will. It will never die out! Its survival, however, is based on readiness to die to those behaviors and institutions that render us indispensable (mainly to ourselves) and a willingness to be open to radical new ways of responding to the needs of the times and the urgent call to serve God's world, particularly through the struggles of the poor and marginalized.

The Religious Life *charism*, therefore, has a double meaning. First, it is the divine gift (charism) to humanity at large, a cultural charism, transcending formal religion, given for the benefit of all humanity. Second, the appropriation of that gift happens through a range of specific Orders and Congregations, many of which have sequestered the notion of charism to themselves in a dangerously exclusive and idolatrous fashion. It seems to me that all individual charisms need to reflect, and be accountable to, the general charism. In terms of the various Orders and Congregations, what we share in common is, culturally and theologically, more significant than what sets us apart.[2]

The cyclic approach helps us to understand the crisis and decline of contemporary Religious Life over the past fifty years. Our diminution is not merely the result of the reforms of Vatican II (voiced by restorationists) or the corrosive influences of the secular world. It belongs to a historical theological process, with the Holy Spirit animating and supporting its unfolding, including the decline experienced today, particularly in the West. We have no choice other than to learn to flow with it. And as I indicate in later chapters, it is that sense of divine abandonment that provides the greatest hope and impetus for a possible future refounding of each of our Orders or Congregations.

All of which seems to suggest that we are victims of historical determinism and that we can do little about it. To the contrary, my argument is that we are the beneficiaries of a historical/parabolic narrative, imbued with the wisdom of providence, interlaced with the paradoxical dynamic of birth-death-new life and capable of empowering and guiding us on a more hope-filled journey into the future. The success of that enterprise, however, is heavily dependent on how we read and discern our historical past, particularly the bedrock inspiration to which I now turn attention.

---

[2] In a previous work I seek to extend this embrace of commonalities to include the Religious Life traditions of the other great religions. Despite cultural differences many of the underlying aspirations show a remarkable similarity (see O'Murchu 1991).

Revisiting the Bedrock Inspiration

When and why did Christian Religious Life come into being? And what can we glean from the foundational wisdom that might inform our discernment as we wrestle with the refounding challenges of the twenty-first century? Here, parable and paradigm coalesce with a quality of shock and surprise that requires a great deal of discernment.

Most historians trace the origins to the middle of the third century (c. 250 CE), when Anthony of Egypt fled to the Judean desert and apparently attracted a large number of co-hermits who exhibited varying degrees of heroic austerity. Legend has it that Anthony one day visited a church seeking God in his life and experienced a distinctive call in the words "If you would be perfect, go sell all you have, give to the poor and come follow me" (Matt 19:21). Taking these words literally, Anthony left all to follow Christ—as a desert anchorite—and was quickly joined by many others inspired by his example.

Anthony's option has been interpreted broadly along four lines:

1. Alongside the mainline Christian faith is a more noble ideal requiring Christian devotees to abandon all earthly cares to dedicate themselves exclusively to a spiritual alliance with Christ. This tends to be interpreted as abandoning all earthly cares and eliminating from their life all attachments to earthly and bodily welfare. One easily detects the then-popular split between sacred and secular, resolved by fleeing the latter in order to obtain for reassurance of salvation in a life hereafter. Not surprisingly, in every Christian generation questions have been raised on how this extreme asceticism can be reconciled with the earth-centered vision of bringing about the kingdom of God on earth, a clash of paradigms requiring a more nuanced discernment and a more responsible understanding of ancient history (as suggested by Goehring 1996; 1999; Rubenson 1998).

2. In times of persecution the readiness to shed one's blood as a martyr was viewed as another ideal of Christian witness. Since this was not everybody's calling, religious scholars of the time developed the notion of a "second baptism," often identified with martyrdom and applied to the early Christian ascetics in a form known as white martyrdom, which became another rationale for the Religious Life option. How prevalent the practice of martyrdom was, and the complexities of the practice, ecclesiastically and politically, are reviewed by Candida Moss (2013), requiring in our time a more nuanced interpretation of a phenomenon that merits a more in-depth evaluation and a more cautious admiration.

3. When Roman Emperor Constantine (272–337) adopted Christianity as the official religion of the empire, many gospel ideals were reframed as imperial values (power, domination, structure, control, and others). For some Christians, this was an unacceptable compromise from which they fled, initially to the desert areas and later to the monasteries established by Pachomius and others. This notion of the vowed life as a countercultural protest movement against the growing institutionalization of Christianity (a new paradigm) has never been given the discerning attention it deserves. It may well be one of the more authentic reasons why Religious Life arose in the Christian tradition (for a contrary view, see Joest 2010, 159).

4. Nor have we done responsible historical discernment around the lay foundations of the vowed life. The late Benedictine monk R. Kevin Seasoltz claims that Christian monastic life began as a pre-canonical experience (1997, 28–34). The first monks did not seek orders. (In fact, Pachomius seems to have avoided meeting a bishop lest he be coerced into priesthood.) Rather, the early monks saw themselves outside the hierarchical structure of the church. They understood themselves to be lay people, based on their baptismal call. In the ancient Rule of the Master (chap. 83), the abbot is identified as a lay man.

As indicated above, Christian historians have long favored the heroic patriarchal paradigm, thus ignoring or bypassing other historical developments that should inform both our research and our discernment. Some researchers suggest pre-Christian precedents such as the Therapeutae and the Qumran community. Within the Gospels themselves, both Eusebius and John Cassian regarded the Twelve as the first monks. Among the other models of discipleship we note that of the Beloved Disciple, documented at length by the late Johannine scholar Raymond Brown (1979), suggesting another form of discipleship, with a focus on contemplative, non-imperial values. According to Christof Joest, community asceticism characterizes Christian faith from the beginning, "providing early Christians with the possibility to follow Christ in different stages of radicalism" (2010, 178).

The Apotactic Movement

Under the impetus of American monastic scholar James E. Goehring, our understanding of early Christian monasticism has changed dramatically: "Thus the old theory that traced the monastic impulse in all corners of the empire back to an original Egyptian inspiration has proven to be a literary fiction" (Goehring 1999, 32). The *Life of St. Antony,* written by St. Athanasius, depicts an ideal ascetic hero, now understood to be of limited historical worth. The movement to the desert, popularly acclaimed as the *fuga mundi,* is a complex social and historical phenomenon embraced by a minority rather than by a majority of ascetics at the time.

The developments of Pachomius, along the Nile, should not be portrayed as a simple shift from the eremitical to the coenobitic. Pachomius's unique contribution is that of a monastic organizer (rather than an originator), and his most reputable foundation was a deserted village called Pbow rather than Tabennisi (for more, see Rousseau 1985). Increasingly, evidence from archeology and ancient literary sources suggest that there may have been no direct link between the Pachomian monasteries and the desert hermits. The link belongs to a third group known as the *apotactic movement* (Goehring 1999, 26, 31, 45, 54ff., 212), often referred to as the village ascetics, and the first group to which the term *monachos* (monk) was applied (Goehring 1999, 21, 45).

St. Jerome effectively denounced the village ascetics as heretics (the *remnouth*), because they did not measure up to his ascetical ideals as did the postulated desert hermits. The apotactic movement adopted a life of simplicity and celibacy and lived in small clusters in towns and cities, not merely in Egypt but also in Syria and Palestine. Some lived in family homes or rented houses, meeting frequently for prayer and the study of scripture. They also seem to have been involved in local church communities. Most important, however, is their immersion in *every aspect of secular life,* experiencing, it seems, no conflict between the sacred and the secular. This involvement in the lives of ordinary people became an integrated aspect of the communal movement associated with Pachomius.[3]

When, where, and how did the apotactics come into being? Thus far we don't have the scholarly evidence to answer that question. Meanwhile, Australian scholar of ancient history Edwin A. Judge (2010, 162–63), as well as Goehring (1999, 213), suggests that the

---

[3] Goehring notes the oldest version of the *Life of Pachomius* was published in Bohairic, an Arabic dialect, largely devoid of any of the dualistic splitting between the holy and profane that inundates the later Greek version, and more specifically, the Latin text used and promoted by St. Jerome (1996, 26n.56, 58). "In the aftermath of Chalcedon and the eventual Arabic domination, knowledge of Coptic developments mostly vanished outside of Egypt. Egyptian monasticism was defined through the monastic texts that had appeared in Greek and Latin" (92n.12).

virgins were the *first* apotactics. Later, the men adopted the structures that the females had evolved and developed. The *virgins,* known to have existed throughout the second and third centuries, have been popularly hailed as ascetical, asexual heroines, fleeing the world and the temptations of the flesh, a depiction elaborated at length by church fathers such as Tertullian, Jerome, Origen, and Augustine. But as Elizabeth Castelli argues at length, this is a dangerously misleading description, reflecting male misogyny and the irrational patriarchal fear of women's embodiment, rather than the intuitive prophetic counterculture of the virginity movement itself, infused with much parabolic wisdom and a paradigmatic significance that merits more responsible and discerning attention (1996).

In the dominant patriarchal culture women were viewed essentially as biological organisms designed by God for the primary purpose of biological reproduction. A woman obtained status and dignity by being somebody's wife or mother. The virgins saw through the oppressive misogyny and decided to change things for themselves. By opting for the virginal state, they sought to transcend—and ultimately transform—the cultural oppression. Most lived singly and in their homes, meeting frequently for dialogue and prayer. Some dressed unconventionally, probably as a mark of protest, and they excelled in devoted care to the poor and suffering. McNamara captures the mood when she writes:

> The free movement of women who simply desired not to marry, to live alone or together with other women and pursue a vocation of charity and religious devotion in the midst of normal urban life, may have scandalized pagans and provoked persecution. It definitely scandalized male clerics and provoked their resentment. (1996, 38)

The political and sociological implications of this movement are cryptically stated by Sandra Schneiders:

> The consecrated virgins made a radical choice against not only reproduction for the empire but also reproduction for the family. In the virgin the family died out historically, something the virgin considered not a tragedy (like barrenness in the Jewish community) or a curse (like being born or made a eunuch), but a triumphal espousal of the Resurrection as a present, intra-historical but history-transcending reality. (2013, 8)

Inviting all historical researchers into this more discerning mode that can sense the parabolic shift and the paradigmatic breakthrough we detect in this foundational strand of the vowed life, Irish scholar Bernadette Flanagan writes:

> I do not intend to get involved in the sociocultural meaning of the ascetic behavior of women in the ancient Greco-Roman world. Instead, I accept the work of a wide community of scholars that has argued that the solitary, celibate choice of women in this era was not a private religious choice but an embodied protest against the social roles to which women were assigned. Lastly, I will read the available fragmentary material in the awareness that while the textual sources are limited, the overall conclusion of contemporary scholarship is that in this era, "women's asceticism had sizeable numbers, varied lifestyles, and considerable vigor" [William Harmless, SJ]. At all times the originality of the imagery in the text witnesses to a vivid personal voice behind the author's inscriptions. (2014, 49)[4]

While church history generally gives prior attention to the male developments of early monasticism, I devote considerable attention to the more loosely federated female story. This is the alternative paradigm with a distinctive parabolic flavor. It is not merely a case of trying to balance the gender emphasis. To engage responsibly with the several challenges of refounding, and above all to be receptive to the guiding wisdom of the Spirit, we need to reclaim and reconnect

---

[4] Flanagan goes on to describe a parallel countercultural movement among early Irish monastic women, which was also consigned to historical distortion and misrepresentation. She writes: "What we read then in the lives of early Irish women innovators is a socially androcentric perspective on women's new spiritual engagements. Within this perspective two approaches characterize the biographies: minimalist reporting of women religious innovators; robust reporting of the negative reception of the new spiritual autonomy claimed by women through frequent accounts of the abduction, rape, and murder of the virgins; and positive reporting of women who displayed 'manly' virtues in their new lives" (Flanagan 2014, 61). Throughout much of Christendom, outstanding holiness in women, and the internal genius of its aetiology, was attributed to a psychic and spiritual makeup that belonged primarily to men, but somehow became possessed by some women. Consistently, when it comes to the spiritual realm, women are viewed as frail, fickle, and unreliable, incapable of reaching the spiritual maturity of the male. Thus emerged the concept of the virile woman, who features strongly in medieval spirituality (see Newman 1995). For a comprehensive overview of this historical and cultural distortion, see Gillian Cloke (1995).

with historical developments that are likely to be more authentic in terms of the Spirit's creative freedom and bold originality. It strikes me that the early female strand briefly reviewed above is a long-neglected example of the Spirit, who blows where she will, forever surprising us with parabolic breakthrough. For me, at least, the story of the early virgins illustrates this in a vividly inspiring way, providing an invaluable resource for the discerning task of refounding the vowed life in our time. The historical and theological significance for the work of refounding can scarcely be exaggerated.

The Male Tradition

As already indicated, the *apotactic movement* was not merely an Egyptian development; in fact, it seems to have arisen simultaneously in various geographical locations, Syria possibly being the place of origin. What some scholars claim to be an earlier communal strand in Syria, popularly known as the Qeiama/Covenanters (Voobos 1958; 1961; Gribomont 1965; Nedungatt 1973), deserves more discerning attention than it has thus far received. These groups may have prevailed in more peaceful times, before being forced to scatter as persecution became widespread. The Basilian communities (Gribomont 1965; Fedwick 1979) are often considered to be a direct offspring of the Covenanters, with a more moderate quality of asceticism and a lack of the Hellenistic split between sacred and secular. As already indicated, the Pachomian developments in the Upper Nile probably drew much of their inspiration from this same ancient source.

Initially, the Covenanters consisted of baptized members of the Christian Church, at a stage when, apparently, baptism involved commitment to an ascetical life, including celibacy and a degree of communal living (Leclercq 1968, 63–70). With the expansion of Christianity, however, baptism became synonymous with membership of the Christian Church, and those formerly committed to a "special" lifestyle became a group apart. Their commitment came to be known as the *second baptism,* a term frequently used in Christian literature to describe Religious profession.

The following are some of the outstanding features of the Covenanters:

1. Nedungatt claims that they did not leave their towns or cities in search of seclusion (1973, 444). Veilleux (1971) and Gribomont (1965) are of the opinion that the anchorites and hermits were unknown at this early stage. The available evidence suggests that the

communal ascetical movement predates the eremitical one popularly
associated with the traditional Egyptian model.

2. Celibacy and singleness of heart are the distinguishing features
of these groups. Although commitment to the Qeiama was considered
to be lifelong, apparently vows did not exist at this early stage.

3. This was a lay organization and seems to have been well integrated with the local church, coexisting with ordinary Christians,
and, like the latter, subject to the local bishop. Superiors and internal
governance do not seem to have existed among the Covenanters.
There is some evidence to suggest that a leading charismatic figure,
the spiritual father, held an honored place within the group, providing
spiritual guidance rather than juridical leadership. Both women and
men constituted the membership of this early group.

4. In terms of service to the local church, the Covenanters seem to
have functioned mainly in the preparation of liturgical celebrations
and in the service and care of the sick and needy. Burkitt describes
them as the backbone of the Syrian Church, which probably tells us
little about their functional role; instead, it may be indicative of the
high respect in which they were held among the people (Burkitt 1904,
130, 150).

5. In contrast to the conventional emphasis on extreme asceticism,
practice of excessive mortification, long fasting, and social isolation
seem to be largely unknown among the Covenanters. "The rule of
life which he (Aphrahat) sketches out is quite dignified and temper-
ate, with no special features of observance of asceticism" (Nedungatt
1973, 428).

6. Worthy of note, too, is their attitude toward celibacy. While
regarded as superior to marriage, they did not consider marriage as
an attachment to a passing sinful world, as in the conventional understanding of Egyptian monasticism. The Syrian attitude to celibacy
(and to virginity) is beautifully portrayed in these words of Aphrahat:

> For those who obtain this portion there waits a great reward,
> because it is in our freedom that we bring it to fulfillment and
> not in slavery or under the compulsion of any commandment;
> for we are not forced thereto under law. Its model and type we
> find in Scripture. And we see in the triumphant the likeness of an-
> gels; on earth it is acquired as a gift. This is a possession, which
> if lost cannot be recovered, nor can one obtain it for money. The
> one who has it loses it and does not find it again. The one who
> does not have it can never race to pick it. Love, my beloved, this

charism (*machabta:* gift) which is unique in the whole world. (in Nedungatt 1973, 431–32)

The Covenant groups, with their distinctively communal lifestyle and the other features outlined above, flourished during the third century of the Christian era, and seem to be another variation of the apotactic movement noted earlier. A long phase of persecution under three successive emperors—Shaphur (309–79), Vahram IV (388–99), and Jazgard (399–421)—had a negative impact on the Covenanters. Because of their benevolent attitude to slaves and other oppressed groups, they became the focus of violent attack. Many of their foundations were destroyed, their lifestyle was disrupted, and many fled to the mountains for shelter and safety. Thus began a new strand of Syrian monasticism that in due course seems to have accommodated to the Egyptian desert influence; it became much more individualistic and ascetical in its orientation.

Fortunately, this was not the end of the Covenanters. In time, they morphed into the Basilian monastic upsurge, with a little-known Christian ascetic, Eusthatius of Sebaste, as the crucial link. Basil's monasteries exhibit many of the key features of the Covenant groups: brotherly love, simplicity, moderation, and compassionate care for the sick and underprivileged (see Gribomont 1965; Fedwick 1979).

According to popular history, it was the ascetical Egyptian model that entered the West, mainly through the initiative of John Cassian (360–435). When Cassian came to Europe early in the fifth century, he encountered a rather chaotic scene populated by wandering monks for whom he sought to establish a uniform and universal structure. He modeled this structure on the Christian Church in Egypt, especially as evidenced in Alexandria, and not on the Pachomian communities, as is often presumed. In fact, Cassian seems never to have visited the Pachomian monasteries. Having devised a structure, he sought to enliven it spiritually with the principles and lifestyle of Egyptian eremiticism, which he undoubtedly admired, although it is unclear how much he knew from firsthand experience.[5]

---

[5] As with other revisions of ancient history highlighted in this book, it is difficult to distinguish fact from fiction in our knowledge of Cassian. Steven Driver (2002) provides a critical overview while prioritizing the value of Cassian's overall inspiration. More problematic is the recent debate on whether Cassian was actually the fifth-century monk, later resident in Gaul, or the sixth-century figurehead Cassian the Sabaite, linked with the Mar Saba Monastery in Palestine (Stewart 2015).

As a monastic organizer, Cassian cannot be faulted. However, he can no longer be regarded as an authentic representative of Pachomian monasticism. It is now more widely accepted that the Pachomian developments in Egypt were in both spirit and lifestyle similar in many ways to Basilian monasteries. The long-assumed progression from eremiticism to cenobitism in Egypt is no longer tenable. Instead, it seems that Religious Life initially flourished in a variety of forms with a strong communal ethos, an egalitarian involvement with local peoples (politically and commercially), and a quality of ascetical living far less extreme than formerly understood and much more integrated with adult Christian faith.

Returning to the Archetype

For the purposes of refounding, this original strand embodies a set of values that constitute the creativity and empowering vision for every new breakthrough that happens across the centuries. Throughout this book we encounter time and again something of that original communal and prophetic inspiration; obviously, it is expressed differently in each new historical epoch. At its source is what Sandra Schneiders aptly describes as the "God quest," a mystical fascination with and allegiance to the divine mystery at the heart of all existence; in Christian spirituality this came to be known as the *Sequela Christi* (the following of Christ).

As already indicated, the *Sequela Christi* in the twenty-first century needs to be reinterpreted and realigned with the monastic archetype. Popularly understood throughout much of Christian history as a heroic patriarchal endeavor to emulate an ascetical heroic Christ and to procure individual salvation, we must now wrestle with the cultural contingency of that view, its defective historical appropriation, and its distorted biblical application.

First, the historical context. The solitary eremitical ideal was in many ways a patriarchal projection of excessive individualized heroism. In reality, the evidence points to something much less dramatic and more integrated with the cultural norms of the times. As noted earlier, archeological research is posing the greatest challenges for a review of what we have for long taken to be the norm. Darlene L. Brooks Hedstrom provides an up-to-date evaluation:

> The accounts of the monastic residences at the Cells (Kellia)
> suggest monks resided in one room structures that served as the
> place for prayer, daily work and sleeping. The accounts suggested

that the monks lived in relative isolation from one another and had need of few possessions. But when archaeologists began uncovering massive settlements that looked more like densely settled villages and towns, with multi-room residences, at Saqqara, Bawit, and Kellia, it was difficult to maintain the long-held notion of ascetic simplicity. The archetype of monastic habitations as isolated, solitary, and wholly non-material, is no longer a tenable interpretation of Egyptian monastic history. (2013, 300)[6]

Brooks Hedstrom goes on to claim that the archeological research also indicates that "monks owned property, involved themselves in legal disputes, and were, in large part, very much engaged in the world around them" (2013, 300n.3; see also Goehring 1999, 46–47, 95, 106). To this, Christof Joest adds the observation that while the monks renounced marriage, and were more committed to spiritual practice, they were nonetheless very much integrated into the daily life of town and village, engaging in commercial business and social engagement (2010, 162ff.).

Second, to recapture briefly the material outlined in Chapter 3 above. We need to reappropriate the *Sequela Christi* within the context of how we understand the Christ event today, biblically and theologically. Christian discipleship is not about following a divine patriarchal hero over against the world, but rather about being co-disciples with Jesus in serving the new companionship in the midst of God's creation. Religious Life exists not as a special mode of consecration to engender more salvific holiness, but rather to expedite the wholesomeness of all God's creation through serving the empowering companionship of the gospel, God's new reign on earth. Religious Life involves consecration for mission—beyond the dualistic split of sacred versus secular—and not merely a more selective route for anthropocentric salvation.

The history of the vowed life involves a great deal more than a nostalgic admiration for ascetical heroes whose understanding of incarnational growth arose from cultural, religious, and anthropological influences that have long outgrown their usefulness. Even in their own historical context we now deem them to have been one-sided and, at times, exaggerated. The following of Christ today is not focused on a patriarch-like ascetical hero, but rather on the human and earthly

---

[6] Other researchers documented by Darlene L. Brooks Hedstrom highlight that contrary to the traditional emphasis on fasting for ascetical purposes, the monks seem to have enjoyed a mixed diet of vegetables, fish, and meat (2013, 313ff.). All of this requires us to adopt a more critically discerning approach to ancient literary sources, as suggested by the monastic scholar Malcolm Choat (2013).

transformation required by our appropriation of the Companionship of Empowerment, inspired by Jesus as the first disciple of the new dispensation.

Yet, there is continuity with the past, but it is at a subtle rather than overt level. The virgins, the village ascetics, and the ancient monks, when revisioned within the communal and ecclesial endeavors of their day, were agents for the flourishing of the new companionship and serve as an enduring source of inspiration. Their flight from the world for the exclusive salvation of their souls, pursued through penance and asceticism, is merely one aspect, and certainly not a major one, of their exemplary witness. It was their courageous witness to making God's world a better place for all that singles them out as an enduring and inspiring source for Religious across the ages.

☙

Study Questions

1. How would you imagine the "underside" of Religious Life?

2. How do you see the "God quest" getting lost in the history of Religious Life?

3. "The following of Christ today is not focused on a patriarch-like ascetical hero, but rather on the human and earthly transformation required by our appropriation of the Companionship of Empowerment, inspired by Jesus as the first disciple of the new dispensation." How do you resonate with this statement? Write two or three sentences to expand on your reaction to its challenge.

Chapter 5

Overcoming the Monastic-Apostolic Split

*Change and transformation are not the same.
Change happens at a point in time; transformation happens over time. Change is a new beginning; transformation begins with an ending.*
—BROTHER SEAN SAMMON, FMS

*A responsiveness rich in creative initiative is emi-
nently compatible with the charismatic nature of
the Religious Life.*
—MUTUAE RELATIONES, NO. 19 (MAY 1978)

Official church teaching, as well as spiritual/theological commentaries, tend to distinguish between those vowed to Religious
Life in monasteries (and enclosed convents) and those more directly
involved in ministerial service, whether within or outside the formal
church. Much of the relevant literature views the monastic realm as
superior in holiness and in its dedication to God. Apostolic Religious
Life tends to be regarded as lacking in that exemplary holiness that is
more transparent through the monastic and enclosed life.

In this binary distinction one readily detects that *fuga mundi* (flee the
world) still carries overtones, as does the Atonement influence of the
God who suffers to rid the world of sin, a strategy perceived to be adopted more forthrightly in monastic living. The refounding discernment
relevant for the twenty-first century requires us to focus our attention
on commonalities rather than differences. Both monks and apostolic
Religious share a great deal, particularly the monastic archetype highlighted in Chapter 2 above. The values shared by both groups are rooted
in the Companionship of Empowerment (or at least should be), as is
our mission of value radiation (more in Chapter 8 below), prayerful
discernment, and witness to the gospel throughout God's creation.

79

In Chapter 4, I briefly described the pioneering figures—female and male—on whose shoulders rests the tradition of the vowed life. Those origins are much more complex than the analyses provided by conventional historians. In many ways their true heroism was not invested in their ascetical achievements but in their exemplary service among ordinary people and in their countercultural (prophetic) witness against the values of domination and respectability of their time. That same immersion in the world, with a distinctive countercultural impact, is noticeable in the first major strand of monastic witness, namely, the rise of early Benedictinism.

Structured Monasticism

St. Benedict of Nursia (480–547) created a formal structure for the vowed life that was to last for several centuries. His rule is not merely the basis for several spiritual classics but to this day is referenced for its humanity, moderation, and spiritual inspiration.

Frequently, scholars describe Benedict's endeavor as an attack on the phenomenon of the wandering monks, and they cite his vow of stability as the instrument used to rein them in. This is a rather superficial interpretation of a vision aimed at cultural transformation rather than disciplinary living. Benedict did not withdraw into a remote, ascetical enclosure; instead, he co-created a prophetic movement with an enduring influence on church and world alike.

Scholarship has neither honored nor adequately studied the huge cultural impact of early Christian monasticism. We have scarcely begun to explore how the Benedictines integrated their spiritual lives with intense secular engagement, nor have we explored the rich liminal witness that ensued from their integration of the sacred and the secular. Dualistic splitting has once again hindered and undermined our capacity for deeper discernment.

After the collapse of the Roman Empire it was primarily the monks who restored and advanced European civilization. They did it primarily through the vast tracts of land they inherited and the financial support of the political powers through which they created schools, centers for sacred learning, and a range of commercial enterprises with local lords. But their influence went far beyond the monastery walls, co-creating the earthly and cultural development that in time would make Europe among the most advanced cultures on the planet.

It was this same cultural impact, with its growing accumulation of status, privilege, and wealth, that led to decadence and internal crisis. The crisis was noted by the secular powers, such as Charlemagne, rather than by the monks themselves. It was Charlemagne, at the beginning of the ninth century, who appointed Benedict of Aniane (747–821) to lead a reform of the monasteries and their values. Benedict began his reform in 817, but despite a temporary measure of success, the cultural and spiritual decline continued, reinforced to no small degree by the political turmoil in Europe at that time. One wonders if this might be yet another example of the predictable decline that characterizes the downward movement in each historical cycle. At a conscious level, everything is being done to halt the decline and reverse the group's good fortunes, yet a serious disintegration ensues.

It would take a far more formidable force to bring about the needed reform, indeed, a new phase of refounding, in what can be described as the second Benedictine wave. In the early tenth century Western monasticism was experiencing a severe decline due to unstable political and social conditions. The instability was due largely to continuous Viking raids, widespread poverty, and especially, the dependence of abbeys on the local nobles, who controlled all that belonged to the territories under their jurisdiction. Clearly, the secular interference in the monasteries, along with the church's own collusion with the feudal and manorial systems, needed to be addressed.

To rectify the problem, William, Duke of Aquitane, in 909 donated one of his domains for the founding of a new Benedictine monastery; this marked the initiation of the Cluniac reform. The reform movement opted for a highly centralized form of government entirely foreign to Benedictine tradition. The reform quickly spread beyond the limits of Cluny by the founding of new houses and by the incorporation of those already existing. The focus was on a retrieval of the more authentic spirit of Benedictinism through a strict observance of prayer, liturgy, silence, and solitude. During its height (c.950–c.1130) the Cluniac movement was one of the largest religious forces in Europe, with more than one thousand affiliated monasteries.

The ensuing purification and reawakening of monastic fervor enriched the life of the church throughout the whole of Europe at the time, and several bishops and popes arose from its ranks. The wider society also benefited because the monasteries catered for wayfarers, pilgrims, and the destitute poor. Two Cluniac developments—known as the Truce of God and the Peace of God—brought much-needed healing of the violence and revenge that had become endemic in feudal rivalries. The Cluniac monasteries also revived the Benedictine tradition of learning and art, while making available to local peoples the fruit and benefices of the monastery lands.

However, the achievements of this period were primarily liturgical and devotional. In the words of historian Elizabeth Rapley, "What Cluny came to offer was the most elaborate, the most sumptuous, form of liturgical prayer" (2011, 16). That, combined with its ever-expanding ecclesiastical power, would eventually result in its decline and fragmentation. The prophetic counterculture was being compromised by a devotional spirituality focused more on procuring salvation in a world beyond rather than transforming earth for the sake of the kingdom of God. In the beginning of the eleventh century yet another attempt was made to rescue the pure Benedictine vision, leading to the birth of the Cistercian Order. It enjoyed a one hundred year period of growth and expansion before yielding pride of place to a whole new articulation of the vowed life, the rise of the Mendicant Orders in the early thirteenth century.

What were the women monastics doing during those early centuries? The virgins were a formidable cultural force, denouncing and challenging many of society's misogynist values of the day and helping to co-create the original communal flair of the vowed life in what is now known as the apotactic movement. And according to Jo Ann McNamara, women throughout the first millennium continued to honor an eco-feminist prophetic view, the grounding of which is extremely difficult to retrieve (1996). From the time of Pachomius, female monastics lived in separate buildings with varying degrees of supervision from bishops and clergy, and with more restricted access to ministerial outreach.

From the time of the Mendicant Orders, male Religious were able to translate their prophetic, countercultural endeavors into more explicit and structured forms of ministry, such as preaching and teaching. For women, it was different. In 1298, Pope Boniface VII promulgated the bull *Periculoso*, decreeing that all women Religious everywhere must be cloistered. The bull was reiterated at the Council of Trent (1545–63) and again at Vatican I in the nineteenth century.

The Mendicant Era

Throughout the twelfth and thirteenth centuries seismic shifts were happening around the *monastic archetype*. The significant male developments—Franciscans, Dominicans—are extensively researched and documented, while the subversive female presence has been largely suppressed and neglected. Jo Ann Kay McNamara captures the mood of women at this time when she writes: "Like it or not, women Religious in this age of massive institutional reform had to struggle with the paradox of an unwanted subjection to episcopal authority (e.g., cloistering) coupled with an unwanted liberty from the organizing efforts of the monastic networks" (1996, 215).

Best known among such networks were the Beguines. They usually were located in Northern Europe. They did not take formal vows and could leave if they wanted to get married. They had to work to support themselves because most of their members were not from the wealthy classes. Some made lace; others were fullers, washing wool in the canals for weavers. Still others took care of the elderly and sick, and some operated schools. In some of the towns the Beguines even had citizenship rights, despite the fact that citizenship was usually reserved for men. In other towns the Beguines did not pay taxes on their earnings, making them persona non grata with the guilds, whose members did pay taxes. Most controversial of all, some Beguines translated the Bible into German and French, while others openly debated questions of faith and theology, to the ire of church authority at the time. One of their outstanding visionaries, scholar and mystic Margaret Porete, was denounced as a heretic and burned at the stake in 1310.[1]

The twelfth century saw great changes in Western Europe. As commerce revived, urban centers arose, and with them an urban middle class. New directions in spirituality were called for. Ecclesiastical reform became a major theme of the cultural revival of this era. Religious Life for women in the Middle Ages was more complex than is usually imagined. The nuns and hermitesses of the eleventh and twelfth centuries; the anchoresses of the twelfth and thirteenth; the Beguines and Tertiaries of the thirteenth and fourteenth; the Observant nuns of the fifteenth—all were in the forefront of the religious mood of their days. As cultural catalysts, they integrated a genuine love for God and for God's creation; to them, the nunnery was indeed an earthly paradise.

While I am seeking to honor this enduring female legacy amid the significant male developments that characterize each major cycle, I do not wish to understate the estimable mendicant breakthrough of the twelfth and thirteenth centuries: the Franciscans and Dominicans, as well as the Carmelites, Augustinians, and Servites, who also made notable contributions. In 1210 and 1215, respectively, Pope Innocent III received in Rome two visionaries with strikingly different dreams for the evangelization of Europe. The first visit was from Francis of Assisi

---

[1] For more information on the Beguines, see Malone 2014, 73ff.; and Flanagan 2014, 70ff.

(1181–1226) and eleven of his companions. They were lay men who had given up their worldly possessions. They wanted to live among the poor, particularly in the rapidly growing towns, preaching and bearing witness to the Christian life. Five years later Innocent's visitor was a Spaniard, Dominic de Guzman (1170–1221), who, challenged by his preaching among the Cathars, was acutely aware of the need for a more empowering theological vision amid the intellectual questioning of the time. He was given Innocent's blessing to launch the Order of Preachers.

The papal endorsement of both the Franciscans and Dominicans proved to be something of a mixed blessing. Basically, they were given the freedom to travel and preach wherever they discerned a need, largely exempt from episcopal control. By 1246, there were a number of angry bishops seeking the abolition of all Mendicants. The resentment simmered till 1274, when the Council of Lyons proposed to close down all mendicant missionary endeavors. The attempt came to naught.

The courageous and daring initiatives of Francis, Dominic, and the entire mendicant movement in its foundation phase has important implications for crisis periods in Religious Life (the present one included); that is, *no matter how entrenched Religious Life becomes in any one historical, cultural, or spiritual mold, the Spirit will call forth prophetic leadership to pioneer new possibilities in response to new needs.* Unfortunately, old, well-established groups rarely seem to be prepared for this moment and so fade into oblivion. Yet the vowed life continues to flourish.

In 1217, there were five thousand more members of the Franciscan Order. The Franciscans spread rapidly, inspiring many through their devotion to the humanity of Christ and their compassionate care for the poor and oppressed. Francis died in 1226, leaving his followers with many unresolved problems, their interpretation of poverty being the most acute. For the following three hundred years poverty was to remain divisive among the Franciscans, leading to the emergence of many splinter groups, including the Spirituals, the Laxists, the Moderates, and the Capuchins.

Despite the internal crisis that existed almost from the beginning, and the explicit resentment from many bishops, the Franciscans grew and expanded in numerical strength and cultural impact, counting thirty-five thousand members in 1347, on the eve of the Black Death. This observation seems to suggest that no crisis, whatever its intensity, can offset the upward growth and expansion that the Spirit generates in the opening decades of each historical cycle. At this juncture the discerning person cannot avoid asking: Are we dealing with a form of historical determinism—some kind of predictable growth rate in the first half-cycle, and a predetermined decline in the second half? How do we discern truth here? Presumably through contemplative wisdom and graced discernment, rather than through the rational intelligence with which we conventionally read history.

The Dominicans, while also endorsing poverty and a simple life, adopted a more ecclesiastical role, with a focus on informed preaching and doctrinal rectitude, a stance that later would ensnare the Order in the violent suppression that marked the Inquisition. By the time of Dominic's death in 1221, the Order had spread through Western Europe, hundreds of young men had joined, and the Dominicans became a powerful intellectual and theological force throughout the major universities of contemporary Europe.

Despite six hundred years of monastic stability, the Mendicants made the innovative decision to relinquish the principle of being tied to monasteries or territorial parishes. Instead, they moved freely and extensively, having also obtained freedom from the previously exercised jurisdiction of bishops. Moreover, they adopted different models of internal organization, with the superior exercising more autonomous authority mediated through regional provinces and local communities.

With deep insight the Franciscans and Dominicans put into practice a pastoral strategy suited to the social needs of the day. The emergence of urban centers meant concentrated numbers of homeless and sick. This created problems for the parish churches, who were unable to address those issues adequately. With many people moving from the countryside to the cities, the Mendicants prioritized the urban zones as the primary focus for life and ministry. Secular institutions, such as the labor organizations, the ancient guilds, and civil authorities often had recourse to the spiritual counseling of the Mendicants, seeking their guidance in resolving both internal and external conflicts. The Franciscans and Dominicans became the spiritual animators of the medieval city.

In due course both groups suffered the serious decline that seems to be endemic to the major life cycles of Religious Life. We can identify three factors that contributed to the cultural decline of the Mendicants:

1. The Friars were coopted into the sale of indulgences, seriously undermining their commitment to simplicity of life.

2. The Black Death (1346–53) depleted their numbers and resources in a Europe already devastated by the Hundred Years' War (1337–1453). A sense of mediocrity, along with the fear of a punitive God, pervaded Religious Life for much of this time.

3. After the Great Schism (1378–1417), not only was the papacy divided, but frequently the friars were also split into destructively competing allegiances.

While numbers still remained strong—and in the case of the Franciscans were boosted by the papal approval of the Capuchins in 1528 (reaching a membership of six thousand by 1580)—their cultural impact had lost its original fervor. Religious Life needed a fresh awakening, and as another three hundred year cycle ran its course, the new breakthrough came forth.

Apostolic Zeal

Following the mendicant era we witness a plethora of Congregations, both male and female, moving more deeply into the world and integrating the gospel of liberation and empowerment through a range of new services and apostolic outreaches. Despite the mendicant emphasis on poverty and simplicity, their success brought glamour and power of the type that in time seriously eroded the credibility of their cultural witness. As happens so often in the history of Religious Life, it took a new thrust not merely to recapture something of the earlier insertion among the masses, but to give apostolic outreach a relevance appropriate for new needs and demanding circumstances of the time. Into the breach stepped the Orders and Congregations of the apostolic era, among the better known being the Jesuits.

Until the sixteenth century recognition was granted only to institutes with solemn vows. Institutes with simple vows now began to arise and increase in number. After at first being merely tolerated, such groups gradually obtained church approval. They provided specific services or ministries for the church and society, building schools, hospitals, and new missionary enterprises around the world. The period of their greatest growth was in the wake of the French Revolution in early nineteenth-century France and Belgium. Only in 1900 did many of these groups obtain full recognition as Religious Congregations.

The Society of Jesus is an example of an institute that obtained recognition as an Order with solemn vows, although the members were divided into the professed, with solemn vows (a minority), and the coadjutors, with simple vows. The Order was founded by St. Ignatius of Loyola in the wake of the Protestant Reformation, introducing several innovations designed to meet the demands of the sixteenth century. Its members were freed from the commitments of common life, especially common prayer, which allowed them to minister individually in distant places.

Elizabeth Rapley describes their visionary organizational skill:

> The Society organized itself to be effective and flexible; it attracted men of intelligence and imagination, then trained them in obedience and sent them out on mission across the known world. They took on the more forbidding adversaries, and often paid heavily in blood. . . . Without them it is hard to see how the Catholic Church of the early modern period could have made its successful comeback." (2011, 132)

Throughout the sixteenth and seventeenth centuries the Jesuits also created lay sodalities, involving thousands of lay people in Christian witness at a range of different levels.

In the entire history of Religious Life the Jesuits stand out as an indomitable religious and cultural force. In 1750, the Society of Jesus numbered over twenty-two thousand members spread throughout the entire known world from the Orient to the Americas. Their power was immense. They held a virtual monopoly on higher education; their sodalities and secret societies were still drawing in men and women by the thousands; they exercised influence in many of the princely courts of Europe; they were active as missionaries at home and abroad. Within their ranks could be found brilliant theologians, scientists, mathematicians, diplomats, polemicists. There was not a Religious Order that could compete with the Jesuits in talent, training, and discipline.

At many moments in history the Jesuits were both the pride and the bane of the hierarchical church, while frequently held in wary regard by European political powers. Between 1704 and 1715, they were denounced several times by Pope Clement XI. Eventually, they were barred from China (along with other Christian missionaries). In 1764 they were banished from France, and from all Spanish-held territories in 1767. In 1773, Pope Clement XIV, determined to extinguish the Jesuit flame, suppressed the entire Order. Nonetheless, the scattered members retained enough vision and force to survive underground till they were reinstated by Pope Pius VII in 1814.

Although the Jesuits tend to be the most frequently cited example of the apostolic groups, the insertion and integration of the vowed life among the rank and file of society, particularly among the poor and marginalized, became the prerogative of a vast range of groups, both male and female. We meet some of the first efforts of female groups breaking through the restrictions of enclosure (for example, Clare of Assisi and Angela Merici). We encounter some of the first groups of brothers in education (La Salle) and in the care of the sick (Alexians). Vincent de Paul became a seminal figure for a vast range of new clerical Congregations.

As already noted, the late nineteenth century marked a drastic decline in European Religious life, from an estimated 400,000 to a mere 40,000 in a timespan of forty years. Classical historians lay the blame at the feet of the French Revolution, resulting in the routing of many monasteries, the scattering of several Religious communities, and the massacre of large numbers of Religious. All this transpired at the end of a three hundred year cycle. But for the classical historian the end of such a cycle is of no significance; the destruction wrought by the French Revolution is the only explanatory factor necessary.

Presumably, then, if the French Revolution had not happened, all would have been well with Religious Life, and its impact would have continued to grow and develop without interruption. Here we face a formidable example of historical discernment arising from our understanding of the cyclic approach to history. *Even if the French Revolution had not happened, I believe we would have had a similar decline in the Religious Life of the day.* Why?

Two factors in particular suggest that an internal malaise had set in:

1. *An introverted spirituality.* An ascetical individual sense of devotion prevailed, heavily tinged with the Calvanistic emphasis on human depravity and the ensuing alienation from God. Hence, Religious, despite their admirable apostolic endeavors, exhibited low morale, a great deal of internal squabbling, and an insipid spirituality preoccupied with individual salvation within the sanctity of their closed communities.

2. *Excessive church control.* It was during this era, too, that Religious Life was first subjected to a "canonical" form of papal and episcopal control (hence, the distinction between Orders and Congregations), thus generating a new identity for Religious Life as an institution within the church: "Religious are seen as an elite of dedicated and militant servants of the church with a high level of individual holiness, and a readiness to defend the church on any front" (Fitz and Cada 1975, 698).

Chronologically, the suppression of Religious by the French Revolution coincides with the breakdown phase of all previous cycles. The French Revolution is the external trigger but not the entire explanation. This kind of breakdown, the diminution that characterizes each historical cycle, results from a combination of internal stagnation and external pressure. *In most cases, I suspect that the internal disintegration far outweighs the external influences.*

Accompanying the introverted, myopic kind of spirituality described above (historically inherited from Jansenism) was the progressive clericalization of the vowed life arising from the enforced ecclesiastical authority demanded by the legislation from the Council of Trent in the sixteenth century, along with the emergence of a number of Congregations with the sole focus of improving the quality of the priesthood itself—the Theatines (1524), the Barnabites (1530), the Somachi (1532), and perhaps best known of all, the Oratorians (1564).

By the end of the eighteenth century the apostolic model had become comfortable and complacent, relishing its guarantee of individual salvation. In its zeal for a holy church it had seriously compromised the wholeness of the new reign of God (the new companionship). It had lost its originality and prophetic boldness. A new impetus of the Spirit was needed. It would come to birth—and flourish—within the broad strokes of the global missionary movement of the nineteenth century.

Already by the late 1500s the horizon had begun to stretch beyond Europe to the distant lands of the Americas and China. The nineteenth century would add Africa as a new and challenging missionary horizon. A plethora of new Religious Congregations would take up this challenge, despite the fact that several had been founded to address issues of acute need within Europe, especially within France. Despite the frequent colonial undercurrents, the Religious Life witness never entirely betrayed its bold, prophetic focus, and while it consciously embraced the call to mission in the name of the church, somehow the flourishing of the kingdom took precedence. That priority seems endemic to the growing and flourishing of the vowed life in every era.

Apart from the Jesuits, few of the older groups were restored to their former numerical strength. The missionary vision was carried to the ends of the earth predominantly by new groups. The revitalization of the vowed life always seems to need a fresh birthing as its primary impetus for refounding. By 1850, the missionary cycle was already recording a membership of 80,000, accelerating its growth to a massive 1,330,000 (one million female and 330,000 male) in 1960. Predictably, the utopian flaw was already at work, and from 1960 onward we can trace the declining pattern that has prevailed since then.

The missionary endeavor has itself been transformed in recent decades. The Caucasian missionaries from Europe, the United States, and Australia have declined significantly in number, being replaced in all cases by resources from the local indigenous churches. Bringing the gospel to the pagans, and ensuring that they are baptized for salvation, has given way to salvation for the whole person through education and development, and further evolved into the work of peace, justice, and the integrity of creation. Additionally, contemporary missionaries are committed more explicitly to establishing God's kingdom on earth; seeking justice and liberation for refugees and asylum seekers and victims of sex trafficking; and bringing about reconciliation beyond the violence of our time. In the early years of the twenty-first century the nature of the missionary endeavor is itself being refounded. Indeed, several factors related to a future refounding of Religious are already visible in the revamping and redefining of the missionary undertaking.

Discerning through History

The historical overview of the vowed life provided in this book stretches the meaning of both history and the vowed life itself. In both cases the truth of parable expands the mere recording of historical events and remarkable feats of patriarchal heroes. The wisdom accrued through the study of paradigm shifts invites us to look at history not merely as a kind of Darwinian survival of the fittest, succeeding by repeating the triumphs of the past, but rather as a paradoxical evolving cycle, driven and lured by the dynamic of birth-death-rebirth.

In this blending of parable and paradigm we more readily detect the fidelity of thousands of vowed Religious to the great Christian enterprise of the Companionship of Empowerment. There has always been a close affiliation with the church, and I expect there always will be. But when the Orders and Congregations become embedded in canonical structures and lured into an ecclesiastical power enclave, they rapidly lose their dynamism, the prophetic empowerment they are called to embody for and mediate with the people of God.

The history of Religious Life can be read as a sequence of events, with triumphs and failures. This standard approach misses the sense of mystery and mystique, and much more seriously, it highlights the achievement of heroic characters over and above the many rank-and-file members who frequently are the ones rendering the greater service—both to God and to humanity. Even in times of serious decline,

Religious still retain something of that mystical lure, the enduring archetype, which can never be reduced to the dualistic split between the monastic and the apostolic.

In February 1790 the French National Assembly legislated that solemn vows were to be banned definitively. Novices of all monastic Orders, male and female, were ordered to go home. This did not lead to the intended abolition of the vowed life. On the contrary, the monks regained a fresh vitality inspired by the missionary endeavor that was to characterize the refounding revitalization of the nineteenth century.

The commonalities held jointly by the monastic Orders, on the one hand, and the apostolic Congregations, on the other, far outweigh the differences between the two groups. Both represent the same monastic archetype, giving it a variety of expression at different times in history in accordance with the demands of various cultural epochs. *What we should be highlighting are the complementary features and not the canonical distinctions.* Ideally, the apostolic groups need to embrace more explicitly the solitude and prayerfulness of the monastery, while the "monks" need to engage the cultural spiritual hunger with more creative forms of outreach. In the twenty-first century, groups like Taize in France, the Community of Sant'Egidio in Italy, the L'Arche communities around the world, along with various groups representing the new monasticism, seem to be embodying such a creative integration.

Something of that same creative synthesis can be seen in the vision and exemplary courage of the many great female foundresses. Although several history books don't even name them, for the present work they are primordial examples for the new refounding envisaged in the late twenty-first century. Their long subverted story will be broken open in the next chapter.

ട

Study Questions

1. As you read through this evolving history, a litany of imagination and vision, what is your *personal response* to how Religious Life has emerged and is still emerging?

2. The monastic and apostolic dimensions of the vowed life tend to be explained in terms of significant differences. What do you consider to be the *commonalities* shared by both forms?

Chapter 6

The Parable
of Paradigmatic Foundresses

Despite the variety of their activities, women's experience of the Religious Life, as it came to be called, had profoundly different lineaments from men's, and merits a separate history stressing the unity of that experience.
—JO ANN KAY MCNAMARA

As insiders to their own suffering, women must be attentive to the power of their emotional authority, as well as the ways in which harm diminishes a woman's capacity to carry out an analysis of her oppression.
—BEVERLY J. LANZETTA

In Christian Religious Life today, women outnumber men three to one. Yet, practically all the laws governing the vowed life are drawn up by men and are based upon masculine values of rationality, exclusion, heroism, and control. Most women Religious work in apostolates where the masculine urge to master and dominate still prevails. In both male and female forms, the more feminine qualities of feeling, imagination, creativity, inclusion, the freedom to evolve, and a passion for justice are largely subverted.

Religious Life in its popular historical depiction presents not merely a misleading picture, but one that is grossly distorted and unjust. Most of the historical records were compiled by men, themselves schooled almost exclusively in a culture saturated in masculine values. By addressing a feminine frame of reference, I am attempting to retrieve and reclaim one of the oldest, richest, and culturally significant strands of liminal experience.

The dilemma under review has a long and disturbing history in which women have been side-lined and suppressed by the dominant patriarchal church. Throughout the latter half of the twentieth century, scholars—both male and female—have highlighted this imbalance (see, for example, Malone 2014).

Historical Precedent

I have already alluded to the significance of the virgins in early Christian times. Although popularly construed as devotional recluses, in fact they confronted the prevailing patriarchal culture with bold, alternative ideals of empowerment and gospel liberation (Malone 2014, 34ff.; McNamara 1996, 23ff.). And despite the lack of concrete historical evidence, I support the emerging conviction that it was the early apotactic movement—specifically, the female village ascetics—that became the springboard for the subsequent developments in the monastic life for males and females alike. Next, we note that many of the outstanding founders, from Anthony of Egypt, through Benedict, and up to Francis in the early thirteenth century, had mothers, sisters, or close female relatives in the Religious Life. Although Scholastica was only allowed into the male monastery at Monte Casino on the death of her brother, Benedict, her non-enclosed status gave her the freedom to exercise a life of generous service to the many needy people of her time.

In the West, alongside the desert fathers were the desert mothers, of whom Syncletica and Theodora seem to have enjoyed a reputation on a par with Anthony and Pachomius (Cameron 1993; Earle 2007). Our first evidence for the existence of ecclesiastically based female communities is that of St. Augustine, who, during his episcopate at Hippo, addressed a treatise to the virgins of the city. The nature of religious consecration at this time was determined according to the rubrics of each local church. Our first evidence for a more universal formula comes from the *Gelasian Sacramentary* in the sixth century.

Meanwhile, an Irish monastic woman known as Bridget of Kildare (451–525) seems to have been a generic figure in a Religious Life development largely unknown till the latter half of the twentieth century. According to claims advanced by Medieval art historian Pamela Berger (1985), Christian monks took the ancient figure of the mother goddess and grafted her name and functions onto her Christian counterpart. Berger suggests that believers have syncretized St. Bridget with the pagan goddess Brighid. Whatever the origin of her fame, Bridget came to be known as a zealous leader and one of the first (it seems) to develop the concept of the double monastery, with male and female groups living adjacently.[1]

About one hundred years later we learn of another outstanding abbess, Hilda of Whitby (614–80), with influence even more extensive than that of Bridget. According to her biography, written by St. Bede, she was a skilled administrator and teacher. As a landowner she had many in her workforce to care for sheep and cattle, farm, and cut wood. Such was her reputation that kings and princes often sought her advice.

Throughout the first millennium, across mainland Europe, women ruled monastic communities. As abbess, such women exercised both religious and secular power that required many of them to learn Latin, normally reserved to bishops, male monks, and clergy. In the mid-seventh century, Salaberga of Laon, France, founded seven churches and took responsibility for three hundred nuns. Her contemporary, Fara, founded a joint community at Brie in the north of France, governed as abbess, and assumed priestly and episcopal power, hearing confessions and even excommunicating members.

In the eighth century we learn of such outstanding monastic women as Hrotsvit of Gandersheim (c.930–90), poet, historian, and the only person to write drama in Europe between the fourth and eleventh centuries. Harrad of Lanndsberg, abbess of Hohenberg in Alsace (1167–95), founded a community of canons, a community of nuns, and a hospital; she excelled in knowledge of the church fathers and other classical sources.

Of all these abbesses perhaps the most widely known is Hildegarde of Bingen (1098–1179), whose scientific treatises impressed both popes and emperors. She was also a doctor, pharmacist, playwright, poet, painter, and musician.

> The life of the astonishing Hildegarde of Bingen can be seen as a bridge from the hidden lives of most women in the early middle ages to the full flowering of mysticism in the thirteenth and fourteenth century. . . . The life of Hildegarde, while astonishing in its intellectual and scientific output, also sets down several

---

[1] Jo Ann Kay McNamara adds this witty remark: "So powerful was her position, and so strong the memory of her, that a ninth-century biography, probably intended to limit the influence of women in the Irish church, claimed that Bishop Mel recited the wrong liturgy when he gave her the veil and consecrated her a bishop by mistake. The point of the story seems to be in the bishop's ensuing proclamation that it was an honor no other woman would ever share" (1996, 121).

markers for the further development of women's mystical life. (Malone 2014, 63, 66)

Mechtilde of Magdeburg, Marguerite Porete, Gertrude of Helfta, Julian of Norwich, Catherine of Siena, and Teresa of Avila are among the other outstanding names in this fertile mystical wave of the High Middle Ages.

Hildegarde exhibits many of the outstanding qualities of the great foundresses, transgressing the cloister as a space of female confinement and earning a unique reputation as a female rhetorician, and also transcending bans on women's social participation, interpretation of scripture, and theological learning. The acceptance of public preaching by a woman, even a well-connected abbess and acknowledged prophet, does not fit the stereotype of her time. She conducted four preaching tours throughout Germany, speaking to both clergy and laity in chapter houses and in public, mainly denouncing clerical corruption and calling for reform. She used the curative powers of natural objects for healing, and she wrote treatises about natural history and medicinal uses of plants, animals, trees, and stones.

Many abbots and abbesses asked her for prayers and sought her advice on a range of issues. She corresponded with popes, emperors, and other notable figures, such as St. Bernard of Clairvaux, who supported and advanced her work. Her name entered the Roman martyrology at the end of the sixteenth century. After four failed attempts, she was eventually canonized by Pope Benedict XVI in May 2012, and in October of the same year she was declared a doctor of the church.

Her character was steely and determined—overbearing at times—exhibiting a patriarchal approach that would win little approval in our time. But the nuns who flourished under her unorthodox regime were allowed extraordinary freedoms, such as wearing their hair long, uncovered, and even crowned with flowers. Nevertheless, Hildegarde's transformative and prophetic life commanded the respect of the church and political leaders of the day.

The Great Foundresses

As we enter the second Christian millennium, female Religious Life takes a kind of quantum leap that has received scant historical attention, leaving us with a seriously unjust historical imbalance. According to the Fourth Lateran Council of 1215, new Religious foundations had to adopt either the rule of Benedict or that of Augustine. Moreover, the bull *Periculoso*, issued by Pope Boniface in 1298, decreed that women Religious everywhere must be cloistered; it was further extended by Clement V to include consecrated women, such as the Beguines, Tertiaries, and other less formally consecrated women. The decree on female cloistered living was reinforced at the Council of Trent and at Vatican I in the late nineteenth century. Realizing the acute needs of the time, and eager to respond within a spiritual context, women began to circumvent the enclosed regulations, leading to one of the most empowering and inspired developments in the richly textured story of women and men Religious across the ages.

Leading the way is Clare of Assisi (1193–1253), articulating a female flavor of the vowed life with women themselves creating the environment. Despite opposition of successive popes (Honorius III, Gregory IX, and Innocent IV), Clare persevered in her endeavor and shortly before her death won pontifical approval for the rule she had written: *The Form of Life of Clare of Assisi*. This was the first rule written by a woman to receive papal approval.

Another pioneering figure is that of St. Bridget of Sweden (1303–73), a patron of a double monastery but also the foundress of a group of sisters whose healing service to the victims of the Black Plague required breaching the laws of enclosure. Both Clare and Bridget set a new precedent, a more open, apostolic thrust that would define the outstanding contribution of female Religious for subsequent centuries. Both dented the patriarchal monopoly, circumventing and transcending the value system of domination and control that had characterized the hierarchical church itself for several centuries (McNamara 1996, 317ff.).

The great foundresses populate the evolving landscape, particularly from the fifteenth century onward. I have selected a small sample to indicate the unique prophetic witness initiated by these women. What I want to highlight particularly is their bold countercultural stance, due to which they often endured disapproval and rebuttal from secular and ecclesiastical powers alike. On a few occasions it took over one hundred years to exonerate and approve their radical vision—a new paradigm with subversive parabolic undercurrents.

I am well aware of the risks of making the kind of selection I present here. Every female group is rightly proud of its foundress—or of the outstanding early devotees, when the founding person was male rather than female. I hope the stories I present also represent the prophetic visionary endeavor of the many I don't name yet whose contributions are also such an integral part of our sacred history.

St. Angela Merici (1470–1540)

Foundress of the Ursulines, Angela was born c. 1470 in Desenzano, a small town near Lake Garda in Lombardy. Angela's religious imagination appears to be rooted in the numinous experiences she had as a young girl. Her love for scripture; her ability to contemplate and discern the lives of saints, particularly Ursula and Catherine of Alexandria; her desire for prayer and fasting; and her intrinsic need to serve others—all were woven into a mystical sense of faith, described by Bernadette Flanagan as "the mystic journey from which deep change emerges" (2014, 97).

In 1516, Angela, now forty-two years of age, moved to Brescia (Lombardy, Northern Italy) and offered spiritual support to a reform movement known as Divino Amore (Company of Divine Love). The company established infirmaries for those suffering from syphilis, cared for widows and their families, and founded an orphanage and a shelter for former prostitutes. It was, however, the attraction to mystical prayer and devotion that united the group, which in due course attracted both men and women, all seeking Angela's spiritual wisdom and guidance.

By 1532, Angela had assembled a small group of female followers (drawn from the Company of Divine Love), and together they embarked on the formation of Angela's community. In 1535, she chose twenty-eight virgins and started the foundation of the Company of St. Ursula. By 1536, Angela drew up a rule for the new group, one of the first to be written by a woman for a community of women. Angela instructed her sisters to live in their own homes, retaining their lay identity. They met in small groups to pray and support one another in their mystical devotion to Christ and some charitable outreach to people in need. Angela died in 1540, five years after founding the Company of St. Ursula. Her final words include a plea to her sisters to retain adaptability as a key virtue for the future.

In 1544, Pope Paul III granted papal approval to the group. Many members became involved in catechetical teaching arising from the Council of Trent, and Cardinal Charles Borromeo quickly recognized the value of their contribution. While deeply admiring the lifestyle and work of these women, Borromeo was uneasy about the sense of self-determination of their rule, particularly the expressed reliance on the Holy Spirit without any reference to clergy or church authority. Eventually, in 1582, Borromeo drew up a "revised, reformed and re-written" rule, bringing the sisters—most but not all—directly under church authority and effectively changing the company into a canonical Religious Order, one branch of which became identified with an educational ministry.[2]

While Angela never intended to found a Religious Order/Congregation, she merits her place among the great foundresses for these reasons:

- Angela Merici's foundational wisdom prioritized a quality of mystical vision that Sandra Schneiders claims to be distinctively unique to the experience of women Religious of every era. Schneiders describes it as the God quest, an underlying and enduring female characteristic largely ignored by male commentators, and by the official church itself (2000, 297; 2001, 187ff.; 2013, 96–98).
- With this same integrated sense of mystical devotion, Angela was able to transcend the more ascetical influence of fleeing and abandoning God's world. For Angela, the spousal relationship with God happened in and through God's world, not in spite of it.
- Angela was a pioneering figure in the movement to outgrow female enclosure, with its oppressive restrictions for so many holy and heroic women.
- Angela's desire for a more feminine mode of governance within Religious Life characterized by fluidity, flexibility, and a diminished sense of institutionalization is clearly a prophetic challenge not merely for her own historical context, but for our time as well.
- The eventual taming and institutionalization of most of Angela's group (and her original rule) alerts us to the need for a more informed mode of discernment in the refounding that will engage all our Orders and Congregations in the later decades of the twenty-first century.

Louise de Marillac (1591–1660)

Louise was born to a noble family near Meux in Paris in 1591. She did not know her mother but was loved and cared for by her father until his death when Louise was sixteen years old. Her desire to become a nun was discouraged by her confessor, and a marriage to Antoine Le Gras was arranged. She soon found herself nursing her husband through a long illness that led to his death.

---

[2] For more information on this Order, see Durkin 2005.

Louise was fortunate to have a wise and sympathetic counselor, St. Francis de Sales, but it was a Fr. Vincent, later known as St. Vincent de Paul, who influenced her profoundly and introduced her to his Confraternities of Charity, ladies of social status who were helping him nurse the poor and look after neglected children. Despite her continuing feeble health, Louise threw herself wholeheartedly into care for the needy and began to organize the female coworkers into apostolic groups in order to provide a better quality of care for those she sought to serve.

Sensitive to the plight of the marginalized and prepared to break rank with the nobility of the time, Louise found the help she needed in young, humble countrywomen who had the energy and the proper attitude to deal with people weighed down by destitution and suffering. As she began working with them, she saw a need for common life and formation. Consequently, she invited four of these women to live in her home in the Rue des Fosses-Saint-Victor and began training them in the spiritual life and in the care for those in need, thus establishing, in 1633, the Congregation known today as the Daughters of Charity.

Popular history tends to construe Louise as one who was heavily influenced by Vincent, while in fact she was a woman of vision and passion, with an unstinting sense of service to the disenfranchised masses of her day. In terms of the emergence of the new Congregation, I suspect Louise took many of the bold initiatives, concurring with Vincent's wish not to found a formal Religious Congregation, opting instead for her own home as the base for ministering to the sick and needy, adopting the parish church for her chapel, the streets of the city or the wards of the hospital as her cloister. The adopted dress was that of the peasant women.

In order to continue working directly with the poor in their own homes and avoid enclosure in convents, Louise and her coworkers remained a community of lay women. Later, they began to take vows of poverty, chastity, obedience, and service to the poor for one year at a time; to this day the Daughters of Charity renew their vows annually. In 1655, the Company of the Daughters of Charity was formally approved by Rome and placed under the direction of Vincent's own congregation of priests, known as the Congregation of the Mission or Vincentians.

Meanwhile, despite her poor health Louise traveled throughout France, establishing her community members in hospitals, orphanages, and other institutions set up to care for the mentally ill, prisoners, and those wounded in battle. The Daughters of Charity became renowned for their flexibility and for mobility in responding to acute need. This mobility was a major innovation in an era when consecrated women were officially bound by enclosure and expected to reside in a monastic context of relative stability.

As a wife, mother, teacher, nurse, social worker, mystic, and Religious foundress, she serves as a model for all liminal, prophetic women. At her death in March 1660, the Congregation had more than forty houses in France and one house in Spain. Louise de Marillac was canonized in 1934 and declared patroness of social workers in 1960. Today, her inspiration continues to flourish in the eighteen thousand Daughters of Charity serving throughout the world, along with a large cohort of lay collaborators.

Mary Ward (1585–1645)

At a time when Catholics in the United Kingdom were being persecuted, Mary Ward was born in Ripon, North Yorkshire. At the age of fifteen Mary felt called to the Religious Life and became a Poor Clare in the convent at St. Omer, Flanders. In 1609, after a period of discernment, she decided to leave the Poor Clares and return to England, where she worked with the underground church, undertaking prison visitations, tending the sick and catechesis. Condemned to death for this work, she left London with a small group of companions in the late autumn of 1609 and returned to St. Omer.

Mary wanted to create a group of women dedicated to service in the church on a par with the Jesuits. Her bold initiative, which evoked praise from certain ranks of laity and approval from some Jesuits, provoked an angry and negative reaction from clerics and church authorities, leading to a series of censures against Mary and her companions.

For her newly emerging group Mary sought a degree of autonomy unheard of in those times. Her women were to be dressed in ordinary clothes, would not be confined by monastic enclosure, and most controversial, were not to be under any male Order but were to be self-governing. These demands were in contradiction to the norms of the Council of Trent and presented great difficulty for the leadership of the post-Reformation church.

Pope Pius V (1566–72) had declared solemn vows and strict papal enclosure to be essential to all communities of women Religious. When she applied to the Holy See for formal approbation for the propagation of her institute in Flanders, Bavaria, Austria, and Italy, this ruling was a major problem. In 1629, she was allowed to plead her cause in person before the congregation of cardinals appointed by Urban to examine the situation. Mary had traveled throughout Europe on foot, sometimes in extreme poverty and frequently ill, founding schools in the Netherlands, Italy, Germany, Austria, today's Czech Republic, and Slovakia. Nonetheless, the cardinals of the Inquisition prevailed, and in 1631 a bull of suppression was imposed on Mary and her institute. Although never formally condemned, Mary was imprisoned in Munich as a heretic, schismatic, and rebel. The institute was suppressed, the schools were closed, and the members of the institute dispersed.

Later that year Mary was released from prison and subsequently absolved by Pope Urban VIII. Despite the suppression, some of Mary's companions continued to live together as lay people and, under the patronage of the elector of Bavaria, the school in Munich reopened. In 1639, with letters of introduction from Pope Urban to the queen of France, Mary returned to England and established herself in London. There, she and her companions established free schools for the poor, nursed the sick, and visited prisoners. In 1642 she journeyed northward and established a convent at Heworth, near York, where she died in 1645.

Despite numerous efforts to gain approval for Mary Ward's dream, in 1703 these women acquiesced to a limited rule based on the Ignatian spirit—a begrudging approval with the stipulation that the sisters would not call Mary Ward their foundress. The Loreto Sisters, founded in Dublin in 1822, also count Mary Ward as their foundress, but neither branch of the Congregation gained canonical approval until 1909—by Pope Pius X—some 260 years after the death of Mary Ward.

Of all the foundresses recorded in this book, Mary Ward's story stands out for its uncompromising resilience and prophetic boldness in the face of fierce opposition from petrified ecclesiastics. The fiery zeal of this outstanding reformer, educator, liberator, and mystic serves as a perpetual reminder to all Religious of what authentic gospel empowerment entails. We trust that the creative Spirit will call forth women and men of this prophetic calibre in the closing decades of the twenty-first century.

Nano Nagle (1718–84)

Nano Nagle was born in Ballygriffin, County Cork, in 1718. She lived during a period in Irish history when the English had imposed the Penal Laws. The Irish were denied access economically, politically, socially, and educationally to the rights and means that would have raised them from poverty and oppression. Catholics who dared to teach were subjected to heavy fines, confiscations, and periods of imprisonment. It was equally treasonable for Irish children to be sent overseas for their education.

While living in Cork with her brother, Joseph, Nano set up her first school for poor children in 1745. Such were the oppressive conditions of the time she kept this a secret even from her own brother. In time, and after some intense conflict, he became her ardent supporter as she set up a network of schools in and around Cork city. Nagle began to visit the sick and the elderly after school, bringing them food, medicine, and comfort. She opened a home for aged women and began conducting adult classes. She went from hovel to hovel each day to gather the most needy people for sustenance and basic education. Night ministries to poverty-ridden elderly, to the sick, and to those forced into prostitution in her hometown, gave Nano Nagle the nickname the Lady with the Lantern.

Nano and her female collaborators continued their work without becoming an established Religious Congregation, so they were free to work for the poor without being enclosed. When her uncle Joseph died in 1757, he left her a large sum of money that she devoted to building schools and convents, providing relief for the poor and the infirm. She resisted the local bishop when he expressed fears that the establishment of the convent might provoke a Protestant backlash. On Christmas Eve, 1775, she founded the Society of Charitable Instruction of the Sacred Heart of Jesus in Cork. Initially, all of this work was done in secret; in time, even the political authorities were so impressed by her good works that they chose to overlook her infringement of the prevailing laws.

Her first convent in Ireland was opened in Cork in 1775 and her first group of sisters made vowed commitment in June 1777. Nano enjoyed a long and supportive friendship with the Ursuline Sisters in both France and Ireland (and in earlier years considered becoming an Ursuline), but because of the enclosed restrictions imposed upon the Ursulines in the eighteenth century, Nano continued to honor the call to be available to people in need without the inhibition of legal or religious restrictions.

Such was the depth of her flexibility and creativity that when she died in 1784 she had not drawn up a formal rule for her community. True to the mythic spirit of new foundations, Nano Nagle kept her focus on vision and mission, not on legalities or structures. Retaining such visionary flexibility will always remain central to every new refounding endeavor.[3]

Rose Philippine Duchesne (1769–1852)

Rose Philippine was born in Grenoble, France, in 1769. She was educated by the Visitation nuns and entered the Visitation Order in 1788, as the French Revolution was developing. She was not able to make her profession because of the social and political disruption and had to return home when the Visitation Sisters were expelled from their convents.

During the revolution she cared for the sick and poor, helped fugitive priests, visited prisons, and taught children. After the revolution she tried to reorganize the Visitation community but was unsuccessful, so she offered the empty convent to Madeleine Sophie Barat, foundress of the Society of the Sacred Heart; she entered the Sacred Heart Order herself in 1804. When the bishop of New Orleans, William Dubourg, requested nuns for his huge Louisiana diocese, Philippine and four companions came to the United States, arriving in New Orleans in 1818.

Philippine came to the wilds of North America when much of the country was still an uncharted wilderness. She came up the Mississippi River to the St. Louis area, where she established schools at St. Charles in September 1818; in Florissant, in 1819; and in Saint Louis in 1827.

She also established a school in Grand Coteau, Louisiana, in 1821. The United States had purchased the area from France only fifteen years before the sisters' arrival, and settlers, many poor but others with money and slaves, were streaming in from the East Coast of the United States. Their new foundations faced many struggles, including lack of funds, inadequate housing, hunger, and very cold weather; even learning the English language proved quite a challenge.

With the eagerness and zeal so typical of the great foundresses, Philippine quickly discerned the pressing social and spiritual needs and responded by building convents, orphanages, schools for Indian girls, boarding academies, and a novitiate for her order. Ten years after her arrival there were three houses of the Sacred Heart in Missouri and

---

[3] Bernadette Flanagan, herself a Presentation Sister, provides a more comprehensive overview of Nano Nagle's contribution as a prophetic woman with an enduring sense of inspiration for present and future refounding endeavors (Flanagan 2014, 100–113). Readers can explore the greater depths of Nano's life in Consedine 1977.

three in Louisiana, with twenty-seven sisters—only eleven of whom had come from Europe—and twenty-five American novices.

Philippine was a woman of indomitable character, acutely aware of pressing needs everywhere she went. Her zeal for gospel service was exemplary, with a prodigious outpouring of creative energy and innovative ideas. Central to her resilience was a depth of faith that was as contagious as it was remarkable. When she was seventy-two years old she finally realized her original desire to be with the Indians in a new foundation at Sugar Creek, Kansas. There, she spent much of her time nursing the sick, despite her own increasing fragility. Gradually withdrawing from pastoral ministry, she devoted much time to prayer; among the Potawatomi Indian children she came to be known as the Woman Who Always Prays.

Her last years were spent at St. Charles. To the end she was a model disciple of the companionship of empowerment, exhibiting the evangelical zeal and courageous response to urgent need that have characterized refounding of Religious Life in every age and culture. She died on November 18, 1852, at the age of eighty-three, and she was canonized by Pope John Paul II in 1988.

Catherine McAuley (1778—1841)

Catherine McAuley was born in Dublin in 1778. After the death of her father in 1783, the family faced increasing poverty and separation. When her mother died in 1798, Catherine was living with her Catholic uncle's family; her sister and brother were with Protestant friends or relatives.

In 1803, at the age of twenty-five, Catherine took a step that would deeply affect the rest of her life. She began to live with Catherine and William O'Callaghan, a wealthy, elderly, and childless Protestant couple. After the O'Callaghans died, Catherine McAuley found herself the sole residuary legatee of their estate. She began to use this inherited wealth to implement the gospel dream she had long nurtured. She leased property and built a large House of Mercy on Baggot Street, Dublin, to serve as a free school for poor girls, a shelter for homeless girls and women, and a residence for lay coworkers who joined her in these works of mercy. The house opened on September 24, 1827, the feast of Our Lady of Mercy.

The Baggot Street community was not initially intended to be a Religious Congregation (a feature common among female founders); it was simply a group of Catholic lay women doing the merciful work of the gospel by visiting the sick poor and serving women and girls who were disenfranchised, uneducated, and distressed. Despite the charitable work of the community, criticism, both lay and clerical, quickly erupted: the community was seen as drawing support away from established Religious Orders in Dublin (though not by those Orders themselves); people complained that they looked like nuns and acted like nuns without approval from Rome.

Like several other foundresses, Catherine dreaded the possibility of enclosure, lest it prevent her ministry to the poor and sick in the slums of Dublin. She also desired a convent lifestyle more flexible and adaptable to the needs of mission. Eventually, for the sake of stable continuance of the works of mercy, she established the Sisters of Mercy in December 1831. The early years involved many struggles—various forms of opposition, shortage of money, clerical disputes, a lawsuit, and community illnesses. For Catherine, these were "portions of the cross of Christ" that she tried to embrace with patience and unrelenting trust in divine providence.

Between 1836 and 1841 (when Catherine died), the Sisters of Mercy created eleven foundations in Ireland and England. Catherine had been a Sister of Mercy for only ten years. In that time she worked tirelessly to respond to the need of the poor and sick. In time the sisters translated the mission of mercy into education and healthcare. Today, about seventy-five hundred Sisters of Mercy and five thousand Mercy Associates serve the needy in forty countries of the world.

Catherine McAuley was a woman of bold, prophetic vision. She was an innovator in what she did and also in how she did things. Passionate in her commitment to Christ and the gospel, no challenge to liberate people from oppression was seen as too great. In 1990, in recognition of her outstanding Christian work, Catherine was declared venerable by Pope John Paul II.

Elizabeth Lange (1794–1882)

Little is known about the early years of Elizabeth Lange, a mulatto woman born in Santiago de Cuba in a French-speaking community. Despite receiving an excellent education, young Elizabeth left Cuba to seek peace and security in the United States. It is believed that she first went to Charleston, South Carolina, and then Norfolk, Virginia, finally settling in Baltimore, Maryland, around 1813. Elizabeth lived in an area settled by immigrants, many from French-speaking Haiti.

It did not take Elizabeth long to recognize that the children of her fellow immigrants needed an education. While Maryland was a slave state, it was never illegal to teach people of color, whether slave or free. Elizabeth responded to the urgent needs of her oppressed friends and used her own money and home to open a school to teach black children. For many years Elizabeth and her friend Marie Magdaleine Balas offered a free education to Catholics and non-Catholics alike.

At the same time Elizabeth and Marie were teaching children in their home, a Sulpician priest, Father James Joubert SS, a refugee of the Haitian Revolution, was teaching catechism to French-speaking immigrant children from the Caribbean. Encountering a great deal of illiteracy, Fr. Joubert invited the two women to form a Religious Order to serve the needs of these deprived children. In 1828, they established the Saint Francis School for colored girls, while also starting the novitiate for what was to become the Oblate Sisters of Providence. In July 1829, Elizabeth and three of her colleagues took their first vows. Henceforth, she was known as Mother Mary.

The new Order pledged to educate and evangelize African Americans, yet it would always be open to meeting the needs of the times. Thus, the Oblate Sisters educated youth and provided a home for orphans. Freed slaves were educated and at times admitted into the Order. They nursed the terminally ill during the cholera epidemic of 1832, sheltered the elderly, and helped the local church in a variety of ways.

Elizabeth Lange practiced faith to an extraordinary degree. In fact, it was her deep faith that enabled her to persevere against all odds, including racial injustice and poverty. To her black brothers and sisters she gave of herself and her material possessions. She rose above the social and religious stigmas of her time. She was a woman of vision and selfless commitment, who personally took action to meet the social, religious and educational needs of poor women and children. Her influence is still felt today in the many communities around the world where the Oblate Sisters of Providence minister to young and old alike.[4]

Other significant foundresses of color were Herrietta Delille (d.1862) and her co-foundress, Juliette Gaudin (d.1887), and Theresa Maxis Duchemin (d.1892).

Theodore Guerin (1798–1856)

Anne-Thérèse Guérin was born in Brittany toward the end of the French Revolution. Like many other great foundresses, her early child-

---

[4] An imminent founding model for reading the signs of the times and responding with great generosity of spirit, the evolving story of Elizabeth and the Order she founded is documented in Morrow 2002.

hood was marked by personal tragedy (the death of two younger brothers), social dislocation, and religious persecution. When she was fifteen, tragedy struck the family again with the violent death of her father at the hands of robbers, leaving Anne-Thérèse to look after her grief-stricken mother and sister. At the age of twenty-five she entered the young congregation of the Sisters of Providence of Ruillé-sur-Loir and was given the name Sister St. Theodore. From 1825 to 1839 she taught in various local schools staffed and managed by her Order.

In 1839 the newly consecrated bishop of the Diocese of Vincennes, Indiana, Célestine de la Hailandière, invited the Sisters of Providence to come and minister in Vincennes. Sister Theodore and five companions departed from France, sailing to America in July 1840. After a treacherous journey across the Atlantic Ocean, the six women arrived at Saint Mary-of-the-Woods, Indiana, in October 1840; they opened their first school in July 1841.

This was the beginning of an educational ministry that was to extend across many parts of the United States, but not without numerous trials. The sisters often went hungry, sometimes going without food for days. They experienced the heat, humidity, and mosquitoes of Indiana summers and the heavy snows of winters. They planted crops and raised hogs and other animals on their farm. Once they suffered a fire that destroyed their barn and harvest.

In 1843, Theodore traveled to France to raise money for the community and to solidify the relationship between the sisters in the United States and those in France, only to learn of a decision made to separate the Indiana foundation from the Ruillé motherhouse. This decision caused great grief and consternation for the French sisters in Indiana.

However, between 1843 to 1847 Theodore's greatest challenge was not the welfare of her fledgling community but her relationship with Bishop Hailandière. Even before she left for France, it was clear that the bishop believed that he possessed total control over the Sisters of Providence. While she was in France, the bishop took over the community, admitting novices to vows, closing the school at St. Francisville, receiving three nuns from another community, and calling for the election of a superior. He hoped that the sisters would elect a different superior, but they reelected Mother Theodore.

After her return Theodore's meetings with Bishop Hailandière grew more and more contentious, often lasting for hours. He insisted on an Act of Reparation from the sisters because he believed they had spoken out against him to his superiors. The matter reached a crisis in 1847 when Bishop Hailandière declared that Mother Theodore was no longer the superior, indeed, no longer even a Sister of Providence. He released her from her vows, and he demanded that she leave his diocese and have no communication with her sisters at Saint Mary's. Despite such harsh treatment, Mother Theodore held a respectful sense of integrity.

It was at this point that the Vatican came to the rescue of Mother Theodore, who wasn't the only one having difficulties with Bishop Hailandière. Amid the turmoil in the diocese, Bishop Hailandière submitted his resignation to Rome. Things began to change under Hailandière's successors as the sisters enjoyed a new quality of support and encouragement. By the time Mother Theodore died in 1856, at the age of fifty-eight, more than sixty sisters were running eleven schools throughout Indiana and in Eastern Illinois and also two orphanages. One of the schools is today's Saint Mary-of-the-Woods College.

Canonized a saint by Pope Benedict XVI in 2006, Theodore was a woman of courage, determination, compassion, and deep faith, a pioneering educator, astute business woman, and champion of justice.[5]

Margaret Anna Cusack (1829–99)

Margaret Anna Cusack, known as Mother Francis Clare, the Nun of Kenmare, has long been a legend—one of the most colorful and controversial Irish women who ever lived. Born in Coolock, County Dublin, into a Protestant ascendancy family, she joined an Anglican sisterhood but grew disillusioned. Becoming a Catholic, she entered the Order of the Poor Clares in 1858 and later, from her convent in Kenmare, began to pour out the stream of books and pamphlets that made her famous. Supporting all the great causes of her time—Home Rule, the Land League, Women's Rights, Famine Relief—she incurred the hatred of many Establishment figures. Her life became a continuous struggle to translate her ideals into lived reality. Among the great foundresses she excels in her ability to read the signs of the times.

The famine of 1879 plunged Ireland into a severe crisis. Margaret Anna responded by raising vast sums of money to feed the poor. Her outspoken ways and success at feeding the hungry earned her a reputation that evoked both admiration and resentment. Such was the eventual resistance that she was forced to shut down her Famine Relief Fund. She then focused her efforts in England, feeling betrayed and disillusioned by the response in Ireland.

---

[5] Her inspiring story is further elaborated in Mitchell 2006.

Not content to feed and educate the poor, Cusack wrote justice-oriented books investigating why the poor were hungry and uneducated. She criticized both British and Irish leaders, including Catholic bishops and landlords, who usually treated their subjects in a condescending and patronizing way. In the politically explosive atmosphere that was Ireland in the 1870s and 1880s, such writing gained her enemies who attacked and slandered her, often viciously and anonymously.

After her work in Kenmare she moved to Knock, the site of apparitions in 1879, working with the same missionary zeal—and still making enemies. She also angered the local clergy in Knock by showing that some miracle healings that the clergy had accepted as genuine had not been properly researched. Whenever and wherever she traveled, fearful and disgruntled clergy warned people to avoid her. Despite opposition from some priests and bishops, in 1884 she won papal approval—from Leo XIII—to start a new Religious group, the Congregation of the Sisters of St. Joseph of Peace. Other prelates and priests, allied with powerful political interests, continued to spread rumors against her.

In 1889, weakened, tired, and sick after decades of ministry and continuing battles with some church prelates, Mother Francis resigned from the Order she had founded and continued to love so that her personal struggles would not keep the Order from flourishing. Ten years later she died in England and was buried with Anglican rites. At the Congregation's General Chapter at Nottingham, UK, in July 1970, the sisters sought to reclaim afresh the mission of peace through justice so boldly proclaimed by Mother Francis.

Margaret Anna Cusack was a dogged and compassionate champion of the underprivileged and a pioneering spirit in the cause of equal rights for women. She remains one of the most daring and prophetic among all the great foundresses of Christian Religious Life.

Mary McKillop (1842–1909)

The Sisters of St. Joseph, otherwise known as the Josephites—and colloquially as the Brown Joeys—were the first Religious Order to be founded by an Australian. As well as being extremely compassionate, Mary McKillop was a strong-willed seeker of justice. She stood up for what she believed, which brought her into conflict with the religious authorities of her day.

The Josephites were unusual among Catholic Church ministries in two ways. First, the sisters lived in small communities among the people rather than in convents. Second, the Congregation's constitution required administration by a superior general chosen from within the group rather than by the bishop. The Josephites incurred further disapproval by refusing to teach instrumental music, then considered an essential part of education by the church. The Congregation's work was among working-class children whose parents simply could not afford musical instruments.

Tension escalated into conflict, and in 1871 Mary McKillop was excommunicated by Bishop Shiel for alleged insubordination. The excommunication, which was lifted six months later, was imposed for a number of reasons, chiefly, (1) the sisters adopted a centralized form of governance, very different from European Congregations; (2) most of the sisters came from working-class backgrounds and prioritized working-class people in their ministries; (3) the sisters moved publicly among the people, visiting the homes of the poor, jails, and hospitals; (4) they lived a very simple lifestyle, occasionally relying on begging for their survival.

It was the originality of their witness and their claim to a distinctively female way of organizing and living Religious Life that irritated the bishops. Mary McKillop herself, despite her harsh treatment, always remained loyal to church authority, while not in any way compromising her prophetic vision. Though the Josephites were not disbanded, most of their schools were closed in the wake of the excommunication. Forbidden to have contact with anyone in the church, McKillop lived with a Jewish family and was also sheltered by Jesuit priests.[6]

In later years she traveled throughout Australasia, establishing schools, convents and charitable institutions, coming into conflict with those bishops who preferred diocesan control over the Sisterhood rather than central control from Adelaide. In 1883, Bishop Christopher Reynolds, misunderstanding the extent of his jurisdiction over the Sisterhood, told her to leave his diocese. She then transferred the headquarters of the Congregation to Sydney.

In May 1901 she suffered a stroke at Rotorua, New Zealand. Although retaining her mental faculties, she was an invalid until she died in Sydney in August 1909. Mary was beatified in 1994 and canonized in 2010. Creative, resilient, and courageously prophetic, Mary McKillop is an eminent role model for the refounding of Religious Life in every age.[7]

---

[6] Some of the sisters chose to remain under diocesan control, becoming popularly known as Black Joeys.

[7] For her fuller story, see Gardiner 1993.

Katharine Drexel (1858–1955)

Katharine Drexel was born in Pennsylvania in 1858. In 1889, she left her life as an heiress, when she affiliated with the Sisters of Mercy. In February 1891 she took the name Mother Katharine and, joined by thirteen other women, formally established her Religious Congregation, the Sisters of the Blessed Sacrament. The Congregation was dedicated to work among the American Indians and blacks in the western and southwestern United States. The Congregation was founded twenty-eight years after the Emancipation Proclamation, which freed the slaves, but the reality of a good life for blacks was still bleak in many places. The country was still seventy years away from any widespread notion of civil rights.

In 1894, Katharine and fifteen of her sisters set up a school for Native Americans in Santa Fe, New Mexico. This was followed by the creation of other schools throughout the Southwest, including ones on reservations. But the education of black children became the new Congregation's primary work, incurring the suspicion and unease of a culture still deeply influenced by white supremacy.

Knowing that many blacks were far from free, still living in substandard conditions as sharecroppers or underpaid menials, denied education and constitutional rights enjoyed by others, Katharine dedicated her educational ministry to change racial attitudes throughout the United States. The turn of the twentieth century marked the height of the Jim Crow laws, accompanied by a good deal of anti-Catholic sentiment, particularly in the South. In 1913 the Georgia Legislature, hoping to stop the Blessed Sacrament Sisters from teaching at a Macon school, tried to pass a law that would prohibit white teachers from teaching black students. When Mother Katharine purchased an abandoned university building to open Xavier Preparatory School in New Orleans (in 1915), vandals smashed every window. Despite such opposition, Katherine and her sisters continued with unflinching courage.

In Charlotte, North Carolina, Katharine contributed four thousand dollars to finish construction of two churches with the stipulation that an entire aisle of pews be set aside for use by black parishioners. In Wilmington she funded construction of a new church to replace an old church and be used by both blacks and whites. But when a priest, a transplant from Katharine's home state of Pennsylvania, objected to the plan, blacks got the old church and whites the new one.

Her charitable ways so impressed Congress in the 1920s that several lawyers and congressmen successfully lobbied for an amendment to the federal tax code that would allow an organization that gave at least 90 percent of its income to charity an exemption from income taxes. The law became known as "the Philadelphia Nun Loophole."

By 1942, the sisters had established educational services for black Catholic schools in thirteen states, plus forty mission centers, along with twenty-three rural schools. Over the course of six decades Katharine spent about twenty million dollars of her private fortune building schools and churches, as well as paying the salaries of teachers in rural schools for blacks and Indians, while also contributing to missionary endeavors at home and abroad for the education and enhancement of black and Native American peoples.

Even though she was raised in opulence, Katharine took seriously her vow of poverty, living in utter simplicity and frugal surroundings. An ardent devotee of eucharistic adoration, in the fragility of her last years she fulfilled her lifelong desire for a contemplative life. She died in 1955 at the age of ninety-six and was canonized as a Catholic saint in 2000. Her lifelong commitment to racial justice and equality makes her a champion of gospel inclusivity.

Mary Josephine Rogers (1882–1955)

As founder of the first American mission Congregation of Catholic women, Mary Joseph (or Mollie as she is affectionately known among the Maryknoll Sisters) proved that women were equal to the demands of life and ministry abroad, particularly in places where poverty, ignorance, and oppression prevailed. She was raised in an Irish Catholic family at a time when anti-Catholic discrimination was still rife in the United States. She was sent to public schools to maximize her chances for success in life, and later to Smith College in Northampton, Massachusetts, where she earned her bachelor's degree.

From a young age Mollie seems to have transcended the culture of religious discrimination and may have obtained the original inspiration for a missionary calling by observing the Protestant Student Volunteer Movement for the Foreign Missions that flourished on the Smith College campus. That movement sent idealistic young people overseas as missionaries. There was nothing comparable in the American Catholic Church at the time. Amazing for 1906, Mollie saw Protestants not as rivals but as models. Here was a woman comfortable with religious diversity.

Mollie's close affiliation with Fr. James A. Walsh from 1908 to 1912 led to the creation of a group of female affiliates known as the secretaries. In 1920 that same group, then numbering forty, was recognized as a diocesan Religious Congregation, the Foreign Mission

Sisters of St. Dominic, known today as the Maryknoll Sisters. At the first General Chapter in 1925, Mollie was elected mother general. Mother Mary Joseph (her Religious name) was reelected to that office at subsequent General Chapters until her retirement in 1946 at the age of sixty-four. By that time the Congregation numbered 733, and the sisters were working in Asia (China, Japan, Korea, the Philippines) and in Latin America (Panama, Bolivia, Nicaragua), as well as with ethnic and racial groups in the United States.

In 1908, Rome had declared the United States to be no longer mission territory; it could now send missionaries for evangelization elsewhere. Not only was Mollie Rogers one of the first to heed that missionary endeavor, but she brought to it an empowering vision transcending narrow proselytizing. From the beginning she accepted sisters from any culture of the world where Maryknoll worked, requiring for her sisters a quality of formation necessary to deal with the varieties of racism and ethnicity they encountered within and without.

Mollie's own spirituality exhibits a quality of inclusivity largely unknown at that time. She wanted her sisters to combine and integrate contemplation and action, unity and diversity, individuality and the common good. Even among apostolic female Congregations in the early twentieth century, canonical procedure required sisters to be in their convent or, while outside, to minister collectively, not individually (the imposition of enclosure still haunted female Religious Life). From the beginning the Maryknoll Sisters in China traveled in twos and moved freely in the Chinese towns and villages, a creative liberty adopted by Mollie Rogers long before Rome gave official approval.

Mollie Rogers frequently reminded the sisters to be women of courage, honesty, charity, and courtesy, with a tender love for God and for all God's creatures. She was a woman grounded in the ordinary with a vision that embraced the extraordinary. When she sent the first sisters to China on mission, she was not content to serve as some distant administrator. She followed them to China and spent several months immersed in the culture, experiencing the hardships and culture first hand. By the time of her death on October 9, 1955, there were 1,065 Maryknoll Sisters working in twenty countries and serving minorities in several cities in the United States.

Reclaiming the Subverted Vision

Barbara Newman (2011), in her brief overview of the life of Cornelia Connelly (1809–79), foundress of the Holy Child Sisters, portrays a woman of intense engagement with life—home life, marriage, family responsibilities (she mothered five children), trauma, and struggles, which at times were emotionally, socially and religiously distressing. Several of the same features characterize Elizabeth Seton (1774–1821), foundress of the Sisters of Charity, a pioneering figure in Catholic education in the United States and the first native-born American canonized by the Catholic Church (in 1975). It is important to note that many of the great foundresses were married women who raised children, lost partners to disease or untimely death, knew from firsthand experience the ups and downs of life. Perhaps it was this social and marital immersion that enabled them to read the signs of their times with such acute perception and to respond with such utter dedication, brushing aside all the legal and religious objections they encountered.

In the lives of many of these outstanding women there was no dualistic splitting. In the intimacy and depth of their experience, the sacred and the secular were one. They knew the unity of body, mind, and spirit far ahead of the holistic health movement of the twentieth century. They created a feminist consciousness as prophetic and outstanding as any other, ancient or modern. To them we can emphatically apply the affirmative words used in the "Final Report on the Aposotlic Visitation of Institutes of Women Religious in the United States of America," published on December 16, 2014: "Since the early days of the Catholic Church in their country, women religious have courageously been in the forefront of her evangelizing mission, selflessly tending to the spiritual, moral, educational, physical and social needs of countless individuals." This statement should be heard as an acclamation for what women Religious have achieved, not merely in the United States over recent millennia, but ever since the birth of the vowed life in early Christian times.

The great foundresses were women who broke with the respectable, the influential, the institutional, and the dominant. They read the prevailing winds of economics, politics, religion, and culture, and they smelled the air of death, of manipulation and control, of abuse of power and lack of humanity. At the same time they recognized too the fear and insecurity, the pain, the cries, and the silence of those who were victims and treated inhumanely.[8]

Megan McKenna (2010) summarizes the accomplishments of the women she names under twelve headings that also provide a fine

---

[8] These same characteristics are highlighted in stories of other women who have shaped the world (McKenna 2010). See also Peddigrew 2009; Peddigrew describes the search for a new identity among a sample of vowed women in the closing decades of the twentieth century. For an account of the daring and creative witness of ten contemporary United States sisters, see journalist Piazza 2014.

overview of what the foundresses sought to change and transform in the world and church of their time:

1. Relieve suffering.
2. Stand witness against the taking of life or harming of all sentient others.
3. Name evil, at its roots and sources, pointing out its effects on people.
4. Change and organize for change with no violence; live in solidarity with victims.
5. Ensure healthcare and dignity for all, especially for women and children.
6. Make sure there is fresh water, air, food, shelter and space—for all.
7. Promote education.
8. Engage in wholesome economics, of a type that brings the kingdom of justice and peace.
9. Take special care of the needy: refugees, minorities, victims of violence, victims of pollution.
10. Weep and rail against violence, injustice, and unnecessary death.
11. Share beauty, the arts, spirituality, wisdom, music, earth rituals.
12. And do all this with others across boundaries, borders, religions, genders, and so forth.

All Religious Life foundations—male and female alike—embrace this twelve-point agenda. We see it vividly at work in many of the brothers congregations, which receive even less attention than the female groups, an imbalance Rome sought to address in promulgating the document *Identity and Mission of the Religious Brother in the Church* in December 2015. Today there are an estimated fifty-five thousand brothers in the Catholic Church. John Baptist de La Salle, St. Alexius, St. John of God, St. Louis de Montfort, Peter Joseph Triest, Edmund Rice, Marcellin Champagnat, Daniel Delany, and Mathias Barrett belong to that small but significant cohort of non-clerical vowed males, who, like many of the exemplary female foundresses, sought first the transforming power of the gospel in the generous and radical service to the poor and marginalized.

The great foundresses, individually and collectively, furnish an originality of vision, an intensity of presence, and a prophetic audacity that illuminates the archetypal empowerment of the vowed life. In the words of Gerald A. Arbuckle: "Founders and refounders possess a profound knowledge of the critical needs of the church and society, a proven intimacy with the Lord, imaginative and practical responses to the problems they so sharply see around them" (1996, 12). For the refounding challenges of the twenty-first century the foundresses provide not merely a blueprint we all can emulate, but more important, an inspiring vision to sustain us for the way ahead.

ॐ

Study Questions

1. When you read the first two paragraphs of this chapter, what emotional response does the material evoke in you?

2. Read the Conclusion to Part Two. What implications might this have for your current living of Religious Life?

Conclusion to Part Two

The Discerning Process

History is loaded with patriarchal distortion and infected by the contagion of domination, and so it is not easily integrated into our discerning processes. Yet few can deny that the history of Religious Life, particularly as delineated in the present work, is a rich reservoir for the creative initiatives of the Holy Spirit.

Three observations require additional discerning time and energy. The first is the false and misleading inflation of the ascetical hero in the traditional foundations of the vowed life. This is a patriarchal distortion whereby dominant males seek to replicate their own inflated heroism (itself based on a deluded projection onto a powerful deity), but much more serious, a cultural imposition to keep the masses subdued, silenced in a disempowering sense of unworthiness, guilt, and anomie. This is a cultural perversion that over many centuries has seriously undermined the grace and empowerment of incarnational faith and the healthy sense of disciplined living that accompanies it. A more informed historical awareness will lead us to a different discernment of how the foundational wisdom of the vowed life is to be appropriated for our time

Second, we need to unmask the extensive suppression of female giftedness and the corrosive repression that often accompanied such domination and oppression. While we have much to learn from the enduring legacy of the great founders, the inspiration and empowerment modeled by the great foundresses gives much more direct access to the liminal and prophetic challenges of our vowed calling. By including the foundresses and their inspiring stories in our historical overview, we capture not merely a more discerning engagement with the vowed life, but also evoke a call for justice to undo the often brutal exclusions and oppressions meted out to women throughout the history of Christendom.

Third, the traditional dualistic split between the monastic and the apostolic needs to be bridged and healed. All forms of Religious Life serve discipleship of the new Companionship of Empowerment (the kingdom of God) while seeking to appropriate the foundational archetype outlined in Part One. Different Orders and Congregations may highlight one or more aspects in preference to others, but we are all called to live out of a mystical/contemplative quality of vision. And for all of us, Christian mission requires a set of practical responses in daily living, carrying out the good deeds required by our gospel fidelity to justice, love, liberation, and empowerment. Celebrating our commonalities rather than invoking differences that inflate some groups above others needs to become an integral dimension of how we discern what the Spirit is asking of us in the refounding endeavors of the twenty-first century.

Part Three

Religious Life and Value Radiation

The parable narrator stands on the cusp between two worlds: the imperial consciousness that seeks to immortalize its own existence, and the evolutionary imperative that seeks to make all things new. This is the liminal space, the prophetic cutting edge that seems to me to be the primary sacred space for all Religious. A relatively new concept in the emerging theology of the vowed life, it holds enormous promise for a more authentic and empowering future.

Essentially, the liminality is a space from which we negotiate and radiate the values that empower and liberate. First and foremost, these are the values embedded in the Companionship of Empowerment: justice, love, liberation, compassion, and others highlighted in the Christian gospel. The values have universal significance. Deep down all humans yearn to live lives imbued with deep values; our dismal failure to do so often arises from the dysfunctional and distorted systems (social, political, religious) in which we inculturate such values. It is the prophetic challenge for liminal movements to engage those forces that undermine our creative appropriation of such values, while also discerning how such values can be integrated within different times, places, and cultural contexts.

The liminal context is also the foundation to retrieve the long-suppressed lay identity of our vocation, and to do so in a way that makes close affiliation with other lay people an indispensable dimension of our life and mission. And for those lay people who embrace the challenges of this new partnership, the insights of this chapter are significant. Liminality provides virgin territory for the empowerment of Religious and laity alike.

As I indicate in Chapters 8 and 9, we need to rethink the meaning of the vows in terms of values rather than laws. The three vows can be understood afresh as areas of intense cultural engagement around the key areas of value-appropriation relating to persons, goods, and structures. Such an approach requires, among other things, a renaming of the vows, adopting language and concepts that can speak more coherently and convincingly to the cultural context of the twenty-first century.

Chapter 7

Liminality: The Core Value of Every Paradigm

> *If religious life, by its very structure, involves a certain abnormality, then that life will experience crisis when it seeks to become normal and when it is no longer lived in the desert or on the frontier.*
>
> —Jon Sobrino

> *One of the major challenges facing postconciliar religious has been to rediscover what it means to be in and for the world in accord with their own particular vocational charism.*
>
> —Sandra M. Schneiders

Religious Life as a cultural phenomenon has been around longer than historical records can verify. And despite its numerical decline in recent Catholic history, it is anything but a spent force, doomed to extinction. The historical outline adopted in this book indicates a capacity to rebound, a historical resilience that defies any and every historical explanation. However, it is the cultural significance of the vowed life, rather than its history, that defines its durability, and this is a dimension that has received scant attention till relatively recent times.

The enduring resilience of and fascination with the vowed life seems to relate to its subversive capacity to provide a countercultural quality of spiritual witness unique among mainline religions and, in one sense, transcending them all. In Chapter 2, I described this countercultural aspect as the *monastic archetype*, while also highlighting its distinctive *prophetic* capacities. I now want to deepen and expand the prophetic horizon of Religious, adopting some insights from social and anthropological sciences. Of central importance is the notion of *liminality* as a core parabolic truth in the historical lived experience of the vowed life.

Throughout history, anthropologists have noted a universal trend in which humans mission some of their own members into an alternative, countercultural way of being. The process is largely unconscious but can easily be comprehended under the rubric of Carl G. Jung's *collective unconscious*. According to Jung, a collective intelligence permeates the whole of creation. For Jung, this is a spiritual, divine life-force which we humans appropriate through archetypal yearnings,[1] a creative energy mediated through symbolic behavior, myth, and ritual. Through observing and studying mythic and ritualistic behaviors, we come to know something of the powerful influence of the collective unconscious and how it becomes insinuated in human cultures—usually in complex and subtle ways.

The Liminal Paradigm

Throughout the twentieth century both anthropologists and psychologists became more acutely aware of how archetypal values surface within human cultures and how they become translated into human behavior. At the beginning of the twentieth century a Dutch anthropologist, Arnold Van Gennep, noted something intriguing in his study of African rites of passage (ritual ceremonies). The neophyte (candidate) was often taken apart from the group for a specific or indefinite period of time. The act of separation required a subsequent return to the group, usually in the form of a celebratory ritual. The return happened at a consciously explicit level—everybody knew what was going on and consciously participated in the event. But the separation was

---

[1] In Chapter 2, I introduced archetypes, exploring their significance through the monastic archetype as a recurring energy force in the spiritual awakening of people across time and culture. In the present chapter I add the notion of consciousness, one of the most exciting and controversial issues in modern science, in the social sciences, and also in contemporary spirituality (see Van Lommel 2010). At one end of the controversial debate is scientist Daniel Dennett, for whom consciousness is nothing more than the qualia (atoms of the brain) bouncing off each other in a mechanistic fashion. At the other end is scientist Christof Koch (2004), who posits that consciousness is a fundamental property of all living matter. The spiritual import is beautifully articulated by Medical Mission Sister Miriam Therese Winter, who writes: "Consciousness is the core of an emerging spirituality in this quantum universe, for consciousness, like energy, is mysteriously pervasive. We speak of divine consciousness, yet all consciousness is divine. It is a mode of divinity whereby Spirit is present in and to and through each and every one of us and every aspect of creation" (2009, 94).

often shrouded in mystery, and sometimes in secrecy, and this became the unique focus of Van Gennep's research.

Despite the hidden nature of the separation—or perhaps because of it—Van Gennep detected a powerful, subconscious energy at work, one that had a profound impact not just on the individual but on the whole group. The act of separation paradoxically served as a powerful cohesive experience for the entire group—albeit at a subconscious level. Van Gennep named this act of separation *liminality*, from the Latin word *limen*, which means "threshold, marginal space, new frontier, being at the cutting edge."

Several years later anthropologist Victor Turner (who worked with his wife, Edith) revisited the theory and began to explore its wider implications. The Turners proposed that this behavior is a feature not only of tribal peoples in Africa but a phenomenon that occurs throughout the entire human family. The concept includes all those transitional moments in which we step out of the mainstream of life—recreation, holidays, worship, retreat, pilgrimage, and so forth—so that we become renewed and refreshed for further engagement. Through liminality, a particular mode of human interrelatedness emerges, which Victor Turner (1969) named "communitas," a utopian dimension of liminality, as distinct from "structure," which defines that which procures stability, formality, and rationality. In a subsequent work Victor Turner described the communal endeavor as follows:

> Prophets and artists tend to be liminal and marginal people, "edgemen," who strive with a passionate sincerity to rid themselves of cliches associated with status incumbency and role-playing, in order to enter into vital relations with other men in fact or in imagination. . . . (Communitas) is almost everywhere held to be sacred or "holy," possibly because it transgresses or dissolves the norms that govern structured and institutionalized relationships and is accompanied by experiences of unprecedented potency. (Turner 1974, 128)[2]

---

[2] "Structure," according to Victor and Edith Turner, is "the patterned arrangements of role sets, status sets, and status sequences consciously recognized and regularly operative in a given society and closely bound up with legal and practical norms and sanctions" (Turner 1974, 252). *Communitas,* on the other hand, is "a relational quality of full, unmediated communication, even communion, between definite and determinate identities, which arises spontaneously in all kinds of groups, situations, and circumstances" (Turner 1978, 250). For a valuable overview of Turner's theory of liminality, see Alexander 1991; for a more extensive analysis, see Horvath, Thomassen and Wydra 2015.

For the Turners, liminality carries many cultural expressions—withdrawing in order to engage afresh—but it seems to have one enduring cultural articulation, namely, the *vowed life*. Here more than anywhere else, the liminality assumes a quality of social and cultural expression with implications not merely for the liminal people themselves but for the entire human species.

To appreciate and understand the depth and richness of this concept the reader must forgo, indeed transcend, the dualistic conditioning that is still so prevalent in religious cultures. Beyond the conceptual neatness of binary opposites—such as earth v. heaven, body v. soul, and so on—we must learn to embrace the both/and that facilitates integration and new growth. Religious need to reassess and integrate afresh the *fuga mundi* spirituality, with its often glamorous and utopian eschatological language. Liminality transcends all dualistic splitting. It is unambiguously focused on earthly and cosmic transformation; it is not based on any kind of escape to a world hereafter, nor does it invest hope or meaning in some future return of Christ to earth. We are dealing with a concept that transcends all our dualistic divisions between sacred and secular, holy and profane.

The theory assumes that subconsciously *all* peoples desire deep, authentic values. The origin of this yearning belongs to the God who created us all and, in the Christian context, to the empowering and liberating God of the Companionship of Empowerment. While at the conscious level we may often behave in a way that contradicts this fact, subconsciously we are always yearning for that which is good and wholesome—aptly described by many as wrestling with God. Religious Life, therefore, serves as a perennial model for the integration of key values, *not by the choice of the Religious themselves but by virtue of the fact that the people have called us forth to do this task.*

In undertaking this daunting challenge, it is the struggle and engagement that make us authentic, not the correct or perfect achievement of the task in hand. Liminality is not some modern version of the call to perfection, but rather the call to grow into that fullness of life that forever stretches the yearnings of the human heart, that same fullness of life to which Jesus invites all people (Jn 10:10). There are, of course, substantial risks involved in this undertaking, and if the witness is not creative and constructive, the process can easily result into distortions, addictions, and fetishes (see Eigen 1991, 69).

Liminality and the Vowed Life

Liminality, in the context of Religious Life, therefore, has a treble significance:

1. It describes the unique cultural and spiritual role of those called apart, traditionally known as monks or Religious.

2. Much more important, however, is that the call to be apart is not for the vowed people themselves but rather to serve the wider human community as cultural catalysts.

3. The service rendered is by living out more deeply—in a more spiritually integrated way—the values that carry meaning for all human beings, irrespective of time or culture.

The monastic/Religious Life embodies in a unique way the institutionalized expression of liminal communitas: "Nowhere has this institutionalization been more clearly marked and defined than in monastic and mendicant states in the great world religions" (Turner 1969, 107).[3]

From within Religious Life, Benedictine monk Richard Endress was one of the first to explore Turner's insights and their application to the vowed life, noting that the monasticism elevates the liminality that normally characterizes persons only during certain highly charged but brief periods of change into a permanent lifestyle. For the monk, this life is a transitional state, similar to that of a pilgrim, a wayfarer, in the world but not of it. The monk wavers, so to speak, between two worlds, traditionally described as sacred and profane, without being part of either. In this world, therefore, the position of the monk, like that of a ritually liminal person, is (for outsiders at least) ambiguous and tinged with an aura of sacredness (Endress 1975, 148).

Another Benedictine monk, Cyprian R. Langlois, views the monastic community as endowed with an enduring sense of transition, devoid of the trappings of secular power. On the other hand, the monastic community does possess awesome sacred power (2002, 66–67, 27). Monks are called to be "edge people" whose entire daily witness is centered around ritual liturgical time and space, augmenting the liminal state. Within this unique space-time environment, beliefs are construed and constructed to ground afresh in our world the liberating and empowering wisdom of the gospel of Christ.

While not explicitly invoking the notion of liminality, Australian Cistercian scholar Michael Casey endorses St. Benedict's advice to the monks to "make themselves strangers to the actions of the age"

---

[3] Other scholars who support this understanding of the monastic/Religious Life include Livia Kohn, professor of oriental religions at Boston College, who describes monasticism as an acute manifestation of liminality (Kohn 2003, 15); and the Irish-based, Hungarian sociologist Arpad Szakolczai (2009; 2016).

(see the rule of Benedict 4:20). Monastic living offers an alternative world view involving a great deal more than contempt for the world and its values. For Casey, "Monastic life is the diametric opposite of aimless living" (2005, 5), witnessing to a focused mindfulness on the fuller realization of that incarnational humanity described in earlier chapters as the monastic archetype.

The suggestion that the vowed life is one specific vehicle—yet quite a distinctive one—for the liminality is very much a novel idea, which in my experience awakens a deep resonance for women Religious while often resisted by male clerical Religious. Clearly, it supports the fertile insights of the Spiritan scholar Adrian Van Kaam, who claims that Religious are called to be *cultural catalysts for value radiation*, not merely for the benefit of the church or for religion, but for the entire spectrum of human life and culture. Accordingly, the Religious Life is better viewed as a cultural phenomenon, and not merely a religious movement (1968).

In the 1980s, I first became acquainted with the notion of liminality through the pioneering insights of the priest-anthropologist Gerald A. Arbuckle (1988; 1996), whose primary interest was in the notion of refounding to which we will return in the final chapter of this book. Arbuckle was thoroughly familiar with Turner's research and fully endorsed his conviction that the vowed life carried a distinctive potential for liminal witness. More practically, Arbuckle viewed the liminality at work in the transitional chaos characterizing Religious Life in the late twentieth century as it evolves from an earlier, now-declining paradigm on its way to the birth of something radically new.

Witnessing to Liminal Values

Liminal witness is not merely embodied in the visible structures of liturgy, silence, work, and distinctive lifestyle, as Cyprian Langlois (2002) intimates. It is the foundational values being witnessed, articulated, and mediated afresh—for a range of cultural situations—that constitutes the primary target of liminal witness, ensuing in some significant paradigmatic shifts:

- *Beyond dualisms.* Our inherited distinctions between the sacred and secular no longer make sense. The binary splits between earth and heaven, body and soul, matter and spirit create a kind of fragmentation and adversarial polarization that alienates us from the foundational unity of God's creation. The liminal witness calls us to build bridges across all the false and violent divisions that characterize our inherited worldviews. The wisdom to embrace the dynamic of *both/and* rather than *either/or* constitutes the prophetic wisdom so urgently needed in the world of the twenty-first century.

- *Multicultural and trans religious.* Dominican scholar Donald Goergen claims that Religious Life does not exist simply for the sake of the church but to foster in the world a special attentiveness to the surplus in the gospel. That surplus may be understood as the call to seek *first* the kingdom of God and its justice (Matt 6:33), an undertaking I interpret afresh as discipleship serving the Companionship of Empowerment (O'Murchu 2011; 2014). As we delve deeper into the ancient Hebrew culture of the historical Jesus, we understand that the vision and mission of the kingdom transcend all social, political, and religious enclaves. They transcend all sense of nationality, ethnicity, and denominational distinction.

- *Co-creation.* This new gospel companionship also embraces daring horizons of incarnational empowerment, epitomized in the Johannine call: "I do not call you servants, but friends" (Jn 15:15). In terms of Religious we must no longer envisage ourselves as those who have left all to guarantee the salvation of our immortal souls in a life beyond this vale of tears. Instead, we are called—and missioned—to become co-creators with our creative God, unambiguously committed to co-creating a new heaven and a new earth where the enduring values of the Companionship of Empowerment become the primary focus of our life and mission.

- *Lay identity.* The liminal context of our way of life indicates that—subliminally—our vocational calling arises from the inherent faith of humanity itself. We can regard it as a divine calling, but it is mediated through the people. To understand what is at stake, we need to transcend our inherited understandings of religion and opt instead to discern the innate spiritual yearnings that characterize all humans, although many people may not be consciously aware of these endowments. It is from within this subliminal spiritual yearning that the liminal people and groups are called forth, and it is to those same people—all humanity—that the "liminars" (the vowed Religious) are primarily accountable. Consequently, the vocation to Religious Life is first and foremost a *lay* calling—arising from the people and accountable back to them. Contrary to

Sandra Schneiders's conclusion that Religious constitute "a third group" that is neither clerical nor lay (2000, 218)—as stated in canon law and affirmed in *Vita Consecrata* (1996, no. 60)—I suggest that we, Religious, are *first and foremost lay people.* This close affiliation with laity can be discerned in the words of Pope Francis in a conversation with the Union of Superior General of religious men in Rome on November 29, 2014: "Evangelical radicalness is not only for religious: it is demanded of all. But religious follow the Lord in a special way, in a prophetic way. It is this witness that I expect of you. Religious should be men and women who are able to wake the world up" (in Spadaro 2014).

- *Relationship with religion/church.* Currently, the vowed life— across all the major religions—is understood to be a faith-based movement belonging to, and accountable to, religious institutions or formal churches. A more discerning reading of history will alert us to the dangerously myopic limits of this view. In the early Christian foundations the monastic movement sought to distance itself from much of the ecclesiastical institutionalization. The movement remained fundamentally lay (and was viewed by the church as such) until the early thirteenth century. The progressive clericalization of the vowed life, particularly at the Council of Trent and thereafter, is a feature of the inherited paradigm that needs to be challenged if we stand any hope of embracing in a more authentic way the refounding paradigm of the twenty-first century. Too close an affiliation with institutional Christianity seriously undermines the liminal potential of Religious.

- *Liminality and marginalization.* Sandra Schneiders describes a marginal status that is inherent to the prophetic nature of the vowed life, exemplified in this passage:

> Religious are marginal by choice, but that marginality is in the service of prophesy, not escapism. From the edges of the system there is a view of what the system does to those who are excluded, to those who are made means to other people's ends. To feel the pathos of God is not a warm and comfortable religious experience; it is an experience of the howling wilderness driving one to protest. Marginality is not a safe haven from the complexities of modern life but freely chosen solidarity with those who are excluded against their will. . . . By not undertaking one's species role as reproducer

of the race, by not participating in a capitalist economy by acquisition or use of wealth for personal purposes, by not exercising political power for individual goals, the Religious situates herself at the edges of the systems that makes the culture function. From this marginal position Religious share in the hermeneutical advantage of the poor. The marginality forced on the poor and defenseless is voluntarily chosen by Religious. (Schneiders 2000, 141, 327).

For Schneiders, such marginality is a stance of prophetic solidarity with the poor, and against all that leads to poverty and oppression in the first place. Such marginality is not chosen (as she suggests); rather, *it is chosen for us by virtue of our calling.* In no way is it an escape—rather, it is a deeper mode of engagement. Although she does not use the word, Schneiders is speaking of the liminal challenge described above, with one notable difference: the liminal challenge is addressed to all peoples and not merely to the poor. In fact, in the context of the twenty-first century the perennial challenge for liminal witness is to engage and confront *the rich and powerful*—corporations and governments—so that they face their own complicity with the corruption and exploitation that adversely affects rich and poor alike. Substantial challenges arise here for the refounding of Religious Life in the twenty-first century.

• *Paradoxical vision.* Many years ago British Benedictine monk Cyprian Smith wrote a book on the mysticism of Meister Eckhart, entitled *The Way of Paradox* (Smith 2004). The kind of paradox he describes illuminates the liminal calling, vividly expressed in the Christian notion of being in the world but not of it. Traditionally, that ambiguous presence in the world was understood in dualistic terms and implied an eschatological waiting to escape from this sinful vale of tears to fulfillment beyond. The liminal understanding is very different: the "world" is God's chosen location in which we are called to live out our incarnational mission, seeking to make the world a better place, not merely for all humans, but for all creatures.[4] The liminal perspective

---

[4] Confusion often arises here because of how the word *world* is used in John's Gospel, where it has two meanings: (1) All creation, including all created things, which includes humankind. This is the sense in which the world is used in John 3:16: "For God so loved the world that he gave his only Son, so that everyone who believes in him may not perish but may have eternal life." (2) Everything opposed to God, as in Jesus' prayer for the Apostles in John 17:14–16: "I have given

highlights the fact that we can view and understand our world more deeply from within a mystical horizon, requiring us to be present to creation not merely in an embodied sociological way, but from within a contemplative context that will often set us at variance with the dominant cultural values of our time. Like Jesus, liminal people need to escape to the mountain, precisely in order to return with deeper vision and renewed vitality for more intensely discerning engagement.

Liminality and the Prophetic

When Christians adopt the notion of the prophetic, they are usually referring to the major prophetic figures of the Hebrew scriptures, such as Isaiah, Jeremiah, Baruch, Ezekiel, Hosea, and Amos. Throughout the Hebrew scriptures prophets are variously described as having exceptional status, usually denoting special access to divine wisdom, and frequently challenging the prevailing power of domination. Just as the king represents imperial values of power and control, so the prophet becomes the voice of those unjustly oppressed, disempowered, and marginalized by the prevailing political structures.

The prophet, however, does not adopt violent confrontation; neither does the prophet seek the end of kingship. The prophet wants the king to change his strategy from empire building that favors the select few, to justice building that seeks the good of all—in structures and systems that deliver liberation and empowerment. It is the manner in which the prophet pursues the countercultural values that requires a more careful discernment. The prophet tends not to engage in rational rhetoric, and from a rational point of view can easily be accused of overstatement and wild posturing. The prophet invokes the wisdom of the God of justice, giving voice to God's desire for an alternative way of relating. The prophet adopts a countercultural space seeking to prioritize larger spiritual values that tend to be overlooked or ignored by the imperial forces.

The world of the Old Testament prophets is clearly a patriarchal environment. Prophets like Isaiah, Jeremiah, Ezekiel, Amos, and Hosea

---

them your word, and the world has hated them because they do not belong to the world, just as I do not belong to the world. I am not asking you to take them out of the world, but I ask you to protect them from the evil one. They do not belong to the world, just as I do not belong to the world." St. John Chrysostom writes: "They become attached to the world and relish only the things that are of the world" (*Homilies of St. John*, 7).

deal almost exclusively with the male context and therefore have a limited usefulness for the wider gender horizons of the present work. However, as scripture scholar Michael Crosby points out, the central values exhibited in the ancient prophets, and particularly their unmitigated commitment to justice in society, embrace a value orientation that transcends gender differences and can inspire all Religious, male and female alike (Crosby 2004).

As used in the literature of Religious Life, throughout the latter half of the twentieth century the notion of the prophetic is frequently either set in opposition to the institutional church or viewed as a supplement to it. While the institutional dimension of the church seeks order, structure, hierarchy, and harmony by the observance of law and ecclesiastical expectations, the prophetic dimension tends to emphasize community building, mutuality, empowerment, and justice making. While the former tends to be preoccupied with the preservation of power (understood to be divinely sanctioned), the latter brings to the fore the liberating empowerment of the Christian gospel.

In terms of the Hebrew scriptures, Walter Brueggemann highlights this distinction when he writes:

> The Mosaic tradition tends to be a movement of protest situated among the disinherited and that articulates its theological vision in terms of a God who decisively intrudes, even against seemingly impenetrable institutions and orderings. On the other hand, the Davidic tradition tends to be a movement of consolidation situated among the established and secure and articulates its theological vision in terms of a God who faithfully abides and sustains on behalf of the present ordering. (Brueggemann 1979, 162)

All the formal religions, including Christianity, claim to represent and promote the values of the former (the Mosaic), but in practice, the allurement of power, with its bureaucratic legacy, and the solemnizing of hierarchal structure (the Davidic tradition), undermines the more foundational aspirations—which consciously or otherwise, have been liberally adopted in how Religious live the vowed life.

Much of the writing on Religious Life over the last fifty years (see Azevedo 1995; Boff 1981; Chittister 1995; Crosby 2004; Fiand 2001; Schneiders 2000, 2001, 2013) considers Religious to have a special and unique responsibility for safeguarding the prophetic dimension of the church, sometimes leading to the dismissive accusation that Religious behave like a kind of alternative hierarchy. It is our allegiance to the prophetic dimension, as outlined above, that marks us off, not merely as different, but more important, as the ones who consistently seek another paradigm that transcends the patriarchal imperialism which can only tolerate one dominant vision, overly devoted to power and control.

The prophetic provides a countercultural corrective to the monopoly of patriarchal power, embodying and witnessing to a range of alternative empowering ways of being. Unfortunately, in the church at large, and for many Religious themselves—particularly male clerical Congregations—this interdependent paradigm is more a theoretical construct than a lived reality. The basis for a truly prophetic engagement is not understood, appreciated, or promoted by either side. Religious often perceive themselves as more dedicated workers who promote the gospel *alongside* the institutional church, while the formal church and its leadership view the contribution of Religious in similar functional terms. Each group operates out of a paradigm centered around the lowest common denominator, a reality that painfully surfaced in the investigation of the American women Religious in the early years of the twenty-first century.

In declaring a special year to celebrate the giftedness of Religious to the church, Pope Francis clearly wanted to rectify the inherited tension between members of the hierarchy and Religious Congregations. Addressing Religious leaders in Rome on November 29, 2014, the pope said:

> The fact is: I know the problems, but I also know that the bishops are not always acquainted with the charisms and works of religious. We bishops need to understand that consecrated persons are not functionaries but gifts that enrich dioceses. Dialog between the bishop and religious must be rescued so that, due to a lack of understanding of their charisms, bishops do not view religious simply as useful instruments. (in Spadaro 2014)

Within the Church and beyond It

Liminality denotes a spacious cultural embrace that is unambiguously spiritual (of God's creative Spirit) but cannot be confined to any one religion or Christian denomination. It is a cultural transformative influence requiring a quality of discernment that seems very new for many contemporary Religious. More daunting still are the ensuing challenges for how Religious relate with ecclesiastical/canonical institutions.

For Catholic readers of this book, Religious Life is inconceivable apart from the church. For many Religious today, living the vowed life and exercising a ministry within the church are viewed as concomitant. It is inconceivable that one could exist without the other. Nor can the teaching authority of the church envisage any other scenario; in its eyes Religious Life is first and foremost a canonical structure, officially sanctioned by the church, and aberrant without the protection and guidance of the church.

It seems to me that this is a grossly simplistic view, unduly reliant on law and order rather than theologically and spiritually grounded. A more nuanced and discerning view of history suggests all too clearly that for its first one thousand years Religious Life was essentially a lay movement, loosely affiliated with the official church but not controlled by it. In its bedrock tradition the monastic movement adopted a countercultural stance to the growing institutionalization of the church itself. The escape to the desert was really an option for a non-imperial embrace of God's new reign on earth. It was an option for gospel empowerment and a denunciation of a church deluded by Constantine into the cult of domination.

Increasingly, studies in archeology and ancient history depict the early monks as architects of an intense communal fellowship, exhibiting limited interaction with the formal church of the day. Benedict insisted that all were brothers in mutual solidarity, with only a few priests to provide Eucharist for the community. Even Francis in the thirteenth century wanted a brotherly federation, not a clericalized structure. Despite a gradual clericalization from the fourteenth century onward, it was not until the Council of Trent (1545–63) that the priest became the ideal model for all forms of Christian discipleship. From then on, even apostolic women Religious were expected to dress in the black-and-white of the clerical uniform.

Today, the close affiliation of Religious with the formal church is so taken for granted that most Religious never query its evolution. We assume it has always been that way, when in fact it is a relatively recent development. The unquestioned assumption is often grounded in a kind of practical co-dependency: without the money and resources of the church, Religious would have been unable to function, either in terms of lifestyle or ministry. This has been true not merely in Africa, Asia, and Latin America, but also in the United States, where many female groups live in and work from church-owned properties. This close working relationship often has led to the perception of sisters as pseudo-priests, seriously undermining the liminal, prophetic aspects of vowed witness.

Ever since the Second Vatican Council (1959–64), Catholicism has been wrestling with a diminishing priesthood and a growing consensus that the future of the church will be lay led rather than clerically governed or controlled. Certainly in the West priesthood as we have known it is in deep crisis, and this is increasingly true in the Two-Thirds World also, where clerical control is losing its firm grip. There is much to suggest that the renewal and revitalization of the church will arise from a new lay ferment rather than anything resembling a revitalized priesthood.

In terms of Religious Life the several examples of newly emerging developments (cited in Chapter 10 below) indicate unambiguously a shift to a new quality of membership, with a desire to witness in the presence of God's world and not just in the church. Even groups, like L'Arche and the Sant'Egidio Community, with explicit historical links to the Catholic Church, welcome and include people of all denominations, some from other major faiths, and occasionally people of no particular religious allegiance.

These observations should not be read as anti church or a kind of postmodern free for all. I am trying to honor what I perceive to be a deeper meaning to the vowed life, with a dual perspective:

1.   History itself suggests that a refounded model in the twenty-first century is likely to veer in a much more non-ecclesiastical, non-canonical direction, not in opposition to the church but rather as a deeper commitment to the new reign of God at the heart of the world.

2.   We cannot hope to reclaim the liminal significance of the vowed life if we still want to confine it either to formal religion or to an explicit ecclesiastical context. In more forthright terms Sandra Schneiders asserts: "It seems to me very important for Religious to appropriate and internalize the fact that Religious Life is not an ecclesiastical job corps, a source of cheap labor for the projects of the hierarchy" (2000, 85).

Liminality and the Task of Refounding

In every new cycle Religious Life reclaims afresh its charismatic flavor. New visionary leaders read afresh the signs of the times and respond to a contemporary set of urgent needs. Although historians tend to interpret this novel response to the needs of the church at a particular time and place, a more discerning survey would show that it is a great deal more complex than that. The underlying inspiration arises primarily from within the new reign of God (the companionship) at the heart of the world rather than as a dream to reform or renew the church itself.

History also tends to judge new Religious Life foundations in terms of fidelity to church authorities and their expectations. We are often told of founders seeking out ecclesiastical approval through adaptation of established rules and procedures. This would be more true of the second Christian millennium than the first. And when it did happen it may be more about practical expediency rather than zeal to be fully in tune with church expectations.

The anticipated refounding toward the end of the twenty-first century will carry that same creative originality and daring vision that has characterized many of the original founding endeavors in earlier historical epochs. Some existing groups will be refounded; most, however, will fade into history. And the refounding will embrace the human and cultural realities of the late-twenty-first century in ways that few if any of us can foresee. Time alone will confirm the truthfulness of what will emerge.

We cannot plan for refounding. It is a divine prerogative through which the God of surprises catches us. We can anticipate it, desire it, and pray that we will be rightly disposed to being refounded, if that is God's will for particular Orders and Congregations. Being rightly disposed includes, among other things, acquiring the discerning wisdom and analytical skills to understand better the cultural transformations of our time and to move our resources where they can best serve the urgent needs that will ensue. This is an almost insurmountable challenge for groups undergoing the stages of ethical and/or absolute doubt (described in Chapter 11 below).

Arguably, Religious Life is nowhere more liminal than in its refounding moment. Everything is new, unpredictable, open to possibility, risky, and daring. The threshold predominates, just as in a birthing moment, when delivery cannot be halted. This mythic creativity is the lifeblood of the vowed life. It is what will sustain a group through all the ups and downs of the founding years. It is also the spark of the Spirit through which even a dying group can be rekindled into a refounding response. When the Spirit is at the helm, life will thrive even amid the letting go of death itself.

ॐ

Study Guide

1. What is your experience of *liminality* in your life, or in your personal experience of Religious Life?

2. How do you relate to Religious Life as being "within" the church and "beyond" it?

Chapter 8

Revisioning the Vows in a Refounding Model

> *Questions will more likely lead to deeper questions as intellect yields precedence to heart and we in our thinking leave room for the existential and experiential; for the mystical, the paradoxical. . . . What we vow is open-ended, a process, not a final product.*
>
> —BARBARA FIAND

> *The decision to follow the counsels, far from involving an impoverishment of truly human values, leads instead to their transformation.*
>
> —VITA CONSECRATA, NO. 87

The vows have long been understood as the canonically sanctioned guidelines for upright and responsible behavior among Religious. Any deviation from such right behavior incurs a moral transgression of varying proportion. Over the centuries the vows became associated with the rule, embodied and articulated through canon law and the specific Constitutions of a particular Order or Congregation. Observation of the rule automatically indicated fidelity to the requirements of the vows.

The vows therefore were viewed in canonical, legal terms, often expressed in the statement: "Keep the rule and the rule will keep you." For much of Christendom, fidelity and holiness were judged by how well members observed the law(s). We were dealing with a paradigm emphasizing quantity rather than quality, external norms rather than internal disposition, individual salvation rather than communal wholeness. While many recognize the limitations of such an approach, commentators, nonetheless, are keen to note that it provided a solid basis for growth in holiness and generous service to the church and to the cultural context of various historical epochs. It was based on a kind of cultural conditioning that was widespread for much of Christendom, and it was extensively adopted across several other lifestyles as well.

In the twenty-first century the inherited paradigm—with emphasis on the observation of law, rational explanation, and external criteria for success—has lost a great deal of credibility, with the inevitable swing to another extreme whereby many contemporary Religious are ambiguous on their understanding of vowed commitment. There is so much fluidity of understanding and flexibility in practice that it is difficult to identify a common ground along with a communally shared set of values and expectations. A refounding model cannot hope to take root without a concerted effort to discern afresh what the vows mean and how to live them authentically in the twenty-first century.

The Expansive Vision

In the post–Vatican II era, living the vows in Catholic Religious Life shifted significantly toward a focus on *community life* rather than individual holiness. How we relate to one another in community—in terms of human relationships (celibacy), sharing material resources (poverty), and the exercise of mutual co-responsibility (obedience)— became the new focus, articulated by a number of commentators including Barbara Fiand (1996; 2001) and Sandra Schneiders (2000; 2001; 2013). The communitarian focus required a renaming of the vows more congruent with the novel relational understanding. Although several Religious desired a new and more relevant language, few took the liberty of exploring how this might apply to the vows themselves (see O'Murchu 1999; 2005).

This enlarged communitarian context initiated a range of other extended horizons. Community life came to be understood as the basis for mission and not merely an internal forum for lifestyle and group expectations. A growing sense of ecological sustainability in the closing decades of the twenty-first century evoked for Religious, sisters particularly, a grounding of Religious Life in the natural world in the hope of serving better the eco-justice call for more engaging environmental and ecological accountability. This new orientation is illustrated vividly in a fine study entitled *Green Sisters: A Spiritual Ecology* (McFarland-Taylor 2009). And this was not merely an awakening in the Western world; for many years Religious in the Two-Thirds World were aware of the eco-feminist imbalance between people and their natural environment. In several local endeavors—unpublicized for the greater part—Religious in the Two-Thirds World were addressing the underlying injustices through a range of bold missionary-based enterprises.

The vowed life is returning to earth, precisely where the great foundresses believed it should be grounded. However, earth life itself is being revisioned thanks to the breakthroughs in cosmology and quantum physics. This expanded horizon had a significant impact on people's faith and spirituality throughout the latter half of the twentieth century, marking a transformation that has as yet scarcely been recognized by major Christian churches. Religious, however, being more directly interconnected with the web of life itself, have imbibed and internalized this new global consciousness to a deeper degree than almost any of our members are prepared to acknowledge. It is at the basis of many of the tensions and misunderstandings that prevail among us. Far more significant, it arises from the inescapable inner wisdom of our liminal identity.

Interconnectedness is an indisputable fact of our twenty-first-century culture. It points to a holistic sense of harmony and unity requiring us to reconsider and construe anew our past framing in terms of distinction, difference, isolation, and opposition. Our gospel commitment to live nonviolently requires us to develop whole new ways of interrelating that prioritize pluralism over conformity, commonalities over differences, engagement over a spirituality of escape. Increasingly we realize that the major global problems of our time—ecological, political, economic, social, religious—cannot be resolved by individual nations, tribes or religions, but only by a new global strategy requiring a massive shift in how we view and understand the world in which we live.

From within this enlarged context the vows need to be revisioned afresh, not as set of laws governing and guiding internal behavior, whether understood personally or communally, but as a set of *values* that in liminal terms compel us to engage more authentically with the evolutionary breakthroughs of our time. Vowed living must be seen to belong integrally to the global transformation desired by so many people today. All the vows now take on global significance, inviting Religious of the twenty-first century into modes of engagement for which—thus far—most of us are ill prepared.

Value Orientation

In a work that did not get the attention it deserved, Spiritan priest and psychologist Adrian Van Kaam (1968) described the witness of Religious Life as that of "value radiation." Our primary function is to radiate key values for the surrounding culture, and, for Van Kaam, our living out of the vows is central to that quality of witness. Many Religious will undoubtedly agree but probably miss the deeper nuance of this challenge. It is not simply a case of Religious being exemplary in living their vows through lives that radiate values more strongly than the rest of the human population, which is what Pope John Paul II had in mind when he redefined Religious Life as a *consecrated* way of living. From a liminal perspective, what is at stake are the people's values, rather than some exclusive, superior quality of holiness that only vowed people can attain.

This is one important aspect in the paradigm shift described throughout this book. The context is parabolic rather than rational or linear. It begins with the assumption that *all people, irrespective of culture, time, or space, yearn for a value-imbued and value-inspired way of living.* Along the lines explored by theologian Karl Rahner, we come into the world transparent to holy mystery, and subliminally we are always desiring a deeper connection with the empowering grace of that pervasive mysterious presence. Many strands in contemporary spirituality seek to retrieve, reclaim, and reinstate that deep primordial conviction (see Johnson and Ord 2012; Rowson 2014).

In liminal terms, Religious are called to prophetic thresholds where we engage more deeply with the people's values, incarnate them in more inspiring and empowering ways, and live them out more overtly and passionately. We cannot do that until we first discern the people's yearnings and longings and how those aspirations are sold short, distorted, and undermined by the dominant imperial culture, which has contaminated and distorted religion for far too long.

According to the popular understanding of the vows (and of Religious Life in general) we embrace deeper values to exhibit a stronger sense of holiness and thus guarantee for ourselves—and for others—a better chance of salvation in a life hereafter. That sense of privileged access to salvation cuts short and distorts the deeper meaning of our calling and our cultural prophetic identity. It is essentially a spirituality of *escape*, whereas the heart of liminal witness is about the quality of our *engagement*—in this world rather than in a life hereafter. At our finest moments in history, Religious have been deeply involved in the world, seeking to rectify the unholy conditions in which people were oppressed and being active in creating liberating alternatives offering hope for a better future.

Religious are not about a different set of values but about those values for which all humans yearn in our deeper, truer selves. We,

Religious, are called to take the values more seriously and strive to live them out more authentically, but the ensuing holiness does not result in a privileged position above and beyond everybody else. Our ultimate reward needs to be measured by how we bring the people with us, which is only possible when we live in deep solidarity with them. At this deeper level it will sometimes be a case of the people challenging us rather than of us challenging them, a quality of engagement succinctly articulated through the missiological vision of the 1970s (especially in *Evangelii Nuntiandi*): *We must be open to being evangelized by those we seek to evangelize.*

From the liminal space we strive to discern how values have become inculturated in the surrounding culture, both positively and negatively. We discern in order to name the distortions and possible ways of authentically reclaiming the key values (for Christians these will be the primary values of what the Gospels traditionally call the kingdom of God). Next, we need to discern how best to engage the people of God in a process of reappropriating empowering and liberating values. Dialogue and networking are likely to be key strategies for this undertaking. And we must overcome the corrosive impact of dualistic splitting; we are not simply about doing holy work in a secular world. We will need the skills to engage the political, economic, systemic, and social spheres as these are the locations from which the dominant values originate and prevail. Discerning the appropriate skills and acquiring the appropriate training will be major aspects of the refounding task facing all Religious as we move deeper into the twenty-first century. We return to this topic in Chapter 12.

Three Vows

Although some Religious (Benedictines, Jesuits, Daughters of Vincent de Paul, Sisters of Mercy, Missionaries of Charity of Mother Teresa of Calcutta, among others) have added a fourth vow, three has been the traditional number for a variety of reasons, including the symbolic sacredness of the number itself. Adrian Van Kaam (1968) sought to highlight the cultural significance of the three life contexts, traditionally depicted as the vows of poverty, chastity, and obedience.

This threefold path, Van Kaam suggested, emerged from experiential foundations already incipiently present in the human person and even foreshadowed in animal life. This way of life, he argues, served the culture in a profound threefold attitudinal response to persons, events, and things, a kind of bio-physical predisposition providing a healing program for life formation.

For Van Kaam, obedience denotes a response to changes in both the external and internal environments. Even animals could be said to obey the instinctual drives to eat, sleep, reproduce, and maintain a harmonious relationship with their surroundings. In doing so, they follow certain patterns of behavior present in nature and therefore give themselves the best chance for survival. Similarly, humans can choose those life options and values, thus guaranteeing an obedient attentiveness to our true selves and to our creaturehood. For Van Kaam, chastity (celibacy) is better described as the observance of appropriate sexual activity within a particular value system viewed in terms of balancing appropriate social and personal behaviors for empowering and loving human relationships. Van Kaam sees poverty as the maintenance of a healthy relationship to *things*. In other words, poverty requires both proper dispositions and behaviors in relation to material goods and possessions, such as simplicity of lifestyle, a free and generous attitude toward belongings, and a detachment from excessive materialism.

According to Enzo Bianchi, founding member of the Bose Community, the human sciences also arrive at this triad when they indicate the *three libidos* that constitute the human being in its depths: the libido *amandi* (the desire to love and be loved), the libido *possidendi* (access to the resources to live with dignity), and the libido *dominandi* (a sense of usefulness in our engagement with the world) (2001, 74). As we develop our personalities, we are challenged to become more mature; we become more human in relation to those three interrelated areas, described by Amy Hereford as a triple commitment to an alternate economy, an alternate politics, and an alternate relationality (2013, 122–30).

Both Van Kaam and Bianchi identify three foundational life energies informing much of our daily interaction with self and others. In this case *three* has more of a symbolic rather than a literal value, and as Van Kaam highlights, it should not be restricted merely to the human realm. Even in this explanation, there is still the temptation to view the vows in terms of individual personal behavior, whereas the value orientation being described clearly requires a communal context. It is through the relational appropriation of values that the radiant power of Religious inspires, empowers, and liberates.

In the contemporary world, with so much emphasis on public image and external achievement, the rational mind can make a certain amount of sense of the vows of poverty and obedience. In a threatened planet, surrounded with inescapable evidence of environmental degradation and recurring ecological catastrophes, the call to live simply and sustainably makes rational sense. In terms of the vow of obedience, the chaotic disarray in so many structural situations—political, structural, familial—clearly evokes the need for fresh attempts at order, harmony, and a more engaging sense of mutual participation.

The vow of chastity/celibacy, however, baffles and confuses modern people. When so many people cry out for love and intimacy, and there is such an acute need for more constructive psychosexual behavior, opting out seems a grossly irresponsible thing to do. Historically, the call to celibacy has always had an enigmatic feel to it, while persistently being a source of challenge and inspiration for people in every age and culture. It is a good place to start in our assessment of the vows for the refounding context of the twenty-first century.

The rest of this chapter reviews and reevaluates vowed celibacy, while the next chapter deals with the other two vows, conventionally named poverty and obedience.

Celibate Relatedness

In Catholic tradition celibacy tends to be associated with the non-marital status of priests, a clerical identification that militates seriously against a liminal appropriation of this vow. Clerical celibacy has had quite a checkered history, and today it holds prominence not for any profound theological reasons but as a pragmatic arrangement so that the pastoral availability of the pastor takes precedence to preoccupation with wife/partner, home, and family. Beyond this sociological context the church has long lauded celibacy as a symbol of a total giving of self to God, whereby God, or Christ, becomes the alternative spouse to fulfill all needs, spiritual and emotional alike.

As is widely known, the history of clerical celibacy is marred by several deviations, the most recent being the allegations of sex abuse of minors by priests throughout the closing decades of the twentieth century. However, long before the contemporary problem of clerical sex abuse, a largely unexamined culture of sexual repression impacted the clerical world, right up to the papacy itself (see Peter de Rossa 1989). There is also the less conspicuous emotional toll, a pervasive sexual woundedness, documented by authors such as Eugene Kennedy (2001) and more recently by priest-author Donald Cozzens (2006; 2008).

It is unfortunate that most people understand and judge the celibate calling as evidenced in the lives of diocesan priests. Throughout history people have opted for a non-marital status for a range of noble reasons, and we find a sense of celibate calling in the monastic systems of all the great world religions (see De Dreuille 1999; Launderville 2010). Celibacy is not merely an option to sacrifice marriage and forgo the joys and pleasures of human sexuality, the basic understanding offered by canon law.[1] It denotes a great deal more and should be judged by what it embraces rather than by what it chooses to forgo.

There is also a deep mystical dimension, which Sandra Schneiders (2001) considers to be the central feature of a celibate calling. In classical mystical language it may be described as being so overwhelmed by love for God that that allurement excludes all other forms of loving. I would opt for an alternative explanation, elucidated several years ago by the late Roger Balducelli, OSFS (1975), namely, that the call to celibacy is not something one consciously chooses but rather an inner transformation that happens as a result of being overwhelmed by a divine embrace. Valuable though these insights are, we do need to qualify them lest they are heard as a deluded escape from the challenges and responsibilities of daily life and human loving.

Throughout the closing decades of the twentieth century the call to celibacy was viewed not so much as an individual undertaking expressed in vowed commitment, but rather as a response of relational depth mediated through communal living. I have written extensively on this understanding of the vow (O'Murchu 1991, 118–41) and will not repeat the arguments here. Theological departure points include our faith in the foundational relationality of the Godhead itself (see Johnson 2007, 214–24) and, more important, our Christian commitment to the new reign of God that is calling all Christians to more empowering and liberating ways of relating. Celibacy, therefore, embraces an option not to escape all the intricacies of realizing authentic human love, but rather to engage with greater depth in the critical relational questions of our time. And this brings us to the liminal horizon at which I suggest we need to rename this engagement the *vow for relatedness*.

Liminal Relatedness

From a liminal perspective the Religious are called to embrace deeply the values of love that all humans hold in the depth of their hearts. In archetypal terms, however, we are about something much bigger than

---

[1] "The evangelical counsel of chastity assumed for the sake of the kingdom of heaven, as a sign of the future world and a source of more abundant fruitfulness in an undivided heart, entails the obligation of perfect continence in celibacy" (*Code of Canon Law*, no. 599).

human need or desire. We are invited to probe archetypal depths, the primordial capacity for divine relationality (which became subverted in the doctrine of the Trinity), and scientifically in quantum physics and contemporary cosmology. In a word, we are called to be an iconic emblem forever reminding our world that all life is programmed for relationality, an evolutionary imperative initially born out of the womb of Holy Mystery itself.

In a world so fractured and wounded by violence and warfare, exploitation and oppression, it is difficult to persuade anybody that a more relational, cooperative, and collaborative existence is even possible. This is the enormous liminal undertaking of our time, one that pursues not the holiness of a select few, but the redemption and restoration of cosmic justice itself. It is not a venture for the lighthearted, and the exemplary fortitude of the great foundresses is worth keeping in mind as we walk through these reflections.

At the heart of the Godhead is a foundational eroticism, a deep capacity for intimate bonding, highlighted by several "trinitarian" theologians in the closing decades of the twentieth century (La Cugna 1991; Peters 1993; Fox 2001). We believe in a God whose creativity is not that of a master craftsman, and even less of an imperial divine progenitor, but rather the fruit of a passionately intimate process of erotic intensity that effusively flows out into the cosmic web of life, the primary revelation of our co-creative God. Through this intimate relational energy everything in creation comes into being. In this context the erotic denotes an archetypal intimate capacity for creative becoming.

For the twenty-first century particularly, and for the refounding challenge explored in this book, the liminal horizon of vowed relatedness will need to engage with the following critical issues around the integration of key values:

- *The expansive horizon:* Intimacy and love can no longer be evaluated or discerned purely or exclusively on a human level. Cosmic and planetary dimensions must be embraced. The full potential of human loving and relating cannot be realized while we brutalize and exploit our planetary home. Planet and person are each energized by the same erotic energy infused by the creative Spirit of God, who seeks to draw forth order and harmony from the fragmentation we humans have caused, inviting us into a new symbiosis, the oneness desired by many, if not all, of the great mystics.

- *The eco-feminist horizon:* All human relating is done through bodies, not only human bodies but our daily interaction with all the other embodied creatures who share the planet with us. For much of Christendom we undermined the sacredness of the human body, resorting to the dualistic splitting of soul v. body, matter v. spirit, emotion v. rationality. In turn, that often led us to spurn all other forms of embodiment, particularly that of the animal. And our misogynist attitude to the female body leaves many festering wounds in the contemporary world. We are now called to new integration, primordially modeled on the incarnational faith that the Christian churches have long proclaimed but only practiced in a limited and superficial way.

- *The economic/political horizon:* In the economic/political climate of the twenty-first century everything has become a commodity for purchase and trade, a bartering tool in the hands of exploitative and marauding corporations. Aggressive consumerism knows no space where love, dignity, and intimacy can be respected. Increasingly, therefore, we see bodies—human and nonhuman—being traded for commercial patenting, hedonistic pleasure, and gross scientific experiment. Human trafficking for sex has become a multinational business that some Religious Orders are rightly recognizing as an area in need of urgent redress.

- *Religious petrification:* All the major world religions—through a range of expressions—prize the soul above the body and project onto a heaven hereafter ultimate fulfillment for the soul rather than for the whole person. Over the centuries this spirituality of escape has led to a serious degradation of the human body and the human need for embodied flourishing through meaningful intimacy, eroticism, and an integrated communion with the wider web of life. Many of the religions still operate out of, and inculcate, an irrational fear of the visceral, the emotional, the socially interactive, the embodied person that seeks out a deeper engagement with our co-creative God.

- *The human body:* Today billions of dollars are spent each year on the cult of the body beautiful. Our civilization carries within it a frightening trail of disembodied wreckage. Millions walk our world each day uneasy in their bodies, scared to varying degrees of how they present to the world as embodied creatures. Education on the meaning of our embodied existence and spiritual befriending of embodied growth and development has become one of the most urgent liminal needs of the twenty-first century.

- *The psychosexual dimension:* Human sexuality today is a grossly confused landscape with millions of wounded victims. A promiscuous deviancy crept up on us as a species about twenty-five-hundred years ago when the patriarchal urge to dominate and control designated human sexuality as being primarily, if not exclusively, for the act of procreation. Aristotle refined the new ideology into the gender split of the male with the generative seed, the woman as a biological receptacle to fertilize the seed, and sexuality itself as a reproductive mechanism that guaranteed the superiority of humans over the rest of nature, primarily through the prowess of dominating males. Human sexuality had one purpose only: the procreation of new life.

Two thousand years later, at the Council of Trent (1545–63), the Catholic Church defined marriage to serve one function only: *the procreation of the species.* Human erotic energizing was reduced to a biological imperative and reserved to the exclusive domain of monogamous, heterosexual marriage.[2] That understanding of Catholic marriage remained in force until 1962. It is still the prevalent view despite many cultural shifts, particularly in the latter half of the twentieth century.

Liminality and Contemporary Sexuality

Of all the issues facing liminal celibates in the twenty-first century, how to witness to psychosexual growth in a generic, empowering way is one of the most daunting. It is also likely to remain one of the most

---

[2] Many would argue that the monogamous heterosexual basis for marriage predates Trent by several centuries. What I am trying to highlight here is the elevation of marriage to a sacrament. Going back to the time of the Roman Empire, most Christians were married in the same way as pagans—in common law or free marriages. Christians were usually married in simple public ceremonies without any license or written agreement. After the reign of the Christian emperor Justinian (527–65) Christians were married in more formal civil ceremonies, according to the Justinian Code. But, although prayers and blessings were sometimes added to the ceremony, marriage was not a sacrament of the church, and it did not directly involve the church. The first known instance in the West of a blessing by a priest during a wedding ceremony is the 950 ritual of Durham, England. Although the fourth Lateran Council of 1215 required the blessing of a priest, it was unnecessary for the validity of the marriage. Only after the Council of Trent in 1563 was a ceremony compulsory for Roman Catholics. Today, almost one-third of the *Code of Canon Law* deals with marriage, a canonical preoccupation that evolved from Trent onward.

difficult issues to negotiate for a future refounding movement. Perhaps the single biggest issue facing us is the widely taken-for-granted morality of the major Christian churches and religions, all of which deem heterosexuality, mediated through monogamous unions, to be the normative, divinely mandated way to behave.

The churches and religions cling rigidly to the Aristotelian biological reductionism of human sexuality, a stance that has caused enormous pain and suffering among humans and contributed in no small measure to the several forms of sexual abuse that characterize our world today. It seems to me that sexuality should never have been reduced to such a crude anthropocentric articulation. It is intended to serve a much larger agenda related to human growth, development, flourishing, and spiritual depth. Its biological articulation—with procreation as the main, if not sole, objective—is merely one aspect of a much more complex, spiritually imbued phenomenon.

The new liminal horizon invites us to a radical redefinition of what we understand human sexuality to be about. The biological conditioning still distorts and perverts both our perceptions and behaviors. We need to expose and transform this highly destructive baggage, considered so extensively to be normative and enriching. As we transcend that which has kept us repressed and oppressed for so long, we need to embrace a new definition of human sexuality as the *erotic, creative energy mediated through our feelings, moods, and emotions in all forms of human interaction.* In other words, we must come to terms with the fact that sexuality is the energizing source of all authentic relationality, not merely a biological function for human procreation.

Furthermore, there still prevails a range of pseudo-spiritualized distortions that need to be reformed and, in some cases, totally eradicated. Feminist theologian Beverly J. Lanzetta describes the perverse spirituality in these graphic terms:

> In medieval culture, the classical body was male, harmonious, unified, proportionate, spiritual, and pure; it was free of pain, limitation, or decay. Women, and other marginalized social groups and classes, were associated with the grotesque body and its material orifices, fluids, and filth. As representative of the grotesque body, women were disproportionate, heterogeneous, profane, sinful, congenitally impure, and deserving of punishment. Despite its association with the lower bodily functions, the grotesque body . . . also had the capacity to regenerate. It was unfinished and open to the world, by contrast with the

classical body, represented as sealed and formally perfect. (Lanzetta 2005, 158)

The quotation highlights the baggage left over from our sexually
repressive past, leaving not only celibates but many others with a sense
of sexual woundedness that is not easily embraced and surrendered to
compassionate healing. Nor is it an easy landscape to enter and negotiate in a meaningful way, which makes it difficult for celibates—and
many other people—even to talk intelligently about their psychosexual
growth and well-being. That realm of our personal identity which is so
foundational to other aspects of our lives is the very one we struggle
to engage in a transparent and authentic way.

For celibates, therefore, there is always the risk of either fearful
avoidance that further feeds repression, often through a range of in-
dulgent projections onto the salacious culture that bombards us on every side. The literature on how celibates deal with their psychosexual
development tends to veer in the direction of over-spiritualization,
while the current climate influenced by clerical misbehavior discour-
ages many celibates from any overt attention to their psychosexual
processes. Several contemporary authors (for example, Crosby 1996;
Ezeani 2011; Falkenham 2013; Fiand 1996, 2001; Saffiotti 2011)
highlight features for a more integrated living out of our celibacy,
including meaningful adult friendships, creative human development,
regular spiritual accompaniment, readiness to seek psychotherapeutic
support, and being at ease in a climate of solitude.

The solitude that Lanzetta also highlights is probably the healthiest
antidote of all to the loneliness so characteristic of our time, the trigger
for the false pursuits that derail meaningful psychosexual development—whether for celibates or others. Among other things it includes
the ability to feel at ease with oneself, a healthy cultivation of gifts
and talents, an informed sense of one's body image, when alone and
with others, openness to being nurtured by the beauty of the natural
world, and perhaps most important of all, an integrated awareness of
God's unconditional love.

To be more effectively liminal, however, social and interpersonal
resources are every bit as important as individual resourcefulness. We
cannot be authentically liminal or prophetic on our own. Celibates
for the twenty-first century, particularly those who may be called to
refounding creativity, will need forums where they can converse intelligently and as mutual adults, about the major psychosexual issues of
our age. Without such conversation it is inconceivable that we can
embrace the complex discernments that will need to be done or hope

to cultivate the reflective dialogue so necessary to address and rectify the sexual dysfunctionalities of our age.

Androgenous Liminality

I have long believed that celibate sexuality mediates a set of human and cultural values that have neither been named nor integrated because of the preponderance of biologically driven sexuality. Furthermore, it strikes me that the ensuing liminal embodiment requires a human articulation that cannot be accommodated in our dualistically split construct of heterosexual v. homosexual expression. There is another route to gaining access to the deeper spiritual, psychological, and cultural meaning of human sexuality, namely, the pathway of the *androgyne*. We are entering an almost totally new territory, with the predictable reactions of ridicule, subversion, and denunciation.

Although Barbara Fiand does not name the challenge along these lines, she clearly has similar concerns when she writes:

Celibacy today, celebrated and lived healthily, needs to embrace the flow of sexual energy, to acknowledge it as good—as essential, in fact, to our incarnation. It needs to channel this energy with intent into the numerous creative and life-giving forms of loving that cry out for expression in our love-starved world. (Fiand 1996, 98)

These words are followed by a chapter entitled "The Transmutation of Energy."

In a later work Fiand writes:

Perhaps our celibate chastity has never been lived. It may have been avoided instead. . . . Propriety rather than passion was our guiding principle. . . . The ways of gentleness, mystery, inclusivity, compassion, and vulnerability do not speak in this world, nor in this church. Yet, these are ways of Christ-filled love, the keys to bonding, to mutual empowerment, to companioning, to life-giving community. (Fiand 2001, 136, 140).

I wish to propose that many among us who are called to a life of celibacy are androgynes at heart. Labeled by the medical/psychiatric profession as the ultimate state of confusion—whereby a person is not clear whether he or she is male or female—the notion of *androgyny* is ridiculed rather than clinically dismissed as deviant. Subsumed under the label of the hermaphrodite, it tends to be perceived as an idiosyncratic adoption of maniacs or New Age freaks. Retrieving the positive and more ancient meaning is not an easy task.

Gender is also a contentious issue of our time, and it is difficult to describe androgyny without resorting to gender language. In the androgynous state the biology tends to be clearly demarcated. Contrary to transsexuals, androgynes do not wish to have a sex change; in fact, they tend to be quite comfortable in their gendered identity as male or female. What is different is the *psychic energy* that informs their erotic drives and desires. Perhaps the major stumbling block to understanding androgyny is that the psychosexual focus is about *psychic energy* rather than *biological endowment.*

Psychosexually, androgynous behavior is informed by a stronger desire for psychic wholeness than driven to perform out of stereotypical, biological conditioning. Because it is difficult to internalize this identity in a culture addicted rigidly to sexist and gendered stereotypes, androgynes are often labeled bisexuals or transsexuals, and some people prematurely adopt these labels.[3]

Initially, the desired integration may manifest in a man becoming restless and disillusioned with conventional male roles, no longer wishing to play games of competition and male prowess, but desiring instead a lifestyle of a more cooperative, creative, and nurturing nature. In a woman it will sometimes become manifest in a desire for greater achievement and competence in a commercial or business role. It is not

---

[3] In the confused psychosexual landscape of our time, human sexuality carries several connotations, including these: (a) The primary function of human sexuality is the procreation of new life (a position adopted by many Catholics, Muslims, and religious fundamentalists of other persuasions). Therefore, sexuality can only be expressed through a heterosexual couple, ideally within monogamous marriage. (b) Sexuality is the means through which couples—heterosexual or homosexual—articulate their intimate love for each other, irrespective of human reproduction. Within this understanding are those who see the ideal of a permanent, lifelong relationship; at the other end of spectrum are those who understand sexual expression in more liberal terms and consider its articulation to be fluid and diffuse. (c) In both the above expressions, sexuality is viewed as an embodied, interpersonal set of behaviors. Instead, I am suggesting, it is primarily a form of psychic energy at the basis of every desire for intimacy, the understanding one needs to keep in mind in trying to understand the androgyne. The energy comes first, and its various articulations are, in many ways, culturally determined. For more on this complex subject, one of enormous cultural import, see my book on human desiring (O'Murchu 2007), in which I define human sexuality as the sum total of our feelings, moods, and emotions as mediated through human interaction, asserting that all human behavior is sexual, not merely genitally related interactions.

a case of switching roles or breaking down more conventional boundaries. Both men and women find themselves drawn to engage in interpersonal, social, and professional behavior that tends to transcend the cultural attributes often identified with a specific gender. Irrespective of what society feels about the newly adopted role, deep within the androgyne knows a type of "homecoming" that defies rational explanation.

The inner drive is toward *integration* and *wholeness,* motivated in this case not so much by conscious choice as by an inner, subconscious urge that is fundamentally spiritual in nature. It is not a once-and-for-all achievement; it is a lifelong process that merits the status of a life calling or vocation, as distinct from a goal one reaches through learning and human accomplishment.

The *androgyne* and *mystic* seem to have a lot in common; each aspires to a sense of wholeness that transcends all our manmade distinctions and dualisms. Perhaps St. Paul was alluding to this when he describes the new person in Christ: "There is no longer Jew nor Greek, there is no longer slave or free, there is no longer male and female; for all of you are one in Christ Jesus" (Gal 3:28). The mystical dimension helps to articulate and channel the spiritual meaning that is central to androgynous orientation; this may be subconscious rather than conscious and may not be easily integrated with formal religion.

Celibacy as an Androgynous Call

I suspect that people called to a celibate vocation operate effectively out of an androgynous identity. This is not something they have consciously chosen; more likely it is something that happens in the internal spiritual realm, evoking a particular calling or vocation. Were such people always disposed to this calling—already marked out at birth as several ancient cultures claim? I feel unable to offer a meaningful response to this question. Whatever the preconditions governing the vocational call, the consequences remain the same, and it is the consequences I am exploring in the present work.

Celibacy in its primordial significance seems to arise from a passionate desire to share more closely in the erotic intimacy of the Divine. God is the supreme Lover who allures and captivates the heart of the loved one. This can easily be depicted as a mystical calling for the rare few, one not readily available to the rest of humanity. I suspect that the opposite may be the case. The celibate fulfills a cultural role—perhaps a paradoxical one—exemplifying the ultimacy that is at the heart of all our desiring as a human species, perhaps a central feature of the monastic archetype described in Chapter 2 above. Of course, the vocational motivation may be based on less worthy aspi-rations, some of which may even be pathological; this is an area for profound and comprehensive discernment.

Despite this divine initiative—or perhaps precisely because of it—I suggest that the celibate calling is a highly sexualized one. The celibate may well be the most erotic of all humans, honoring a very ancient understanding of the Divine as a highly eroticized life force, impregnating the whole of creation. That being the case, two impor-tant adjustments need to be made to our thinking. First, God is not asexual (since the God we believe in is a passionate lover of everything in creation), and neither is any organism created by God. Second, the celibate needs expressive outlets for psychosexual energy, which may not be adequately or appropriately channeled through sublimation or total abstinence.

On this complex question ancient cultures may have been far more enlightened than contemporary ones. They provided outlets for the expression and articulation of sexual desire other than those of the mo-nogamous, married relationship. They seem to have understood better the intense and amorphous energy of human sexuality and facilitated its articulation through rituals and ceremonies whereby people were sexually intimate, inclusive of genital expression (not to be reduced to biological intercourse). We glean evidence for this through ancient Chinese and Indian art; through spiritually informed traditions like that of the Tantric philosophy of ancient India; in the iconography of early Hinduism; through a vast range of initiation rites among indigenous peoples; and through the courtly customs of medieval Europe.

That celibacy will involve an option for non-marriage makes a lot of practical and pastoral sense. That it must also imply total ab-stinence from sexual intimacy is less compelling in our time, faced as we are with understandings of human sexuality that transcend biological reproduction. How our culture might provide appropriate outlets for the expression and articulation of celibate sexual intimacy is a further consideration that need not detain us now.[4] Once we get

---

[4] Carl Olson (2008) provides a fine overview of celibacy in different cultures, with ancient and modern examples, noting the fluid and complex observance among Hindu and Buddhist ascetics. Among Hindu monks there is a widespread expectation that the monk first attends to familial duties in the world before opt-ing for permanent celibacy in the monk's older years. In Buddhism the picture is significantly more complex, with many monks marrying but abstaining from sexual relations while officiating in their monasteries. These other traditions and diverse experiences may be useful for a Christian reevaluation of celibacy in the context of our contemporary world.

the underlying vision clear, informed by a larger sense of culture, history, and especially sexuality itself, then it will be easier to initiate the dialogue that will need to take place, delineate necessary boundaries, discern moral guidelines, and generate the good will to provide the necessary support structures. The inevitable fear is that this will release a new wave of promiscuity and make a mockery of sexual morality at every level. My concern is to clear up the immorality and promiscuity that have been far too prevalent, and perversely covered over, for far too long (see Jordan 2000). Honesty and transparency are what I am ultimately pursuing.

In this suggested reframing of the call to vowed celibacy several concepts need a great deal more elaboration than space permits in this volume. First, our contemporary culture needs to clear up the muddled and confused meanings of human sexuality today. Second, as people who claim to be followers of an incarnational, embodied God, we need to transcend the metaphysical claims that God is somehow beyond our sexuality; all our sexual desires and urges come from God, not from Satan. Third, our Christian discipleship is inescapably psychosexual, having an impact for weal or for woe on the millions who need to come home to their embodied psychosexual selves (including celibates) and engage their sexuality in more informed and integrated ways. Fourth, for celibate people themselves there are psychosexual and developmental challenges requiring a quality of discernment largely unknown in earlier times. Without embracing these new horizons and developing the adult capacities to converse intelligibly on these matters, we celibates cannot claim to be liminal or prophetic in any real sense of the word.

Celibacy: The Future?

Margaret A. Farley, herself a Religious and visionary ethicist of our time, provides the following encouraging resume:

> Whatever the aberrations in some past or present historical settings, celibacy has always held the potential of challenging existing power relations, liberating individuals for the unexpected, breaking the bonds of gender stereotypes, and resisting the rigid social constructions of sexual meanings in any era. There is no reason to prevent the option of religiously motivated, life-long celibacy from fulfilling these functions today. (2015, 235)

The call to celibacy has flourished for several millennia; it will continue to flourish despite all the obstacles to its development, most of which are religious in nature. Current evidence suggests that it may become more diffuse in the wider population as growing numbers—women particularly—opt for single living for a large part if not the whole of their lives. This I describe as cultural celibacy, a single lifestyle, frequently adopted in order to be more successful in a career or in another life project.

This is very different from vocational celibacy, in which the underlying motivation—conscious or otherwise—is a desire to serve, typically informed by religious faith. This is the calling that I suspect is closely related to the psychosexual identity of being androgynous. The service at stake is not just to the cloistered life of prayer and asceticism, or, alternatively, to the unstinting commitment to work for the liberation of the poor and oppressed. These are external expressions of something much deeper and more profound.

The service envisaged in the celibate call goes to the very core of the divine erotic energy, releasing and birthing the capacity for right relationships at every level of creation. There are cosmic and planetary dimensions to this call. This is big stuff, and not for the lighthearted! This is not just about human beings, neither must it ever be restricted to one or another religion, church, or denomination.

Like sexuality itself, we have vilified celibacy in a crude, barbaric form of reductionism. That very calling, which is about engagement with the divine erotic in the whole of creation, has been trivialized and domesticated amid the ascetical distortions of a bankrupt sexuality. In order to redeem the true archetypal meaning of this vocation, we first need to reclaim what sexuality itself is about in its true cultural and spiritual meaning. Only then can we hope to understand and appreciate the call to celibacy, not some irresponsible opting out of life, but a liminal life option with profound implications for all humans. This is particularly true at this historical moment, when the meaning of human sexuality needs to be reviewed in depth and understood beyond the crude biological reductionism of the past two thousand years.

Space does not allow for an overview of the sex scandals of recent times and their impact on both male and female Religious. Nearly every critique of this painful issue highlights the abuse of *power* rather than the misuse of sex. However, we cannot avoid the historical fact that human sexuality viewed primarily as a biological propensity is entwined with the male desire to dominate and control, represented in the power to transmit the seed, viewing the woman as a biological receptacle for the development of the seed, in the hope of producing another ideal human being, namely, a male. This perverse ideology continues to prevail, much more extensively than most people want to acknowledge, and it remains a major area for prophetic contestation by those called to the liminal vocation.

᳁

Study Guide

1. How is your experience of living the vows reflected or echoed in this chapter? Have you leaned more toward a choice of values or a keeping of rules?

2. Has your celibate relatedness grown through liminality in the six dimensions explored in this chapter?

3. How has your celibacy embraced the flow of sexual energy? Has it moved you toward integration and wholeness in the different phases of your life?

Chapter 9

Vows for Mutual Empowerment

Corporately, we are totally co-opted, part of the system, enjoying its benefits too much to critique or confront either church or society.
—RICHARD ROHR

The participative structures and collaborative leadership models we have developed have been empowering, life-giving. These models may very well be the gift we now bring to the church and the world. . . . They reflect our post-Vatican II lived experience of communal discernment and decision-making as a faithful form of obedience.
—SR. PAT FARRELL

Most commentators regard the vows of poverty and obedience as separate entities. Renamed here as the *vow for mutual sustainability* (poverty) and *the vow for mutual collaboration* (obedience), I highlight the similarities involved when viewed within a liminal perspective while also clarifying the specific challenges unique to each vow.

Throughout human history *power* and *property* often have been closely related. Domination is frequently exercised through colonization of oppressed others, condemning them to an inferior status by stripping away the resources that sustain and nourish them, including their right to property. The exploitation of natural and material resources is often a corollary to the domination and subjugation of other peoples. Without access to land and property, most people feel diminished, their integrity undermined, and their value stripped away by those seeking to exploit and disempower them.

Some readers may already be wondering what these observations have to do with vowed commitment and the traditional sense of holiness associated with Religious. This is where we need to reconnect with the liminal horizon, making a paradigmatic shift in our understanding of the vows, with the accompanying need for a new narrative (parable) on how we articulate the meaning of the vows.

In liminal terms Religious are called to the critical threshold of the Companionship of Empowerment (the new reign of God) to discern more deeply how values are acculturated in the contemporary world, how the modes of articulation distort and even destroy the more authentic meaning of the values, and what liminal people need to do in order to reclaim what has been subverted and perverted. The call for such value radiation is not merely for the sanctity of vowed people themselves, but for the empowerment of those we are called to serve, along with the ecological and cultural forces that inform the reappropriation of such values.

First, I look briefly at each of the two vows under consideration, and then I illuminate the values jointly held—the interface of power and property briefly outlined above.

The Vow for Mutual Sustainability (Poverty)

In Van Kaam's schema, outlined earlier, the vow for mutual sustainability (poverty) seeks to uncover the values through which we relate to the resources of God's creation, with a view to clarifying how to enhance the growth and development of the material creation in general, and the more responsible and creative usufruct of the goods we use each day. Down through the ages Religious have handled this responsibility with rather mixed fortunes.

Religious Life has long been associated with the challenge to live simply, so that others may simply live. This ideal works well throughout the historical, founding phases of Religious Life, and it is often one of the first victims when decline and disintegration set in. As an Order or Congregation grows and expands, Religious universally do not seem to have evolved a more refined sense of discernment—to notice the subtle move to more comfortable living and, correspondingly, an even more subtle shift from prioritizing justice for the poor and marginalized. These two features seem intimately interconnected, as indicated by several commentators in recent times (see Cussianovich 1979; Azevedo 1995, 49–62).

Religious in our time need to be more unambiguously involved in the struggle to abolish destitution so that, in the words of Sandra Schneiders, material want does not continue depriving the poor of things many of us Religious take for granted: aesthetic enrichment, contemplation, friendship, and meaning in life (2013, 159). Today, we are faced with a double imperative: (1) How to be authentically in solidarity with the poor and oppressed, with the ensuing challenges for those of us who are rich to opt for greater simplicity; and (2) How to challenge and change those forces of oppression that frequently condemn the poor to poverty in the first place and keep them trapped there, sometimes for several generations. Our Christian fidelity to the Companionship of Empowerment and our mission to liminal boldness require of us direct involvement in bringing about systemic changes (political, economic, social) largely unknown in previous times.

To understand and embrace the liminal challenges of this vow, we need to discard our earlier focus on deprivation (of money or material goods), co-dependency (childlike permissions), or the delusion that we live like the poor (Religious tend to be among the most financially secure people on earth). We also need to change the language itself to respect the fact that in biblical terms *poverty is an evil,* not to be embraced in any sense, but to be gotten rid of at every level.

What Religious are called to model in the prophetic liminal context is a more ecological and economic sustainability, challenging all people to a more responsible use of the goods of God's creation. Money is merely one of those goods, grossly inflated and exploited in our time and stripped of its foundational value of a means of mutual gifting (see Eisenstein 2011; Schneiders 2013, 236ff.). But this vow for mutual sustainability is about a great deal more than money. In fact, it is that narrow utilitarian focus that has led to the lack of credibility around how contemporary Religious engage the vow today.

Revisioning the vow for mutual sustainability needs to begin with the created world in which we are all embedded. All around us is *gift,* not mere commodity. Creation flourishes through the gracious, gifted interdependence of the natural world, a process that flourished long before humans evolved, a prodigious fruitfulness that would outlive us were we to become a redundant species. The development of creation is not dependent on us, but we are, every moment of our lives, dependent on it.

The vow for mutual sustainability, therefore, calls us to a paradigm shift in how we understand the creation of which we are an integral part. As a species we live out of an appalling ignorance of our interdependent relationship with the surrounding web of life. According to prevailing economic theories we claim that the goods of creation are *scarce,* when in fact they are *abundant,* and that the goods must be fought for (consumption through fierce competition), when in truth we need to learn afresh how to collaborate creatively with the blessed

resources of creation. Our entire economic system is based on a bla-
tant lie, which brutally disrupts nature's own creative process, creates
highly destructive disparities, and leads all organic creatures—not
merely humans—into a dysfunctional, alienating relationship with
the web of life.

For conventional Religious Life all this feels like a momentous
leap. To some, it will feel like a betrayal of all they have known and
cherished. Instead of fleeing the world *(fuga mundi)*, we are the very
ones who should be modeling renewed, sustainable ways of engaging
with it. Instead of dualistically splitting the sacred and the secular, we
are meant to be the bridge builders, revisioning anew the pervasive
sacredness of all life. Instead of colluding with monetary exploitation
for lucrative investment, we should be developing alternative economic
paradigms to enhance and advance the common good of all.

And what about our preferential option for the poor? For a start, we
need to acknowledge our hypocrisy, that is, having such words inscribed
in our Constitutions while our overall lifestyle is not congruent with
that of the poor and most of our members do not live like poor people.
Nor is it religiously or morally responsible to offer a quality of spiritual,
emotional, or material solidarity to marginalized people, while we do
little or nothing to change their plight. Poverty is an evil to be removed,
not a social condition to be made tolerable, at least on a long-term basis.

Another confusing area where complicity undermines our integrity
is our preference for *charity over justice*. We feed the hungry but rarely
ask why in a world of abundance people are starving in the first place.
We create supportive networks for marginalized minorities, and we
create an elaborate rhetoric about their rights, yet we expend little
energy on rectifying the political and economic structures that rob
millions of the power of agency in the first place. In the Catholic tradition we tend to support the church's tendency to castigate individual
immorality while ignoring or bypassing the systemic injustices that are
often the primary cause of immoral human behavior.

To reactivate a more credible and empowering sense of the vow
for mutual sustainability we need to reclaim the primary communal
foundations (frequently highlighted in the writings of Barbara Fiand,
Michael Crosby, Sandra Schneiders, and others). Internally, we need
communities (ideally combining Religious and lay people) that are
creatively equipped with the skills to do the discernment required for
the revitalization of this vow. Externally, the same principle applies;
we need to cultivate or seek out communal networks to unmask, confront, and challenge the destructive imperial forces that prevail today

particularly in the economic and political domains. The strategy is essentially one of community engaging community, thus challenging and transcending the competitive and brutal individualism that characterizes our contemporary world, leading to exploitation, violence, and injustice.

The quality of networking I have in mind is that employed by agencies like Greenpeace or Friends of the Earth. Greenpeace is a particularly helpful example, known to governments all over the world—and hated by most of them. Yet, when it comes to the formulation of ecological policy and environmental strategy, most governments copy Greenpeace's blueprint. In the contemporary world bottom-up networks tend to be grounded in the real in ways that are far ahead of our major institutions. Our liminal witness is diminished and undermined when we align ourselves too closely with the prevailing religious, political, or economic standards; it is enhanced when we shift our allegiance to those movements that characterize the prophetic cutting edge, seeking justice and deeper truth for all creatures inhabiting the web of life.

The wisdom needed for this new endeavor, and the skills Religious will need for such future refounding, are outlined in Chapter 12 below. In order to move forward in the exercise of more responsible sustainability, and develop more congruent liminal forms of witness, we Religious need to do three things:

1. Outgrow the inherited over-spiritualized, ascetical understanding of the vow of poverty, that of fleeing the world in order to procure salvation in a life hereafter. This simplistic overview has led to several abuses of people, property, money, resources, and the exercise of authority. It undermines incarnational spirituality and is alien to all that constitutes responsible adulthood. Significantly for our time, it leaves Religious at a serious loss about how to engage the urgent ecological issues confronting humanity today.

2. Develop the ability to converse about the meaning of this vow as theologically informed, responsible adults. True to the gospel call to seek first the Companionship of Empowerment (cf. Matt 6:33), we need to explore our liminal responsibilities to model with and for the people of God responsible and creative ways to celebrate and protect the essential giftedness of the planet's resources. Among other things, this will require of us an honest, transparent discernment of our own lifestyle, individually and communally, particularly our slide in recent decades into comfortable middle-class acquiescence.

3. Outgrow the dualistic split between the sacred and the secular so as to embrace the tasks of eco-justice in more forthright and anticipatory ways. Most of the crippling poverty in the contemporary world arises from structural injustice that leads to the exploitation and usurpation of our natural, God-given resources. We cannot bear liminal witness for more sustainable gospel living without the engagement in justice ministry that will enable and empower us to confront the major injustices of our time.

Far from being a vow that keeps us "poor in spirit" and helps us to attain salvation in a life hereafter, this new understanding of the vow of poverty moves us into the realm of enrichment as we seek to build up God's kingdom on earth (the new companionship) and thus contribute prophetically to bringing about the empowering sustainability of a new heaven and a new earth.

The Vow for Mutual Collaboration (Obedience)

Despite the fact that the early Benedictines tried to outgrow the parent-child approach to Religious obedience, opting instead for an adult mutuality mediated through communal discernment, the history of Religious Life exhibits many tragic deviations of the abuse of power in the name of being loyal and obedient. Even today there are many Religious who carry the scars of such abuse, including those who were called to exercise its implementation. Meanwhile, our postmodern world has moved toward an opposite extreme, a type of cultural and behavioral free for all, creating a climate of benign anarchy and a lack of mutual accountability. In this area there is an acute need for liminal witness, much more difficult to translate into action than in the case of the other two vows.

In the third volume of her trilogy on Religious Life, Sandra Schneiders devotes considerable space to the treatment of this vow. Her primary concern is Catholic Religious Life, with its juridical, canonical status within the institutional church. In words echoing the opening quote of Sr. Pat Farrell, Schneiders writes:

Many in the hierarchy are still operating within a premodern model of society, that of the church as a divine right monarchy in which authority flows in one direction only, namely downward, and can be exercised absolutely on the assumption that the subordinates have no rights except those bestowed upon them by the superiors. Religious in general are operating within a different model, one that has developed over the past two centuries in non-totalitarian societies and that was, in principle, enshrined in the documents of Vatican II in its recognition of the equality of all the baptized in their church and the inviolable freedom of conscience. This equality and freedom are the basis for a theology of obedience as an exercise of asymmetrical mutuality rather than abject subordination. (Schneiders 2013, 547)

What Schneiders seeks for Catholic Religious (women Religious, in particular) within the context of the hierarchical church suggests a larger issue regarding the exercise of power and authority, which, in my opinion, cannot be resolved by focusing exclusively on the church. From a liminal, prophetic perspective, Religious must keep a close eye on the wider cultural context, in this case the *culture of patriarchal domination*. This is at the root of many current abuses—personal, social, and systemic—and its impact on the ecclesiastical process cannot be rectified till the dysfunctionality is addressed on the larger societal scale.

One definition/description of the prophetic dimension worth keeping in mind here is that of *speaking truth to power*. This requires a comprehensive analysis of how society adopts, appropriates, and mediates power throughout our major structures and institutions, and why it is done in such a way that restricts empowering outcomes to a minority left disenfranchised and disempowered. That is the foundational crippling injustice that Jesus sought to challenge and rectify by proclaiming a new reign of God as the Companionship of Empowerment. And that too must be the primary vowed undertaking of those who claim to be following Christ at the liminal prophetic threshold of the twenty-first century.

Schneiders expresses the challenge in these words:

Religious life, by its very nature, is a voluntary, egalitarian network of Gospel-based relationships in which power is not exercised hierarchically and therefore cannot normally be exercised coercively. . . . [It is] a theological and spiritual option for the kind of non-hierarchical community Jesus founded and for its collegial rather than monarchical structure and function. (2013, 456, 505)

The words *authority* and *obedience* have often been used interchangeably, with little attention to their specific meanings. The word *obedience* is derived from the Latin *ob-audiere*, which means "to listen attentively." From a liminal perspective this is a valuable starting point, also posited by Adrian Van Kaam when he writes: "Obedience in the widest sense is the total openness of the whole person to the meaning of all events in their life situation" (van Kaam 1968, 25). He elaborates: "Obedience is, therefore, the willingness to listen to reality as the place of revelation of possibilities that one might bring to life. Disobedience disconnects me from that flow (van Kaam 1968, 281–82).

Authority normally means commanding another to carry out a specific task or behave according to expected standards—as exercised in traditional top-down parenting paradigms. When the Gospels inform us that Jesus spoke with authority (Mk 1:22; Matt 7:29; Lk 4:32; Jn 7:17), it is not the exercise of patriarchal power that is meant (although, frequently, that is how the texts have been interpreted); neither is it the right to a more exalted status based on scribal wisdom. Rather, it is the witness to a truthfulness that comes from deep within. Jesus's words ring true, and so do his actions, because they emanate from an inner wisdom that conveys truth and authenticity.

In the theological context, therefore, the exercise of authority, and the obedience that ensues, has nothing to do with a co-dependent relationship between a junior and a senior, in some kind of pseudo-parental construct, but rather a mutual process based on an adult capacity for interrelating within an empowering communal structure, as proposed by Bernard J. Lee (2008, 290–303). And, in terms of Religious Life, its primary function is not the orderly running of a Congregation or the supervision of a ministerial outlay, and less so the management of buildings and structures! Obedience, as mutual collaboration, denotes above all else a group committed to reflective discernment on alternative ways to empower new life among all who are downtrodden, marginalized, and disenfranchised.

Two key notions underpin this understanding: *discernment* and *empowerment*. In liminal terms the group's primary obedience is to God, and God's will for our world now—in terms of how a particular charism can serve the contemporary needs of the world. This requires a primary allegiance to solitude, prayer, study, reflection, dialogue, and social analysis—and those in formal leadership carry a primary responsibility to ensure that the group remains faithful to this primary undertaking.

Second, the discerning eye of the group needs to be continuously vigilant for abuse of power and the ensuing disempowerment that cripples millions of people in our world today. The impact of such destructive power on the environment, the usurpation and exploitation of natural resources for aggrandizement of the few at the cost of the many, needs to be an integral dimension of the sustained critique arising from the group's discernment. The end goal is unambiguously clear: the promotion and grounding of the Companionship of Empowerment, not merely in the church but throughout the whole of God's creation.

All the Talk about Leadership

Of all the issues confronting the commercial and business communities for at least the past half century, leadership tops the bill. Every major text, as well as several web pages, aspire to a new model and a new way of leading. Yet many of these visionary ideals leave the reader with a sense of opacity! Something is amiss, yet it is rarely if ever stated forthrightly. One wonders if it is not the leaders themselves undergoing some collective identity crisis who are projecting their restless confusion while feverishly groping for ways to resolve their confusing dilemma.

Within Religious Life things don't seem a great deal better. Many of us have been through the ritualized process of naming key qualities of prospective leaders, knowing all the while that none of us would measure up; rarely are we prepared to look at the fact that even those among us so richly endowed will probably fail to deliver in an empowering way. There seems to be a kind of systemic blindness within the ecclesiastical realm that prevents us from discerning why so many promising leaders prove such a huge disappointment. It never seems to dawn on us that perhaps we are operating a dysfunctional system that inhibits, or even chokes, the creative potential of those entrusted with a ministry of leadership. More disturbing still is the prospect of having to face the fact that all of us, and not merely those entrusted with formal leadership, are victims of a highly destructive patriarchal system that has long outlived its usefulness.

For many Religious, leadership still denotes the responsibility of being in charge, which includes looking after the members, and ensuring that all are happy and fulfilled, whatever their life status. Managing the members is itself a major part of leadership today in most Orders and Congregations. While in theory there is much talk of delegation and shared responsibilities, an enormous amount still falls on the people in leadership roles. The tasks of management can be so demanding that leaders are left with little time or energy to provide animation and inspiration for the members, to challenge membership into more adult ways of creative collaboration. Vision suffers, and correspondingly problematic issues tend to multiply.

Schneiders, in her elaborate analysis of obedience and leadership in contemporary Religious Life (2013), comments in rather glowing terms of the alternative non-patriarchal modeling Religious provide in the structuring and exercise of authority within the church. Certainly, a lot of women Religious in the United States (with sporadic examples elsewhere around the world) have explored more communal ways of exercising co-responsibility in mutually empowering ways; in this process they inspire and challenge a range of lay people in the secular sphere, but I doubt if they have much influence on church authority, either locally or internationally.

From a liminal perspective this is one area where we fare quite poorly. We are so attached to the institutional church, and so canonically hidebound, that we have few openings to explore and offer alternative models for the creative empowering leadership that millions hunger for in the oppressive world order we inhabit today. In this regard the excessive clericalization of the vowed life has stymied and undermined our prophetic integrity in a substantial way. For this reason alone the refounding vision of the late twenty-first century needs to transcend—in every way it can—the manipulative control of institutional Christianity. A liminal witness, unambiguously focused on God's world and not merely on the church, must resist any efforts to limit this liminal grace. In such an undertaking we can all be challenged and encouraged by Dominican Sister Donna J. Markham:

> This is a moment when we need leaders to call one another and call our communities to heroism; to call us to risk entering into those conflictual conversations that will connect us in trust and in hope to one another . . . to help us to face together the different, the other, the frightening, and the unexpected. We need leaders who call us to discover ever more deeply that the good which we hold in common is nothing less than the participation in the compassionate goodness and mystery of God. (Markham 1999, 168)

What do Religious need to do to reclaim a more authentic liminal witness to the values embodied in what we have traditionally called the vow of obedience and that I suggest should be renamed the *vow for mutual sustainability*? The following might be considered initial steps:

- Postcolonialism highlights the residue that can prevail long after colonialism no longer prevails. Can we, Religious, name those residual elements, the wounds that still hurt, the misunderstandings that fester, and the healing that needs to be embraced?
- Can we begin more adult conversations on how to exercise shared responsibility in mutually creative ways? Can our leaders allow and facilitate this process without looking over their shoulders in fear of incurring ecclesiastic disapproval?
- How do we enable individuals and communities to exercise leadership from the ground up and in the spirit of mutual obedience make community the primary locus for Congregational discernment?
- Can we identify—or co-create—networks that will empower us to confront the systemic injustices of power that reap such havoc in society and church alike?

Vows for the Future

Religious Life, in every culture known to humankind, includes a vowed commitment embracing a remarkably common set of values. One significant difference between East and West is highlighted in the fact that the primary vow in several Eastern religions is *nonviolence (Ahimsa)*. That is a wisdom we in the West could fruitfully embrace. In the case of celibacy, the violence of clerical abuse comes readily to mind, but in fact it is merely one aspect of a much more pervasive oppression, more apparent in the new understanding of the other two views as outlined above.

Most, if not all, the major studies on clerical sex scandals highlight the misuse and abuse of power as the primary underlying problem (Sipe 1995; Keenan 2011). Clerical and/or ecclesiastical power is often singled out as the primary culprit, but rarely is the connection made with the more extensive misuse of such power in other realms above and beyond those of the church. Hence the difference in the liminal approach: it seeks out depth, breadth, and interconnectedness. It seeks to transcend the cause-and-effect explanation in favor of a more discerning understanding of human and earthly complexities. It seeks to move beyond scapegoating to the larger systemic and cultural factors that underpin human motivation and ensuing behavior patterns.

In terms of value radiation we detect several shared values in the areas of life experience related to the vows for mutual sustainability and mutual collaboration. These I have already named in terms of the salacious, compulsive hunger for power, driving several of our patriarchal institutions, culturally mandated, and often sanctioned by religion across the modern world. In the patriarchal worldview, everything (including human beings) is a commodity to be exploited and consumed. Consequently, a more responsible, nonviolent, liberating understanding of these two vows must prioritize the essential giftedness of everything in creation, to be cherished, protected, and nourished by systems and structures that are modeled on the organic, interdependent nature of universal life itself.

In the post–Vatican II renewal, Religious Orders and Congregations sought stronger solidarity with the poor and marginalized. The *preferential option for the poor* was inscribed into several books of Constitutions. In some cases the aspirational rhetoric never went beyond mere words, and when it did, it took several years to realize that the unjust plight of the poor in our world is always entwined with corrupt politics and economics. The failure to empower people to bring themselves out of their poverty was often directly related to the usurpation and abuse of power by the powerful themselves. The vows of poverty and obedience (to use the old language) were, and continue to be, inextricably linked.

Over-spiritualization, expressed in terms such as "being poor for the sake of the gospel" and "being obedient like the suffering Christ," can be dangerously deceptive rationalizations that result neither in empowering holiness for the devotees themselves nor in the liminal value awakening that the vows are meant to serve. It is not just a case of being more Christlike oneself (which in itself requires a theologically informed interpretation), but rather radiating for all "others" the Christ passion for love, justice, liberation, and gospel empowerment. In seeking first the new Companionship of Empowerment, Religious for the twenty-first century will need a multidisciplinary understanding of how all our values (and lack of values) are intertwined in one complex matrix. We cannot hope to witness to empowering and enduring freedom, internally or externally, without appropriating this multidisciplinary way of engaging with life. The practical implications will be reviewed in Chapter 12.

In seeking to integrate the notion of nonviolence into our vowed commitment—in solidarity with Jain, Hindu, and Buddhist monastics—I want to conclude these reflections with some suggestions for embracing the nonviolent approach. First, in the case of the *vow for relatedness,* how do we outgrow the functional and competitive drive that sustains and exploits so much of our human relating, not merely within the human realm, but with the entire web of life? How do we transcend the biological conditioning we have inherited from Aristotle, by which we often reduce the human person, the body, and sexuality to a violently perverse caricature? And how do we transcend centuries of demonizing healthy erotic pleasure so that we can reclaim a nonviolent sense of incarnational dignity for all organic creatures, humans included?

Second, how do we honor the call to *mutual sustainability* through more conscious choices to safeguard and advance the essential giftedness of all God's creation? In a culture of insatiable consumerism, how do we maintain a contemplative sense of vigilance, live uncluttered lives, and prophetically challenge the forces that exploit and brutalize creation's resources? And particularly for those living amid the wealth and imperialism of the West, including all who live by such inflated standards all over the world, how do we use our "blessings" to ensure that those deprived of the good gifts of creation can also begin to experience the meaning of justice, equality, and gospel empowerment?

Third, and perhaps most daunting of all, in a world enmeshed in patriarchal domination, how can we begin to speak truth to power, religiously, politically, and economically? If we sincerely believe in *the vow for mutual collaboration* (the vow of obedience), what is the conversion we need to undergo to rid our hearts of the residue that still ensnares us in the wake of imperial oppression? What is preventing our members—and our various levels of leadership—from putting into place the resources for discernment needed for the mutual engagement to which we vow our allegiance? When are we going to take seriously the liminal challenge to model afresh for our troubled world nonviolent structures to evoke and sustain justice for all organic life?

Throughout the contemporary world serious conversations around the meaning of and the living out of the vows simply do not take place. We don't know how to have these conversations in an adult, informed way—and with the theological wisdom that could both challenge and inspire us. It is to be hoped that these reflections on the vows—in this and the previous chapter—provide some fertile and empowering ideas to raise us out of the malaise in which we seem to be trapped. Without that fresh awakening we cannot hope to be creatively involved in the refounding challenges that face us as we move deeper into the twenty-first century.

∾

Study Guide

1. What inner resonance is there for you with the *vow for mutual sustainability* as the deeper meaning of the traditional vow of poverty?

2. If you consider the vow of obedience as a vow for mutual collaboration, how might this phrase describe your way of living right now?

3. This chapter contains many questions. Which are of particular significance for you at this time?

Conclusion to Part Three

The Discerning Process

In the renewal of Religious Life that followed Vatican II, the preferential option for the poor features in several deliberations and became inscribed in updated Constitutions. Without being consciously aware of it, Religious groups were making a liminal option with a challenge to embrace more radical values—a move that proved too much for many Orders and Congregations.

It is almost instinctive to us, Religious, to be drawn to the margins, to the cutting edge, to the threshold of prophetic witness. The preferential option for the poor had that kind of subliminal attraction. On the one hand, we did make a discerning, liminal option; on the other, we failed to maintain our commitment, possibly because we were not sufficiently aware of what was transpiring within and around us and lacked a more empowering theology to inform and sustain our discernment. Our allegiance to the church may have been more of a hindrance than a help; in a church stuck in the dualistic split between the sacred and the secular, we stood little chance of embracing the political and economic interfacing required to undo the oppressive suffering of the poor and marginalized.

In several groups the preferential option for the poor became almost as contentious an issue as the use of the veil had become a few decades earlier. Nobody wanted to remove it from the Constitutions, yet few had any clear ideas on how to integrate the ideal into the life and ministries of a particular group.

When it comes to understanding the meaning of liminality—and its practical applications—many Religious will be attracted to the ideal of gospel empowerment for those weighed down by the paralyzing injustices of our time. It will take a great deal more discernment—understanding of what is at stake spiritually, theologically, politically, and economically—to move from the ideal to its translation into lifestyle and ministry. The novel quality of engagement with key values is new for many Religious, and a deeper, more discerning acquaintance with what is at stake is necessary if we are to avoid the discouraging ambivalence many of us experienced around the preferential option for the poor. Indeed, the value radiation required for the other two vows is even more complex than what was at stake in our aspiration to be more in solidarity with the impoverished of our world.

In the case of all three vows—and other aspects of our lives as well—the following guidelines for discernment will need close and consistent attention:

- We need to discern more clearly how to live out our liminal calling, and the prophetic options it will entail both for individuals and communities. Inevitably, there will be ensuing tensions between individual aspirations and communal/congregational need; while the community or Congregation will tend to be drawn to maintenance, visionary individuals (and occasional communities) will be animated move toward new expressions of mission.
- Even where a group can reach consensus around a more prophetic shift in mission, there is the further discerning challenge to embrace new values regarding lifestyle, prayer, and spirituality that will be congruent with the new liminal horizons.
- Many of the values related to lifestyle are embedded in our vowed commitment as outlined above. Many communities—particularly male clerical groups—find it difficult to conduct adult conversations on the meaning of the vows in our time. How to support and challenge one another in living out our vows in the context of the twenty-first century is one of the more daunting tasks facing contemporary Religious.
- Ascetical and moralistic influences from our past still interfere in a reappropriation of the vows for the twenty-first century, whereby we wrestle with how to reincarnate the vowed values in the complex cultural settings of the modern world. Individually, we will need good spiritual and psychological resourcefulness for that task; communally, we will need to employ facilitating resources to highlight and resolve the hidden agendas that otherwise will obstruct our liminal witness.

Part Four

Revitalization for Refounding

I open this final part with Chapter 10, a chapter on community, reviewing what the concept means in a range of cultural contexts but,
more important, also highlighting its central role in the evolution of
the vowed life throughout the centuries. The communal significance
has always been to the fore but largely overshadowed and subverted
by the fixation on heroic individualism. In several historical situations Religious Life has been personality driven rather than policy
guided.

Chapter 11 returns to the cyclic unfolding of Religious groups
throughout time, reviewing in greater detail the trajectory that has
been observed in each three-hundred-year historical epoch. I highlight
what enhances growth as well as the dynamics that lead to stagnation,
decline, and death. Significantly, however, each cycle ends with the possibility of revitalization and refounding, and while most groups have
not managed the transition into a new wave of existence, a sufficient
percentage have succeeded, indicating the dispositions and discernments likely to launch a refounding possibility.

It may be one or two outstanding visionaries who are on fire
with a new vision, but it will take a collaborative effort to move
the dream along the trajectory from the initial myth (dream) to the
belief and normative stages. And the more coherent and discerning
the communal dynamic, the more effective the forward movement
is likely to be. Community, not heroic individualism, is the central
catalyst that empowers the birthing and refounding of all Orders
and Congregations.

My concluding chapter is on the process of refounding itself, drawing largely on the pioneering work of Australian priest-anthropologist
Gerald A. Arbuckle. One cannot exaggerate the fact that refounding is

a divine, gratuitous gift. We do not refound our Orders and Congregations; only the creative Spirit can do that. Nonetheless, we do seem to have a say in the matter, depending on our ability to remain radically open to the possibility. Such openness will involve a willingness to let go of what has served us well in the past, diligently attending to the discernment of the acute cultural and spiritual needs of our time, and trusting radically in God's providential care when the eventual outcome is one of death rather than refounding. Even in the face of death, hope and not despair can have the final word.

Chapter 10

Community and All It Signifies

*To build community requires vigilant awareness
of the work we must continually do to undermine all the socialization that leads us to behave
in ways that perpetuate domination.*

—BELL HOOKS

*Healing is impossible in loneliness; it is the
opposite of loneliness. Conviviality is healing.
To be healed we must come with all the other
creatures to the feast of Creation.*

—WENDELL BERRY

As indicated in the opening chapters of this book, communal living
has been an integral dimension of the vowed life from its very
inception. The Covenanters of early Syria, the Basilian foundational
movement, the apotactic village ascetics, and the groups of the Judean
desert all predated the Pachomian option for communal living. In
claiming that the earlier groups were essentially eremitical in nature,
scholars are offering a limited and distorted picture. Even the virgins,
despite living singly within their own families, were federated along
several communal lines in terms of prayer life, discernment, apostolate, and interpersonal support. Historians suggest that Orders and
Congregations were founded by outstanding individuals; they underestimate, and often ignore, the inescapable communal infrastructure to
most, if not all, Religious Life foundations. Community is an enduring
underlying dimension that is likely to remain a central feature of the
refounding breakthroughs of the twenty-first century.

Most Religious groups—and their contemporary Constitutions—
envisage community life as a structured arrangement requiring members to affiliate and interact in a regular, frequent manner. At the more

monastic end of the spectrum is the gathering for recitation of the divine office on a regular daily basis, sharing common meals, at least a broad uniformity of ministry, and a set of congregational expectations around social and religious customs such as celebration of key feast days. Toward the other end is an emphasis on fluidity and flexibility, embracing a variety of ministries (usually individualized) with members often living singly, cherishing individual autonomy, and with links to their Congregation usually of a tenuous nature.

Single living creates a degree of tension for many contemporary groups, including monks operating parishes and involved in a range of individualized ministries. To discern our way through this relatively recent development Sandra Schneiders suggests we distinguish between *common life* (the more structured approach, with a high degree of conformity) and *community living* (capable of embracing a variety of structures including the option for single living):

> What I have proposed is that community life, an intrinsic and constitutive dimension of ministerial religious life, is theologically necessary for all members of the congregation but that it can be embodied on the personal level in a plurality of lifestyles, both group and individual, which are related to each other as equally valid variations. . . . Just as the corporate mission of the congregation is not necessarily subverted by a plurality of ministries, so its community life is not necessarily threatened by a plurality of dwelling lifestyles. . . . It seems to me that any realistic attempt to engage the issue of community from the corporate perspective must start from a clear conception of the nature of ministerial Religious Life itself. . . . The challenge today is to imagine and create something that has not previously existed in religious life, a form of community appropriate for ministerial religious congregations that will both provide for the relational growth and development of the members and facilitate ministry. (Schneiders 2001, 351, 376)

Community as an Archetypal Value

Community is an elusive concept that easily falls between the extremes of strong group conformity and a network so nebulous it is difficult to identify either its sociological structure or its communal potential. We are dealing with an archetype as old as humanity itself, one, in fact, with a primordial significance that predates human evolution. Modern cosmology and quantum physics both highlight the inescapable interdependent and interactive process through which all creation flourishes. *Nothing makes sense in isolation; everything needs everything else.* The foundational relational imprint—which also includes fragmentation and conflict—defies rational explanation and can best be assessed for its profound significance by adopting archetypal wisdom.

Perhaps that wisdom is nowhere more transparent than in the great religions of humankind, all of which adopt a relational understanding of holy Mystery (often subverted into the doctrine of the Trinity). And where the formal religion chooses not to adopt that prototype, it resurfaces in the mystical wing—the Kabbalah in Judaism, and Sufism in Islam—suggesting that we are dealing with something that is essentially irrepressible. Translated into the metaphysical categories adopted by the early church councils (Nicea, Chalcedon, and others), the archetypal meaning becomes seriously distorted and suppressed. What in archetypal terms is an attempt at naming and articulating the foundational relational essence of the Godhead (see La Cugna 1991; Fox 2001; Zizioulas 2004), becomes reduced to a set of anthropocentric, metaphysical distinctions and oppositions that seriously undermines the foundational interdependence of both the Godhead itself and the divine imprint manifested in creation.

It is not surprising, then, that all the religions set out to create a cultural value system based upon the relational flourishing of humans in a convivial relationship with the God who relates primarily through creation. Apart from indigenous groups around our world, most religious believers have lost the plot in terms of that original inspiration. And the diverse movements of the twentieth and twenty-first centuries seeking out a new spirituality are implicitly voicing their disappointment with formal religion's failure to deliver the deeper relational truth.[1]

The religions themselves also struggle to recapture a purer essence, which they know has been dislodged along the way. However, they search for the rediscovery in the wrong places. They seek to set right the underlying doctrinal truths or the external legal practices, when, in fact, the deeper crisis of meaning belongs to the dislodged, suppressed relational matrix at the archetypal level. Fidelity to this search for relational meaning will keep the religions alive and relevant.

---

[1] A vast literature now exists on the merging spiritual trends of the twenty-first century. For a comprehensive overview see Johnson and Ord 2012. How contemporary market forces seek to absorb and sell the new spirituality is critically reviewed in Carrette 2005.

In the early 1960s the Catholic Church attempted a fresh appropriation of this relational undergirding through an event popularly known as Vatican Council II. The Holy Spirit pushed hard and had a measured degree of success in reclaiming the relational context. In its final sessions the council even pushed the relational threshold toward embracing the whole of God's creation *(The Pastoral Constitution on the Church in the Modern World)*, but as many Catholics know, that is precisely the aspect of the council that was seriously compromised in subsequent decades. The teaching authority of the Catholic Church, fearing a threat to its patriarchal male leadership, began to panic as the people's relational creativity evolved into ever enlarging horizons of meaning and engagement. When that expansion joined with the politics of liberation (in Central and South America), Rome became petrified, and extensive entrenchment and reactionary teachings came to the fore.

Sadly, many Religious Orders—male clerical ones particularly—failed to adopt a prophetic critique. The collusion with the institutional church left most Religious floundering in an insipid cooption. In many cases we lost our liminal focus, leading, among other things, to an internal fragmentation that further weakened our prophetic/liminal contribution. A new invasive individualism crept into Religious Life, sometimes spreading most virulently precisely in those groups that retained the veneer of a structured common life. Groups often struggled to obtain consensus on the most basic values of spirituality, simplicity of lifestyle, discernment, their apostolic focus. The declining landmark of *ethical doubt* (see Chapter 11) became ostensibly visible. The problem was that most of our members had neither the historical wisdom nor discerning skills to see what was happening.

In not a few cases the desire for more authentic community morphed into a range of material comforts. We needed en-suite facilities for our increasing elderly members, but in just a short few years everybody was demanding access to en-suite amenities. And we mounted arguments to justify the personal (and often exclusive) use of our own car, computer, bank account, technological accessories; we needed extra space to store our ever-expanding range of belongings. In just a few decades we began to judge the "successful" community by the comfort of living conditions, the support structures for greater personal freedom, and a climate where everybody was nice to everybody else, no matter how serious the issues we needed to confront.

An Alternative Option

In some cases it was the members who had opted for single living who proved to be more authentically liminal and prophetic. Their individual lifestyles provoked them anew to ask foundational questions on why they became Religious in the first place and what was keeping them in Religious Life now. Many adopted a reflective, discerning lifestyle; they became more acutely aware of their liminal mission in the world, and for many it was the *world* rather than the *church* that engaged their process of discernment. They sought out spiritual accompaniment on a frequent basis and took seriously ongoing adult faith formation. With varying degrees of success they sought new patterns of alignment with their respective Congregations. In a few cases—and sadly only a few (to the best of my knowledge)—leadership set up processes through which members living singly brought back to their groups the wisdom and richness of their experiences, creating a mutual enrichment for all members of the Order or Congregation.

Some took an even more radical step, occasionally described as *Intentional communities*, in which a sister of a particular Congregation living singly—that is, on her own and apart from her group—forms a close friendship or working relationship with a sister of another Congregation. Together they seek out a smaller discerning group, sometimes consisting of a local pastor with two or three lay people, and meet on a regular basis for quality time together, including spiritual reflection, prayer, discernment around key life issues, a shared meal, and occasionally a eucharistic celebration. The coming together tends to begin on a monthly basis but frequently evolves into bi-monthly or even weekly meetings. As the commitment grows deeper in terms of support, fellowship, and discernment, there tends to be mutual agreement on how precious such times are and an ensuing commitment to prioritize allegiance to their regular time together.

I have met groups in the United States, Canada, and Australia who have formed intentional communities. Doing so requires a high level of commitment, a skillful approach to mutual discernment, and a quality of integrity around transparency and confidentiality. It tends to embrace a quality of faith sharing and discernment with a depth far in advance of many structured formal Religious communities. And sometimes it can create tension, as with the Religious priest in Australia who informed me that he resided in a conventional community of his Congregation but obtained all his spiritual nourishment from an intentional community that met bi-monthly and of which he had been a member for five years.

When Constitutions of Orders and Congregations describe community life, it tends to be *common life* that is under consideration. There seems to be a largely unarticulated desire among Religious universally for a communal structure with emphasis on being together in the one place, even when the group only meets together for twice-daily prayer and shared meals. It seems to me that most groups have not reflected deeply on the rationale for this arrangement. I suspect there is a subtle desire for security, management of people, and control. *None of these are gospel values*, although they do have a pragmatic usefulness. And, of course, we need to acknowledge that in approving Constitutions church authorities tend to demand that such communal structures are inscribed into our canonical guidelines.

Contemporary Religious, for the greater part, do not seem to have discerned either the archetypal undergirding of communal living (referred to briefly above) or its immense potential for theological and spiritual discernment. Nor do I wish to underestimate the significance of community—variously understood—to provide for the social and emotional needs of healthy growth and development. The key elements have been identified by several writers, seeking the integrated wisdom of psychology, spirituality, and the social sciences. I find the overview of Christine Pohl (2011) to be particularly useful. She highlights four qualities essential for the nourishment and sustenance of empowering communities:

1. *Embracing gratitude*, as people gracefully receive and challenge each other toward growth that will transcend the grumbling discontent that undermines trust and stultifies interpersonal enrichment;

2. *Keeping promises*, inculcating a climate of trust and fidelity while also healing the wounds that may have been incurred through emotional or personal betrayal;

3. *Living truthfully*, with a quality of transparency that offsets the debilitating erosion of deception and dishonesty; and

4. *Practicing hospitality*, where all are welcome, and particularly those who feel alienated or estranged because of painful life experiences.

Even happily married couples, and those with access to the intimacies of family life, often seek communal outlets to further articulate emotional and even intimate issues of human flourishing, as highlighted by Martha Nussbaum (2011) in her several studies of human capabilities.

Ever since Vatican II, Catholic Religious groups, in assemblies and chapters, target community life as an area needing more devoted attention. We have often drawn up strategies to improve the quality of community life. The outcomes rarely prove to be satisfying, so we return to the drawing board and create yet another set of aspirations. Some groups have done that many times without a satisfying outcome. Something seems to be blocking us from reaching our goals.

It may be the baggage we have inherited from the past. It may be the complex nature of the human personalities that constitute an average Religious Order or Congregation today. It may be a cultural shift in which the desire for authentic community is morphing into more eclectic expression, suggested by many new developments of recent decades that will be reviewed in the final part of this chapter. We are dealing with a range of complex and interconnected issues. My concern is that our deliberations around authentic community are frequently too pragmatic, and thus we fail to embrace the more onerous task of discerning the deep aspirations within and behind our desire for meaningful community. The tenor of our discussions and the awareness we bring to the task need to go deeper. Discernment needs to become a more central feature.

Communal Discernment

"For where two or three are gathered in my name, I am there among them" (Matt 18:20). This, I suggest, is a core text for our understanding of Religious Life community from a historical perspective and in its contemporary aspirations. It is not human intimacy that brings us together in Religious communities; nor is it blood ties, social compatibility, or common ministerial skills. We are called into community "in my name" and not merely according to our own preferences or primarily in obedience to an appointment by a Religious superior. Community is intended to be the context from which arise all our lifelong discernments—personal, ministerial, and congregational.

This ideal is deeply embedded in the history of Religious Life, but it has been subverted for a number of historical reasons, which include:

- the tendency in patriarchal historical analysis to highlight individual heroes, encouraging a cult whereby values are driven by personalities rather than by primary allegiance to gospel values.
- the displacement of the foundational communal models of Syria and Egypt in favor of the ascetical anchoritic individual heroes.
- the subversion of the great foundresses, and of female Religious

in general, with their more communal modeling of living out
the vowed life.

- inadequate attention to, and poor discernment of, the communal dynamics that characterized a number of the male orders,
  including the Benedictines, Franciscans, Dominicans. It seems
  that in his own lifetime Ignatius of Loyola, founder of the Jesuits,
  favored a communal approach to discernment (see Futrell 1970),
  but it quickly gave way to a more individualistic, militaristic
  orientation and was adopted by several Congregations—male
  and female—from the sixteenth century onward.
- The Council of Trent (1545–63) created a solid clerical foundation for all forms of Christian life, including the Orders and
  Congregations. The heroic, obedient, individual priest became
  the paragon for all Christian vocations. Just as the priest was accountable directly to the bishop, so the individual Religious was
  accountable to God through the hierarchal chain of command
  (local superior, provincial, and so on). Community life became
  an organizational structure dictated by the rule (Constitutions)
  as interpreted by the leadership of the group. A communal sense
  of discernment was seriously undermined.

Although *Perfectae Caritatis* of Vatican II encouraged all Religious
to embrace the fraternal solidarity exhibited in the early church (no.
15), the prior recommendation that Religious should "live and think
with the Church" (no. 6) suggests hierarchical rather than communal
norms for renewal and adaptation. Although the document *Vita Consecrata* (1996) devotes a whole chapter to the communal dimension
of Religious Life (nos. 41–58), the central motivation seems to be the
need to think and feel in union with the institutional church itself:
"The fraternal life, understood as a life shared in love, is an eloquent
sign of ecclesial communion" (*Vita Consecrata*, no. 42). However
well intended such sentiments may be, echoes of patriarchal control
continue to surface.

We must never forget, of course, that all forms of Religious community must serve the call to mission, frequently asserted in *Vita
Consecrata* but always in an ecclesiastical context. Community life
should never be an end in itself or for our own comfort; rather, it is
a resource that empowers us for mission (not to be confused with
ministry). To that extent we can enrich and enhance the restructuring
of our communities by adopting insights and "good practice" from a
range of other organizations, religious and secular alike. For instance,

Patricia Wittberg (1996) outlines the rich potential of networking (which she calls social movement organizations) as a manner of extending the inner resourcefulness of dynamic community life into the more externalized outreach we have traditionally associated with ministry or apostolate.

Some New Developments

Many new Religious Congregations/communities came into being throughout the course of the twentieth century, and most if not all emphasized *community* as a core value. Allegiance to the institutional church was also a central feature, without which they would not have received public approbation. Despite such canonical strictures many such groups have served the church and the world with outstanding and often unstinting generosity. I briefly review some of the better known developments.

Missionaries of Charity

In Catholic circles many people regard the Missionaries of Charity, founded by Mother Teresa of Calcutta in 1950, as an outstanding example of contemporary Religious Life. Renowned for their frugal lifestyle and unstinting charity to abandoned children, especially in India, the sisters stand out for their heroic commitment to society's abandoned people. Mother Teresa herself became an iconic figure loved by both the poor and the rich and used as a model for unquestioned loyalty to the church and its teachings. Beatified by Pope John Paul II in 2003, and canonized in 2016, she serves as a traditional devotional inspiration for millions of Catholics. As a pioneer for a new model of Religious Life, both her vision and strategy were heavily church centered, thus lacking in prophetic vitality and empowering justice. Despite an unrelenting love and admiration of Mother Teresa herself, Mary Johnson (2011), a member of the community for twenty years, describes an internal regime characterized by authoritarianism, rigidity, and a great deal of human emotional trauma. Despite the strong reinforcement of the church, this modeling of female Religious Life falls well short of the alternative prophetic dynamism characterizing many of the great foundresses.

In the 1960s a complementary male group of brothers was founded (by an Australian Jesuit), and in the 1980s the Missionaries of Charity developed a branch for ordained members. Across the world several thousand lay collaborators assist the missionaries in their work, perhaps an indicator of the collaborative dynamic that is likely to feature strongly in the refounding of the late twenty-first century.

Little Brothers and Sisters of Jesus

Along similar lines, the Little Brothers and Sisters of Jesus draw their founding inspiration from Charles de Foucauld (1858–1916), the heroic priest-hermit who lived among the Tuareg, a nomadic tribe of Bedouin Muslims, in southern Algeria. Charles was murdered at his hermitage in December 1916. He was beatified by Pope Benedict XVI in 2005. When Charles de Foucauld died, there were forty-nine people, including him, on the list of members of the Union of Brothers and Sisters of the Sacred Heart of Jesus, which he had worked to set up during the last years of his life

Charles hoped to start a new Religious community, emulating closely the poverty and simplicity of Jesus's home in Nazareth. He wrote a basic rule for the Little Brothers of the Sacred Heart of Jesus, but the canonical congregation was not established during his lifetime. In 1933, several years after his death, a French priest, Rene Voillaume, accompanied by a few brothers, went to the desert to follow in his footsteps. This was the start of the Congregation of the Little Brothers of Jesus and, several years later, in 1956, the Little Brothers of the Gospel.

The Association now holds its general assembly every two years. That is an opportunity for the leaders of the different groups to meet and exchange ideas. An elected team ensures coordination between meetings. It draws together fraternities from some forty countries, with a spiritual vision combining simplicity of life, solitude, and a social commitment to the poor and marginalized. Although there is a clear (and canonically established) distinction between vowed and non-vowed members, a strong lay identity permeates the entire group, providing an inspiring and empowering model of the kind of collaboration likely to characterize the refounding of Religious Life in the twenty-first century.

The Taizé Community

Much more liminal and emblematic for the new models likely to erupt in the late twenty-first century is the international, ecumenical community of Taizé in France. Founded by Brother Roger Schutz in 1940 to address, among other things, the plight of displaced refugees from the Second World War, Brother Roger himself was not able to live there until the autumn of 1944, when France was liberated. On

Easter Sunday, 1949, seven brothers committed themselves to a life following Christ in simplicity, celibacy, and community. The slow and often tedious growth took another fifteen years (early 1960s) before young people discovered Taizé, gradually shaping it into the place of pilgrimage for which it is widely known today.

The community has grown to over one hundred brothers, Protestant and Catholic, about half of whom at any one time live in fraternities around the world. The fraternities witness to the power of peace and reconciliation among differing religions and in a range of circumstances where the resolution of conflict and division is acutely needed. The original appeal of Taizé for young people has now been espoused by peoples of all ages and cultures, attracted to the chantlike prayer, blending ancient monastic style with more modern expression.

As an inspiring model for Religious, Taizé transcends the ancient lure of the *fuga mundi* (flee the world), replacing it with a simple life affiliated with a vast range of spiritual seekers and prepared to establish a communal presence wherever witness to peace and reconciliation is needed. Taizé exerts a liminal attraction, difficult to define precisely but clearly exhibiting a zeal reminiscent of many of the great founding myths in the Christian history of the vowed life.

Monastic Community of Bose

Somewhat similar to Taizé is the ecumenical Monastic Community of Bose (Monastero di Bose), established at Bose (a province in Biella, Italy) by Catholic lay man Enzo Bianchi in 1965. The community has grown to number over eighty brothers and sisters of various Christian traditions, and it receives thousands of visitors annually.

Christian-Hindu Ashrams

Thanks to the popularity of the Benedictine monk Bede Griffiths (1906–93), interest in Christian ashrams, particularly in India, peaked in the closing decades of the twentieth century. However, the Christian Ashram movement already had flourished for some four hundred years, with the Italian Jesuit Roberto de Nobili (1577–1656) adopting the various forms of a Hindu sannyasi in his missionary work in India. In 1938, French priest Jules Monchanin and a French Benedictine monk, Henri le Saux (who later adopted the name Abhishiktananda), co-founded Saccidananda Ashram at Tamil Nadu, a site that was further popularized by Bede Griffiths.

Today, there are an estimated eighty Christian ashrams spread throughout India. Inspired by the Methodist missionary E. Stanley Jones (1884–1973), eighteen Christian ashrams flourish in the United States, and a further six in Canada. In the West ashrams are associated with retreat-time of a quiet, contemplative nature, but in India they are sought out for a range of different purposes, which the Czech researcher Zdenek Stipl has categorized as follows:

1) *Seva* or service ashrams, incorporating charitable service ranging from healthcare to education; 2) *Bhakti* or devotion ashrams, expressing faith typically through prayer meetings with the singing of chants or devotional songs; 3) *Dhyana* or meditation ashrams, promoting silence and contemplative practices; 4) *Gyana* or knowledge ashrams, largely devoted to religious and Hindu cultural research; 5) *Matha* or monastic ashrams, seeking to integrate the Western idea of a monastery into the Hindu religious context; 6) *Kala* or art ashrams, exploring spirituality through various artistic media; 7) *Vidyalaya* or educational ashrams, a kind of forest university where typically a small community organizes regular courses on Indian-Christian spirituality; 8) *Kutir* ashrams, which are hermitages, accommodating one or two disciples. (2013, 207)

Undoubtedly, many visitors may be dismissed as mere tourists, and it is difficult to establish today the spiritual impact of ashrams—in India particularly. Stipl offers this view on the current situation:

To judge the ultimate impact of the Christian Ashram movement is a rather difficult task. While at the beginning there was great enthusiasm linked with hope, at present it seems as if the Movement has reached a dead end or at least has been in the doldrums. This is evident from the desperation and doubts about the contribution and meaning of ashrams following from reflections of ashramites themselves, very often after they have spent some happy decades of their lives in their respective ashrams. The Movement has failed to form the identity of Indian Christians anew. (2013, 209)

Sounds like a crisis similar to that of Religious Life itself! Undoubtedly, the decline is partially due to the negative evaluation over many years by both Christian and Hindu fundamentalists. Nonetheless, this is a movement with enormous potential for refounding experiments in Religious Life, embracing the healing and reconciliation that is so desperately needed at a time when religious-based conflict causes such havoc in our world. While multi-faith dialogue has become embroiled in ecclesiastical politics, the mutual engagement facilitated by the ashram movement embodies aspirations for peace and justice that are likely to be central to the liminal witness of Religious in the latter half of the twenty-first century.

Local Foundations

Throughout the twentieth century a plethora of small female groups (and a few male ones) arose across the southern hemisphere, mainly in Africa. Many of these female Congregations were founded by either bishops or expatriate missionaries. They were called into being to serve local needs, often among the poor and marginalized; typically their service has been in education, medical/healthcare, and social ministry.

While many of these women did heroic work (often with very limited resources) and helped to uphold indigenous struggling communities, their preparation for service and the living conditions to which they have been subjected have been heavily criticized. Their formation—initial and ongoing—often has been of very poor quality. Under the guidance and protection of local bishops they have served as cheap labor, devoid of the dignity and human development every person deserves. Theologically and spiritually, they have been poorly treated.

It is impossible to discern what contribution such groups will make to the refounding of the later twenty-first century as outlined in this book. Many are likely to experience the decline already affecting Religious Life throughout the wider world. And because they are so poorly resourced, that diminution is likely to have a negative impact much more deleterious than experienced by more established groups in the West. It is unlikely that they will contribute actively to the new refounding wave of the vowed life.

The New Monasticism

As we enter the twenty-first century, one of the more exciting developments is that of the new monasticism.[2] The concept was initially developed by Jonathan Wilson (1998), who like many contemporary

---

[2] For overviews, see Bucko and McEntee 2015 and Flanagan 2014. For a more critical sociological analysis, see Ponzetti 2014.

proponents, quotes from a letter written in 1935 by Dietrich Bonhoeffer to his brother, Karl Friedrick:

> The restoration of the church will surely come only from a new type of monasticism which has nothing in common with the old, but a complete lack of compromise in a life lived in accordance with the Sermon on the Mount in the discipleship of Christ." (More in Hereford 2013, 40–49)

Wilson also built on ideas of the philosopher Alasdair MacIntyre. Noting the decline of local community so necessary to sustain the moral life, MacIntyre ended his book *After Virtue* by voicing a longing for "another St. Benedict." By this, he meant someone in the present age to lead another renewal of morality and civility through the process of empowering community. Sharing similar aspirations, Wilson outlined a vision for spiritual renewal within the Protestant Christian tradition.

Calling the vision a "new monasticism," Wilson proposed four characteristics that such a movement would entail: (1) it will be "marked by a recovery of the *telos* of this world" revealed in Jesus, and aimed at the healing of fragmentation, bringing the whole of life under the lordship of Christ; (2) it will be aimed at the "whole people of God," who live and work in all kinds of contexts, and not create a distinction between those with sacred and secular vocations; (3) it will be disciplined, not by a recovery of old monastic rules, but by the joyful discipline achieved by a small group of disciples practicing mutual exhortation, correction, and reconciliation; and (4) it will be "undergirded by deep theological reflection and commitment," by which the church may recover its life and witness in the world.[3]

Groups inspired by this new vision include Chiara Lubich's Focolare movement; Catherine de Hueck Doherty's Friendship House in New York and Madonna House in Canada; George McLeod's Iona Community in Scotland; the Community of the Transformation at Geelong, Victoria, Australia; The Ark Community of Northriding, South Africa; the Manquehue Community in Santiago, Chile; and

---

[3] The summer of 2004 became a defining moment for the movement, when a number of existing communities and academics gathered in Durham, North Carolina and drew together something like a "rule of life," referred to as the "12 marks" of the new monasticism. The gathering took place at a new monastic community called Rutba House, of which some founding members were Jonathan and Leah Wilson-Hartgrove, the latter being a daughter of Jonathan Wilson, referred to above.

the Christian-Hindu Shantivanum Ashram in India. David Janzen (2012) provides a comprehensive list of similarly inspired groups in the United States and Canada.

The new monastic communities constitute not only community life in a more formal sense—some residential, others intentional—but also more loosely federated associations, and even a number of individuals who adopt the values in daily life, and are usually linked to one or more groups identified within this new development. What all strive to follow and translate into daily living are the *twelve marks* that have come to be seen as the hallmarks of the new monasticism:

- Relocation to the "abandoned places of Empire," that is, solidarity with those living at the margins of society.
- Sharing economic resources with fellow community members and with the needy among us.
- Hospitality to the stranger.
- Lament for racial divisions within the church and our communities combined with the active pursuit of a just reconciliation.
- Humble submission to Christ's body, the church.
- Intentional formation in the way of Christ and the rule of the community along the lines of the old novitiate.
- Nurturing common life among members of an intentional community.
- Support for celibate singles alongside monogamous married couples and their children.
- Geographical proximity to community members who share a common rule of life.
- Care for the plot of God's earth given to us along with support of our local economies.
- Peacemaking in the midst of violence and conflict resolution within communities where violence or division prevails.
- Commitment to a disciplined contemplative life.[4]

While the new monasticism is certainly a paradigm in the making, it may need to attend further to what I call its parabolic integrity. It clearly arises from a yearning to transcend all the dualistic splitting of the past while aiming for a new integration of the sacred and secular. Yet, it seems to include a strong allegiance to official Christian churches, the very thing that could both inhibit and undermine the

---

[4] For a valuable commentary on the twelve marks of the new monasticism, see Hereford 2013, 132–52.

integration to which it aspires.[5] It seems to me that a refounding of Religious Life in the twenty-first century needs to transcend inherited aspects of ecclesiastical allegiance precisely to serve unambiguously the priority of God's new reign throughout the entire creation.

New Liminal Endeavors

Sandra Schneiders has made a bold prophetic claim, namely, that the credibility of the vowed life in the future will depend on its ability to hold together (integrate) *contemplation* and *justice-making*: "The active and effective commitment of our members to social justice is going to continue to shake up Religious Congregations as nothing else except contemplation itself can shake them up" (1986, 16). I suspect this aptly describes a key feature of the refounding facing Religious in the twenty-first century. For Schneiders, the contemplation in question is the *God quest* often alluded to in her key writings, a mystical allegiance to God as the sole preoccupation of all we embrace as Religious.

More helpful for the discernment of the present work is Thomas Merton's understanding of contemplation as the keen awareness of the interdependence of all things under God (Merton 1992). It is the ability to see deeply, and understand in greater depth, the complex unraveling of divine revelation across time and culture. It is precisely this deeper awareness that in and of itself leads to justice-making, that is, seeking out the right relationships—liberating and empowering—to make transparent on earth God's new reign, described throughout this book as the Companionship of Empowerment.

A range of contemporary movements embrace these aspirations, with the double dynamic of contemplation and justice providing the core inspiration. Some seem to be explicitly secular, including networks such as Greenpeace, Friends of the Earth, Habitat for Humanity, and Doctors without Borders. Others are more explicitly religious, two of which I will highlight for the purposes of the present study, namely, Jean Vanier's L'Arche Communities and the Community of Sant'Egidio, which is officially recognized by the Catholic Church as a church public lay association.

---

[5] Describing these new communities, Patricia Wittberg remarks: "Many of these new communities are strongly conservative in their theology of Religious Life, and appear to be replacing the traditional model" (1994, 270). In one case, at least, the Protestant Community of Jesus (in the United States) has been tarnished by allegations of cult-like behavior (Carrette 2005).

L'Arche

In 1964, Jean Vanier experienced a divine call to provide an alternative facility for people with developmental disabilities confined to or heavily reliant on institutional care. Beginning with an ordinary household in Trosly-Breuil, France, he named the project L'Arche, which is French for The Ark, as in Noah's Ark. The year 2014 marked the fiftieth anniversary of L'Arche, during which it was noted that the movement now consists of five thousand people, living in 147 communities, in thirty-five countries spread across all five continents.

In pursuit of its mission, L'Arche strives to create small, faith-based communities of friendship and mutuality among people of differing abilities; to develop lifelong support systems for the benefit of all, especially those who are highly vulnerable due to old age and/or multiple disabilities; and to highlight the unique capacity of persons with disabilities to enrich relationships and to build communities where the values of compassion, inclusion, and diversity are upheld and lived by each person.

On concluding her study on the history of monasticism, Canadian historian Elizabeth Rapley makes this perceptive observation:

> Where in past history can we find a greater dedication to Christian principles than in Jean Vanier and his communities of L'Arche where handicapped and non-handicapped care for each other and young volunteers are always welcome? The Catholic laity, that sturdy multitude of souls who for many years were content only to "pray, pay, and obey," have now become fully activate participants in the work of the Gospel. (2011, 323)

Several Religious Congregations participate in the work of L'Arche, not merely as a gesture of goodwill, or as a token of social solidarity, but because of an intuitive sense that L'Arche articulates—for the twenty-first century—many of the deeper aspirations embodied in the lives of Religious throughout time, a view also endorsed by Amy Hereford (2013, 60–75). Hospitality, with varied articulations, is one of the urgent needs of our time identified by Jean Vanier, and clearly he has Religious Congregations in mind when he writes: "In the past, Christians who wanted to follow Jesus opened hospitals and schools. Now that there are so many of these, Christians must commit themselves to the new communities of welcome" (Vanier 1989, 283).

In a world of so much personal and social dislocation—refugees, asylum seekers, immigrant workers, displaced persons of many types—

the hunger for genuine hospitality ranks as one of the most urgent needs of our time. Vanier challenges all our communal endeavors to prioritize our response to such vagrancy when he writes: "Communities that have trouble making room for strangers because they have grown so insulated, or so preoccupied with their own needs and struggles, are communities that are dying" (Vanier 1989, 267). With such challenging and prophetic words, Religious in the twenty-first century can be in little doubt that the revisioning of community life will be central to all our refounding endeavors.

The Community of Sant'Egidio

The Community of Sant'Egidio was founded in Rome in 1968 by a group of Roman high-school students led by Andrea Riccardi. It is named after the Roman Church of Sant'Egidio (Italian for St. Giles) in Trastevere, its first permanent meeting place. Since 1968, the community has gathered each night to pray and read from the Bible, reflecting on the gospel. It has now spread throughout the world, into more than seventy countries, and has fifty thousand members. The mission of the community is to help those in need.

Its apostolic outreach includes setting up refuges for homeless people, for the elderly, along with hospices for AIDS patients, particularly throughout the African subcontinent. Each year, in a different country, the community organizes the International Prayer for Peace, an annual gathering facilitating dialogue among a vast number of faiths and cultures. Beyond its courageous work for charity, the community is now better known for its commitment to peace and reconciliation in situations where social conflict and war prevail. It has had some remarkable achievements in countries such as Mozambique, Lebanon, El Salvador, Guatemala, Romania, Albania, Armenia, the Horn of Africa, and Algeria.

The community acted as a mediator in the talks for peace in Mozambique (1990–92) and more recently played a key role in resolving the Algerian crisis of 1994–95. If there is a hot spot in the world, Sant'Egidio is probably involved somehow—including in Nigeria, where in 2014 community members gathered to discern how best to deal with the threat of Boko Haram in that country. Members of the community are, at any given moment, involved in dozens of secret negotiations, explorations with warring parties, and formal mediation and reconciliation work.

The community of Sant'Egidio opposes the death penalty. It maintains "penpalships" with many convicts on death row, collects signatures for a moratorium on executions, and invites cities around the world to take part in Cities for Life Day.

Sant'Egidio is not a Religious Order in any sense. In fact, it is often described as a movement rather than an organization. Yet, its vision and outreach programs prove immensely attractive to Religious Orders and Congregations. The monastic archetype seems to be particularly alive in the Community of Sant'Egidio. It exemplifies a kind of prophetic breakthrough that has an impact upon poor and rich alike, resulting in a quality of cultural and spiritual transformation remarkably similar to the great founding eras of Religious Life. Without a shadow of doubt, Sant'Egidio is a movement with a vastly inspiring potential for the refounding challenges of the twenty-first century.

Community and Egalitarian Networking

Paul Hawken is an American social theorist with a discerning eye for emerging trends, particularly those that may well determine humanity's survival in the twenty-first century. He has spent over a decade researching organizations dedicated to restoring the environment and fostering social justice (Hawken 2007). These groups collectively compose the largest movement on earth, a movement that has no name, leader, or location, and that has gone largely ignored by politicians and the media. Like nature itself, it is organizing from the bottom up, in every city, town, and culture, and it is becoming an extraordinary and creative expression of people's needs on a worldwide scale. Fundamentally, it is a description of humanity's collective genius and the unstoppable movement to reimagine our relationship to the environment and to one another.

Describing this emerging phenomenon, Hawken writes:

> The movement can't be divided because it is so atomized—a collection of small pieces, loosely joined. It forms, dissipates, and then re-gathers quickly, without central leadership, command, or control. Rather than seeking dominance, this unnamed movement strives to disperse concentrations of power. It has been capable of bringing down governments, companies, and leaders through witnessing, informing, and massing. The quickening of the movement in recent years has come about through information technologies becoming increasingly accessible and affordable to people everywhere. Its clout resides in its ideas, not in force. . . . The movement has three basic roots: environmental activism, social justice initiatives, and indigenous

cultures' resistance to globalization, all of which have become intertwined. (2007, 12)

The great founders of Religious Life—male and female alike—had an impact on the culture of their time precisely because of their ability to discern the urgent needs and respond with originality and ingenuity. The research of Paul Hawken and his co-workers in networks such as Bioneers alerts us to a major shift in global strategies that, in all probability, will be crucial to the refounding envisaged in the present work. Several social and political theorists of our time aver that our conventional institutions are not designed to meet the magnitude and complexity of today's globalized world. The daunting realities facing us—economically, ecologically, politically, systemically—require new forms of organization and leadership anchored in collaboration, teamwork, diversity, and networking models. Beyond the ever increasing dysfunctionality of our bureaucratically burdened institutions, we need alternative ways to engage the world of the twenty-first century.

With their long history of communally inspired initiatives, Religious will once more be required to bring a liminal freshness into the tired and wearied pseudo-culture of our time. Our response will need to be relevant to the complex and rapidly evolving world we now experience; to that extent we must offer something that is relevant and transformative for this time. Past models and modes of behavior, no matter how sanctioned by time, will probably not be of much use. What will remain useful is that mystical daring faith that inspired earlier historical refounding efforts. What the great foundresses and founders attempted one time in the past, by the grace of God and the empowerment of the Spirit, we can do in the world of the twenty-first century.

To affirm us in that endeavor, I conclude this chapter with encouraging words from American Sister of St. Joseph Amy Hereford:

The day is finally dawning, and the new form is beginning to emerge in our spirits, imaginations, and conversations. The reinvention of religious life for today is a renewed commitment to the choice of radical Christian community that inspired, attracted, and sustained the religious of every age. . . . Jesus is the foundation, the gospel is the task, and community is the process. In small, local communities we can share life that is undifferentiated, immediate, and egalitarian. These communities can network to share services while affording each community the freedom and versatility to adapt to its local reality. Resisting the drive toward centralization, they can become circles of gospel living, peace, and justice. They can be mystics and prophets in a world desperately in need of them. (Hereford 2013, 194–95)

ॐ

Study Guide

1. How does the quotation from Wendell Berry at the opening of the chapter invite you to expand your own experience (not merely your notion) of community?

2. Various manifestations of religious community are illuminated in this chapter. Do they enlighten and deepen your comprehension and experience of this way of life?

3. Reread the quotation that concludes this chapter. How does it speak to your heart?

Chapter 11

The Vitality Curve and the New Paradigm

*The important thing for this age to remember is
that there is nothing wrong with death with dignity, provided that it is ringed with resignation,
rather than with denial. In fact, this acknowl-
edgement of services ended may be the last great
gift these groups can give.*

—Joan D. Chittister

*Christian community, and in a distinctive way
religious community, is ultimately for the world.
. . . In some respects, religious have been more
consistent and coherent in their turn to the
world than has the institutional church itself.*

—Sandra M. Schneiders

In 1979, Brother Lawrence Cada and some colleagues wrote an
important book seeking to supplement the historical insights of
Raymond Hostie with contemporary sociological understandings on
the rise and fall of institutions or social movements. Of particular
significance is their use of the Vitality Curve and its application to the
evolution of the Religious state in each of the historical cycles outlined
in Chapter 4 above (Cada et al. 1979).[1]

Today, Religious Orders and Congregations are transitioning
through experiences that the Vitality Curve will help us to identify.

---

[1] Throughout the 1980s and 1990s, business management also adopted a
structural notion of the vitality curve—Forced Distribution (Bell Curving Em-
ployee Performance Appraisals)—popularly described as ranking and yanking.
I am employing the concept in an organic rather than technical fashion with
an application extending over a longer timespan than employed in the business
models.

Most groups in contemporary Religious Life seem to adopt an attitude of "business as usual" that tends to translate into serving the church and spreading the gospel. The declining pattern, particularly in the West, is usually attributed to external forces such as secularization, postmodernism, or simply loss of nerve. The reluctance to look within, at our own collusion with the forces of corrosion, is easier to confront when we understand and accept the insights gleaned from the Vitality Curve.

Some groups rationalize the declining trend in the West by pointing to the new life arising in the church of the South, the surge in vocations coming from Vietnam, African countries, and parts of South and Central America. In most cases the formation process belongs to a highly clericalized culture preoccupied with individual salvation rather than service of God's new reign on earth (the new companionship). As indicated in previous chapters, this successful blip in the midst of a declining cycle is deceptively misleading; viewed historically, it reinforces rather than reverses the gradual diminishment of the group.

The Vitality Curve invites us to a place of truth and honesty. It enables us to make sense of what is transpiring, while illuminating the conversion that needs to take place if we are to become transparent and open to what the Spirit of the future has in store for us. It may be something close to "mission accomplished" in the sense that we have sown the seeds of a new endeavor that can now be carried forward by others (often by lay people). If that is the case, the challenge may be one of transcending our compulsive need for immortality (very common among clerical groups) and learn to die with dignity. And if it is God's will for us to be refounded, then the Vitality Curve illuminates many of the painful transitions we must be prepared to undergo while also adopting a defying sense of discerning creativity.

The Vitality Curve identifies five major phases characteristic of many movements, secular and religious alike: *foundation, expansion, stabilization, decline,* and *extinction/refounding.* The six historical cycles described in Chapter 4 above exhibit these stages, some with greater clarity in different historical epochs. At the present time in the West we clearly are undergoing a period of serious decline, with a drastic reduction in numbers, pastoral impact, and cultural presence. It appears to be different elsewhere, as in Africa and Asia. My understanding of the history of Religious Life suggests that the growth in the South will not endure and that, by the end of the twenty-first century, Catholic Religious Life universally will be in a serious state of decline and disintegration.

The Foundational Phase

The foundational developments in each historical cycle evolve along three consecutive trajectories: *myth*, *beliefs*, and *norms*. The mythic stage is typically described as the founding charism, normally associated with an outstanding founding person such as Benedict, Francis, Dominic, Ignatius of Loyola. Historians are far too hasty in categorizing founding myths into neat conceptual ideas that readily translate into concrete action. The mythic stage is fueled by a kind of wild creative energy, characteristic of the Spirit who blows where she wills. Energy and enthusiasm abound. Vision and hope are the driving forces.

The Myth

We associate the initial charism with an individual person who tends to be depicted in heroic, inflated terms. This is the patriarchal way of engaging with history. In truth, none of the great Orders or Congregations would have come into being without a support group for the founding visionary, colleagues who proved every bit as crucial as the founder. It seems to me that Ignatius would never have founded the Jesuits without the seven companions. And the eleven brothers who first accompanied Francis to Rome seem to have been crucial to the launching of the new group. A more careful analysis of history will reveal the significance of this close group of companions without whose help the founding dream would not have caught fire or have evolved into the cultural and spiritual force that marked its historical impact.

Strictly speaking, therefore, most if not all our Orders/Congregations were *founded by communities rather than by outstanding individuals*. The communal infrastructure of Religious Life is endemic not merely to the countercultural witness it provides (its liminality), but also to a more authentic reading of the vowed life as a prophetic movement for world and church alike. As indicated in previous chapters, historians tend to depict our historical origins in terms of heroic, ascetical individuals, like Antony and Pachomious, largely bypassing the earlier communal structures of the virgins, the village ascetics (apotactics), and the Covenanters/Qeiama groups of Syria. Already by the fifth century the Basilian communities and the Pachomian developments in the Upper Nile were characterized by an unambiguous communal structure, both in terms of internal organization and in their extensive participation in the life and well-being of local human communities.[2]

The myth describes that initial outburst of creative empowering energy, an awakening of the Spirit, that cannot be resisted, and the channeling of which requires vision and the grace of discernment (see Arbuckle 1988, 11ff., 66ff.). Such is the enthusiasm and fervor of this original launching—lasting usually just a few decades—that it requires the discerning and supportive context of a small group rather than an outstanding individual to see the dream come to birth to a degree that will enable it to survive into the next stage of an enduring vision (described by Cada et al. 1979 as the "belief" stage).

Belief

For the original vision to endure, the wild creative energy must be channeled into what today we might call a *mission statement*. Essentially, this is a consensual agreement around a set of key values that the group will be called to embrace. Rarely are the values explicitly named, yet there is sufficient internal coherence to generate a group commitment to a set of values that progressively becomes clearer and more precise.

What this consciousness around key values generates is not a group strategy but a deeper maturation and integration of the illusive energy that animates and sustains the original mythic vision. The vision has now been insinuated into the members' hearts, creating a bonding and unity even where external disagreements may prevail.

As an example, almost from the time of their initial foundation the Franciscans embodied a wide range of feeling and understanding around the issue of poverty—and within one hundred years had already splintered into diverse groups; nonetheless, the Franciscan ideal enjoyed rapid and accelerated growth for its first 150 years, proving to

---

[2] Most historians depict the foundational strand of the vowed life as a predominantly eremitical movement, highlighting the heroic achievements of the devotees. Rarely is equal attention given to the *lavrae*, a Greek term that was extensively employed throughout the fourth and fifth centuries to describe the networks in the Judean desert consisting of a cluster of cells or caves for hermits, with a church and sometimes a refectory at the center. According to Derwas J. Chitty (1966) the lavrae were often structured in groups of three, further evidence for an underlying communal orientation even where the monks lived in hermitages. Graham Gould (1993) documents at some length the communal foundations of the monastic life, indicating that the communal was always seen as more foundational than the eremitical, although popular history fails to acknowledge this fact.

be not merely a prophetic spiritual force but also a highly significant cultural influence throughout the High Middle Ages.

The Dominicans took the beliefs in a different direction. Initially committed to ridding the diocese of Toulouse of heresy; within a few years Dominic was dispersing his brothers to Paris, Madrid, and other parts of Europe. Consolidation is not a characteristic of this early vibrancy; vision and mission dictate both the strategy and pace of movement.

Like the myth, the belief stage must also morph into further growth and consolidation. Otherwise, the emerging vision will tend to become incestuous. The infant movement will implode, and in time fragment. In these early decades there is usually enough idealism, flexibility, and creativity to sustain a healthy momentum, moving the group along the gradient of greater complexity and an evolving sense of faith and mission.

Norms

In time the group arrives at a stage where formality and structure become important. Already the visionary values are indicating particularly ministries and forms of outreach felt to be congenial with how these values can be translated into action. This is a maturation in mission and not just the espousal of specific ministries. The apostolic trust is not merely action driven, but also visionary inspired.

Then comes a series of pragmatic developments, including structural outlets for ministry, along with the creation of legal and procedural processes. We have not yet arrived at the stage of Constitutions, but we are getting there. The Cistercians were in existence for eighty years before they developed their first Constitutions. Although the Jesuits were founded in 1540, their first written Constitutions did not appear till 1559.

Even when a group is expected to adopt a formal Constitutions before gaining church approval, as has been the case with most groups from the thirteenth century onward, the Constitutions carry little significance throughout the opening decades of the group's life. In fact, too close a focus on the Constitutions can undermine the primacy of the founding myth and sideline the significant role of the key values of the belief stage. Similarly, in the refounding, explored at greater length in Chapter 12, an undue preoccupation with legal rectitude is likely to undermine the potential for refounding. Excessive institutionalization has been a killer throughout much of the history of Religious Life.

The Utopian Flaw

All this leads readily to the aptly named aspect of the Vitality Curve known as the utopian flaw. The utopian dimension is the legitimate and admirable zeal and enthusiasm within which vowed members live out their commitment to God and to the world. *The utopian flaw is a subtle and largely undetected shift toward self-inflation at the cost of service to the other.*

Without any intended offense to my Dominican friends around the world, we consider how the utopian flaw might manifest in the Dominican tradition. The subconscious aspiration might sound something like this: We the Dominican Order take great pride and joy in our call to break open the word of God through preaching, teaching and catechesis of the word. We do this through the example of our evangelical lives and our ministries, as we embrace learning, education and a range of pastoral programs. We seek to bring to everything we do a quality of zeal, enthusiasm, and professionalism. *And we believe that we provide a quality of presence and mission exceeding any other Order or Congregation.*

It is that last sentence, rarely if ever articulated in an overt way, that characterizes the utopian flaw. It is an underlying arrogance and self-inflation that has crept up on the group, thus distorting the visionary founding mission into an ideology serving the self-perpetuation of the group rather than prioritizing the proclamation of the new reign of God. At a subconscious level group survival has taken over, and the seeds of corruption are being sown in the life cycle of the group.

This marks the beginning of the downward stretch of the cycle. To all who analyze the Vitality Curve, this is a truly baffling feature. A downward process has commenced that seems impossible to reverse. Something close to determinism seems to be at work whereby the group or movement has to face either extinction or radical refounding.[3]

Logically and rationally, we would expect the group to recognize the signs and symptoms of decline and betrayal of the founding inspiration and to take corrective action to get back on course. This is

---

[3] External factors, such as the Black Death in the mid fourteenth century, or the draconian laws introduced by the French Republic in the early years of the eighteenth century, can certainly trigger the crisis we associate with the utopian flaw. It seems to be the internal malaise, however, that creates the impasse, marking an irretrievable loss of the original founding grace and thus an inescapable decline into progressive disintegration.

precisely what Benedict of Aniane did in the early ninth century and the Cistercians did in the twelfth century—to reclaim the original purity and vitality of the Benedictine charism. Temporarily, both attempts seemed to activate some significant reform. In order to avoid the lure of secular immersion and devote themselves unambiguously to prayer and contemplation, the Cistercians only accepted wild, marshy land on which to build their monasteries. And they developed a new category of membership, the lay brother, to attend to the domestic and commercial affairs of the monastery. These brothers were men of mighty muscle and indomitable strength, whose Trojan work converted the wild terrain into more and more arable land, accumulating wealth and secular influence sometimes in excess of what former Benedictines had achieved. The purity of the Benedictine ideal had become more illusive than ever. It was not the reformed Benedictines, but the new mendicant groups—Franciscans, Dominicans, Carmelites, and others—who regained for the vowed life more authentic expressions of its prophetic vision.

Psychological, sociological, and systemic insights enable us to understand the resistances within a group or movement that prevent it from recognizing the impending decline and addressing it. Today, some of these insights are well understood. In an average group, however, resistances can be so varied, complex, and difficult to surface that it is unlikely that most groups can confront this shadow material and deal responsibly with it. It takes a great deal of discerning wisdom to assume that undertaking. It also requires rare gifts of leadership, whether mediated through reformist leaders or a reawakening in group membership of the task at hand. A greater awareness of history and the strange spiritual dynamics at work in the history of Religious would certainly help to reawaken the consciousness desirable for a more active quality of discernment, particularly as the group slides—largely unaware—into a state of progressive decline.

The Downward Curve

I briefly review here the various stages through which groups fall into decline and disintegration. While there is little consensus on why decline happens (in fact, little serious discernment)—and less agreement on whether or not we can reverse it at the various stages of decline—we have some insight and understanding on what goes wrong and why the erosion of meaning and faith takes place. The four stages or levels of doubt are *operational, ideological, ethical,* and *absolute.*

Operational Doubt

Tensions and disagreements arise based on external issues, typically customs that over time have assumed unquestionable significance. Examples include the arrangement of furniture in a community room; time structures for prayer, meals, and so forth; or manual duties within a household. Suggestions for change or alteration tend to be resisted or opposed, usually for reasons that are not apparent and rarely articulated. It is this lack of dialogue, the inability to offer reasonable and rational reasons, that begins to erode authenticity in how a group lives and functions. An indefinable sense of malaise is eating into the group. On the surface it does not seem destructive or worthy of serious attention. In fact, it is like a festering wound; if left unattended, it can in time become a corrosive cancer.

Much of the uneasiness around the habit—in the 1960s and 1970s—belongs to the stage of operational doubt. Although this is a sensitive issue with a long tradition, it is nonetheless an external feature that can evoke huge emotion and distract from several more substantial issues of mission and lifestyle. In the case of women Religious' habits, we went through adjustments about color of garment, length of hemline, amount of visible hair. One wonders what all this has to do with proclaiming the new reign of God on earth?

Ideological Doubt

Here we note a shift from external arrangements to internal values. Poverty tends to be the big loser here. Inadvertently, the group accumulates more wealth, comfort, and unnecessary appliances. A subconscious, unarticulated drive for security seems to be underlying the group value system. Trust in material resilience undermines reliance on God's providence. This in turn affects how much apostolic risk and creativity the group members will embrace.

Amid such "insecurity" the spiritual quality of the group also deteriorates. Group members will exhibit various levels of acknowledgment around this fact but are either unwilling or unable to address the malaise. As long as the group attends to its horarium—daily Eucharist, Divine Office, annual retreat—it is assumed that there is really nothing to worry about. But all the time, a spiritual crisis is deepening, and this can be the beginning of the unhealthy individualism, which has been noted in Religious Life by many commentators in the closing decades of the twentieth century.

Ethical Doubt

Those of us involved in facilitating assemblies and chapters in the 1980s began to notice how groups were raising new questions: "Is it right for us to be *(teaching in schools, running hospitals . . .)* primarily for the rich?" "Is it right for us to be adopting lifestyles identical to those of the middle and upper classes of society?" Some Religious were even asking: "Is it right for us to be so closely aligned with the institutional church?" When one hears that question being articulated—even by only a few members—the group is entering the stage of ethical doubt; in fact, it may already be well into it.

On more careful observation it is the visionary, disturbing members who initially raise such concerns. And because these are frequently regarded as the maverick members, their observations are dismissed, perhaps even ridiculed, by the majority, thus creating a rationalization whereby the serious nature of the decline is neither acknowledged nor addressed. Moreover, the cumulative resistance to genuine dialogue arising from the previous stages of operational and ideological doubt now makes it extremely difficult for the group to make an active choice to engage their deepening crisis. Instead, the group is likely to deflect attention toward the usefulness of the members, still doing good work for the church (and the world). Still "being useful" becomes the rationale that holds some semblance of meaning. At this stage the group is in deep crises.

Absolute Doubt

At this stage survival rather than reform has taken over as the basic energy driving and sustaining the group. Being "nice" to one another and not disturbing the precarious peace leads to several subconscious collusions. The creative energy can be so low that some groups will not even consider amalgamating with others (provinces or groups); instead, they will choose to "go it alone"—till the end. On the surface, group members and even entire communities can look happy and contented—as long as nobody talks about the call of the gospel in the world of the twenty-first century.

It is difficult to describe accurately what is transpiring at this stage, because nobody is likely to record the process of dying out. That feels too morbid an undertaking in a culture that dreads decline and death, and in a church overly preoccupied with human immortality. To one degree or another everybody is in denial, while desperately trying to put on a brave face. The group is facing extinction, but very few are willing to explore what that actually entails.

Extinction

Approximately 75 percent of all Religious Orders or Congregations ever founded have become extinct. It is a universal law of all creation that new life arises from death according to the cyclic process of birth-death-new life. All major religions tend to problematize death as some kind of an evil we need to get rid of, as a plight to be avoided, a limitation to be overcome. As a human species we need to come to terms with the universality of death as a God-given feature of all organic life, human death included.

Without death, we cannot come to the radical newness at the heart of the Christian notion of resurrection. Even Jesus had to endure death to experience the great breakthrough. We stand little hope of coming to terms with the meaning of death at organizational and institutional levels until we first face our distorted, dishonest understanding of human death and dying. As a species we suffer from an arrogant, inflated sense of immortality, which is the basis of several of our contemporary crises—environmental, political, economic, and religious.

Religious Orders and Congregations finding our way through the twenty-first century need to acknowledge the "writing on the wall" for many of our groups. The historical process outlined in previous chapters alerts us to the need for a more informed discernment, as the declining numbers and aging profile—especially in the West—indicate that the missionary model is entering its terminal stages. In all probability this is God's will and desire for Religious of our time.

It is possible to die with dignity and even with a sense of resurrection hope. The five stages of death and dying—denial, anger, bargaining, depression, and acceptance—initially documented by the renowned psychologist Elisabeth Kübler-Ross (1969), deserve close and prayerful attention. Several social commentators have noted that these five stages are also detectable in the decline of organizations and institutions and that they require the same quality of understanding and discernment as the dying process of an individual person.

A responsible acknowledgment of these dynamics enables us to look back with gratitude for what has been, equanimity for what has not been achieved, and may even empower the group to turn its attention to a anticipatory handing on of the sacred wisdom that has sustained and animated the group. Metaphorically, this is often described as "passing on the torch." The charism that has inspired and guided the group may still have an enduring inspiration that can be picked up by others—that is, perhaps, by lay people—and adopted to reinvigorate or launch anew a ministerial expression. This may or may not be in the apostolic tradition of a particular group. Any viable charism can translate into a range of apostolic options, depending on the critical needs of a particular situation or cultural epoch. However, a group that has not attempted a meaningful discernment around its death and dying is unlikely to embark upon this anticipatory process of passing on the torch.

Revitalization

The oldest Order in the Christian Church, the Benedictines, has been revitalized on a number of occasions. In the process it morphed into different groups, as has also happened with the Franciscan family. Other groups that have been revitalized on more than one occasion include the Dominicans, Jesuits, Ursuline Sisters, and the Alexian Brothers.

Cada highlights three elements that are central to the revitalization process:

1. a transforming response to the signs of the times
2. a reappropriation of the founding charism
3. a profound renewal in the life of prayer, faith, and centered-ness in Christ. (Cada et al. 1979, 60)

Worthy of note is the order in which these guidelines are outlined. If the group is concerned mainly with its own survival and seeks to hold on to the glory of its past achievements, then it is unlikely to undergo revitalization. By the same token, if it seeks to reclaim the original charism with a sense of pristine purity, it may not enjoy a fresh rebirth. Here we need to recall that the primary purpose of all Christian life is to serve Christian mission (not to be reduced to ministry). This requires us to look out to God's world and not stare persistently at our own treasury, no matter how sacred it may seem.

The revitalization process begins with *discernment of the signs of the times*, including a survey of urgent needs, particularly the plight of the poor and marginalized. This should be viewed not merely as a philanthropic gesture, but rather as a core element in the witness value of the vowed life itself: "So crucial is this issue of justice for the poor that the revitalization of Religious Life cannot be considered today, if there is no concern for the exploited and the 'little people' of this world. . . . There can be no radicalness without concern for the poor" (Arbuckle 1988, 67).

This is a complex undertaking, requiring a degree of resilience and consensus that declining/dying groups tend not to possess. Therefore, the creative energy of revitalization will always be embodied in *new groups* rather than in those that have been sanctioned by time and tradition. It is primarily the new groups that bring vitality, originality, and creativity to responding to the signs of the times at the beginning of each new historical cycle.

There then follows a critically important observation: *The revitalization of former groups depends largely on how deeply they can embrace the contemporary vision being articulated by new groups and can follow the creative dynamic espoused by these new groups rather than the well-trodden path of the past.* The monastic and mendicant groups that survived through the apostolic cycle were precisely those that could incorporate the novel apostolic energy into their modus operandi. Those that survived through the missionary era (1800–), were those groups that identified with the missionary spirit and integrated it into their revitalized vision.[4]

Two parallel movements are at work: *revitalization* and *refounding*. In my opinion there can be no refounding without significant revitalization. And the revitalization, as defined here, belongs largely if not exclusively to new groups and charismatic movements. The refounding is made possible when older groups adopt the new vision and use it as a barometer for their response to the urgent needs of the moment. Unfortunately, we once again have little historical precedent to fall back on, but I suspect that the discernment process involved in refounding is subconscious rather than one that easily translates into rational discourse. Embracing new vision by older groups is done in subtle, perhaps subversive ways that only make sense as a creative initiative of the wild Spirit—the proverbial wind and fire of the primordial Pentecost.

Consequently, I would rearrange the order of the three guidelines suggested by Cada. Reading the signs of the times certainly has priority. But I suggest that that guideline should be followed by *a profound renewal in the life of prayer, faith, and centeredness in*

---

[4] Historians have not dealt well with this transitional renewal. As already noted, most of our information is inherited through male clerical historians with a tendency to exalt the past, inflate outstanding male heroes, and prioritize traditional approaches to life and ministry.

Christ, relocating to third place *the reappropriating of the original charism*. The discerning response to the signs of the times cannot be done without a deep contemplative resourcefulness. Nor is it possible without an informed interiorization of discipleship in the Companionship of Empowerment (explained in Chapter 3). When these foundational requirements are invoked and well integrated into the life of a specific group, then the group stands a much better chance of making the contemporary creative response. After this comes the timely moment to reclaim the energy of the original charism.

A critical question then arises: *How do we understand the original charism?* Once more, modern Religious are bedeviled by a historical literalism that can be a major hindrance to empowering discernment. Frequently, we reduce charism to particular apostolates, and since Vatican II we have often confused charism with the inflated importance of the founder's birthplace and other historical artifacts or locations associated with the founder's life story. We easily forget, or to our peril we ignore, the fiery launching vision described above as the original myth.

Let's consider two examples. First, from my home country of Ireland is the story of Blessed Edmund Ignatius Rice, who in 1802 founded the Irish Christian Brothers, which quickly established a school system for educating boys. Boys' schools became synonymous with the Christian Brothers in Ireland and elsewhere. Many brothers themselves regarded the education of boys as their charism, forgetting that the founder focused on young boys roaming aimlessly in very poor parts of Ireland and that the meeting the educational needs of girls was already in place thanks to the pioneering work of Nano Nagle and others. A more discerning eye will observe that the foundational charism of the Christian Brothers is a preferential option for the poorest of the poor, with education being a primary means for gospel liberation and empowerment. We must not confuse the founding vision with the means used to translate it into action.

Consequently, for the Christian Brothers now living in the twenty-first century, the primary discerning question needs to be this: *What are the areas of acute need today awaiting gospel liberation and empowerment?* Most countries where the Christian Brothers have ministered have thriving educational systems, thanks in many ways to the brothers' pioneering zeal. In all probability, education of children and teenagers is no longer the domain for urgent prophetic witness—although adult education might be! Revitalization of the charism of Edmund Ignatius Rice might lead the Christian Brothers today toward a very different apostolic response to that which has preoccupied them for the past two hundred years.

My second example, inspired by groups like the Sisters of Mercy (founded by Catherine McCauley), is that of the several female Congregations that assumed healthcare in homes and hospitals as their charism-based response to urgent needs throughout the nineteenth and twentieth centuries. This often ensued in creating clinics and opening hospitals where there was a dire lack of such facilities. Thanks again to the pioneering work of such women, we now have in all Western countries, and in some poorer countries, a large cohort of lay specialists highly skilled in the healthcare of humanity.

And yet, in many Western nations healthcare is still a hugely problematic issue, as shown in the hurdles Barack Obama had to negotiate in his first term as president of the United States (2009–13). The obstacles he encountered were not about the lack of skilled healthcare workers, but about the bureaucracy that now characterizes health services. This, I suggest, is one area of acute need today requiring prophetic contestation. In several cases transnational pharmaceutical corporations control a great deal of medical and healthcare resources, promoting values of power and financial prowess quite alien to the values of the new reign of God.

In this context a revitalization of charism carries challenges that are totally new and quite daunting for those Congregations that still consider healthcare to be central to their historical identity. In such groups, continuing to train members to become nurses, doctors, or social workers is not likely to be an adequate response for revitalization or refounding in the twenty-first century. Instead, they may need to focus on acquiring the skills and training for justice ministry, so that they can confront the oppression and injustice arising from corporate aggression and manipulation. In such cases those ministering on behalf of the gospel may need systemic, political, legal, and economic skills rather than those traditionally associated with the care and administration of health services.

A closer analysis of the history of Religious Life reveals that each new cycle brings levels of engagement with life that tend to be more expansive and more complex than those of the previous cycle. Such is the nature of evolutionary growth and development. The wisdom and skills appropriate for an earlier time may still have relevance and in some cultural contexts will still be acutely needed—basic education and healthcare, for example—but the technological, commercial, systemic, and political developments of our time dictate the prevailing values and, as indicated earlier, it is the liminal witness to *values* that evokes the prophetic cutting edge for which Religious are uniquely endowed. It is the values we represent, foster, and promote, more than anything else, that determine our cultural credibility and our potential for spiritual transformation.

Formation for the Paradigm Shift

How do we prepare our members for the challenges and undertakings that refounding is likely to involve? Many will balk at the very prospect of such a radical paradigm shift. Not only does it seem a step too far, but for many it verges on betrayal of what we perceive to be foundational to the meaning of Religious Life itself. The critical issue here is likely to be what we have conventionally called *ongoing formation*.

Formation in contemporary Religious Life tends to be identified with the initial process of acquaintance with a particular Order or Congregation, admission to novitiate, and accompaniment over a number of years till the candidate takes final vows. Across the contemporary world a vast range of approaches and practices are adapted. In the southern hemisphere candidates are often admitted at a young age—early twenties or occasionally in their teens—and programs of initial formation still adopt the dualistic split between sacred and secular; this quality of spiritual formation leaves people ill prepared for the complex challenges of the twenty-first century.

Throughout the Catholic world initial formation is still strongly focused on the church and its needs, often preoccupied with how to hold on to the young people or bring them back to the sacramental life of the church. Formation on the new reign of God, and the value radiation of our liminality, is quite sporadic and in many cases only marginally accommodated. We strive to broaden the spiritual foundations, and we seek to integrate accompanying psychological skills with new pastoral exposures, but theologically it is the approach of yesteryear rather than that of the twenty-first century that prevails.

I suggest that when it comes to formation, our greatest area of weakness is in the *ongoing* process rather than the *initial* experience. For several years now we have noted a tension between the wisdom being dispensed in initial formation stages and the vision operative throughout the rest of a particular group's ongoing formation. Deficiencies have been noted in two areas: (1) A sense of novel vision with accompanying spiritual and theological insight imparted to newcomers is not made available to the rest of the membership—either because the larger membership resists such updating or simply is not interested; and (2) Where initial formation follows a more traditional, devotional, and ascetical approach, the larger membership may be embodying a spiritual and theological flexibility at variance with what is being fostered at earlier formative stages. The dilemma in both situations is that initial formation and ongoing formation are viewed as distinct features, when in fact they need to be regarded as interdependently necessary for the evolving growth and development of the group.

Formation programs inevitably become entangled with how a group handles membership in contemporary Orders and Congregations, along with our openness (or lack of it) to future alternative expressions. For several years now the possibility of temporary forms of membership has been raised, and in many cases has been silenced by church authority. Various attempts at reclaiming the primary *lay* identity of Religious Life have rarely won the approval of an entire group, and some attempts at canonical approval have been robustly resisted. Groups that have decided not to seek new members—often after profound discernment—tend to be negatively judged by other Religious families and by church authority. After serious discernment some groups have acknowledged the need for new forms of membership with strong lay identity; very few groups have initiated creative endeavors to make this breakthrough possible.

The confusion, ambivalence, and ambiguity around both membership and recruitment characterize the ethical/absolute stages of the declining Vitality Curve. Faced with our terminal demise, we fail to muster the energy for creative experiment, and in many cases we simply don't have the historical, spiritual, or theological vision to animate our endeavors. Better stay with what feels safe, with what we have always done, with what we need to do to retain some semblance of survival, even when we know it may not be what God is actually asking of us at this transitional threshold. Courage, risk, and a great deal of prophetic imagination may be our most urgently needed virtues for this dark night and the resurrection dawn we still await.

Refounding is not easy: it was never meant to be. And yet it is a possibility for all of us, no matter how stuck we may feel. But it does require a risky, daring sense of openness and a willingness to embrace daunting new horizons of creativity and experiment. The challenges involved are discussed in the concluding chapter of this book.

∾

Study Guide

1. "And if it is God's will for us to be refounded, then the Vitality Curve illuminates many of the painful transitions we must be prepared to undergo while also adopting a defying sense of discerning creativity." How does this statement from the chapter resonate within you? After responding to this question, consider the five phases outlined: foundation, expansion, stabilization, decline, and extinction/refounding.

2. "Without death, we cannot come to the radical newness at the heart of the Christian notion of resurrection." In the context of this chapter, what does this statement stir within you?

Chapter 12

Refounding Is Possible

*True vision always is a gift. When it graces
us, therefore, we do not experience "sight" as
much as the experience of "being sighted," being
drawn, being enticed into depth. Our answers
then will emerge out of that depth.*

—BARBARA FIAND

*Such rethinking is indeed the work of prophetic
imagination that has a calling to walk our society into the crisis where it does not want to go,
and to walk our society out of that crisis into
newness that it does not believe is possible.*

—WALTER BRUEGGEMANN

Central to the reflections in this book is the double dynamic of
parable-type story and paradigm shift. The foundational meaning
of Religious Life cannot be captured merely in historical fact, achievement, or legal status. Nor does it fit the contours of rational discourse.
It consists of a transcultural, trans-religious, Spirit-inspired narrative
with a vast variety of expression and cultural grounding. Like the
gospel parables it does not fit easily into the conventional wisdom of
humankind, including our major religious systems.

Historically, it evolves through cyclic troughs of growth and decline, but not in a predictable sequence subject to human observation
and rational analysis. While the overall cycles seem to embody a
degree of predictability (approximately every three hundred years),
the shift from one cycle to the other is highly unpredictable, exhibiting a kind of quantum leap described in the social sciences as a
paradigm shift.

The breaking down process has been resisted and even denied by Religious down through the ages. The decline that characterizes the late twentieth and early twenty-first centuries in Christian Religious Life has been the subject of several studies, most of which blame the secularizing influences of our time. This overt reason tends to miss the deeper meaning expressed by Patricia Wittberg when she writes:

> The first difficulty is the current lack of a compelling theology which is supportive of religious institutions and, consequently, of a virtuoso spirituality based on institutional service. The 19th century post-millennial theology that had once celebrated Christian institutions as essential building blocks for the coming reign of God . . . is no longer persuasive. In fact, a key component of the late twentieth and early twenty-first century Western society is a profound distrust of all types of institutions. (2006, 260)

As we saw in the previous chapter, the twenty-first century keenly pursues new forms of communal endeavor. Networks replace major institutions; circular formations exert a deeper cultural appeal than pyramid-like structures. The organic takes precedence over the mechanical. So, too, in the history of Religious Life: a radical newness characterizes the breakthrough at each cyclic junction. From a human point of view it has paradox written all over it (the death and rebirthing enigma) and frequently will not make human/rational sense. This is the creative force of the Spirit, who blows where she wills and unceasingly creates new life throughout all creation.

The Process of Refounding

The notion of refounding surfaced in the 1980s, ardently promoted by Marist priest-anthropologist Gerald A. Arbuckle (1988; 1996). He describes the process in these words:

> The road to refounding is a humanly complex and spiritually painful one. . . . No amount of merely human effort or experimentation on our part will bring about the refounding of any Religious congregation. (1988, 6–7)
>
> Refounding is a risk-filled journey of faith and hope, whereby we enter into the heart of the paschal mystery itself, to unite ourselves with Christ and his mission, thus being energized to

be ongoingly creative in bringing the kingdom message to the world of our times. As it is a journey demanding personal and group conversion, it is a slow and hesitant process, the outcome of which is ultimately in the hands of God. (1996, 95)

Arbuckle identifies six main stages in the refounding process, which I summarize this way:

1.   Members of an Order or a Congregation are experiencing the confusion or malaise of chaos, that is, risking to enter into the death experience.
2.   There is some degree of readiness in a group to embrace the pain of loss and death and enter into a process of mourning that will prevent the grief from fossilizing.[1]
3.   The group (or at least an unspecified proportion) acknowledges that new life will not emanate from the old but from within a totally new paradigm. In Arbuckle's words: "The new is elsewhere" (Arbuckle 1988, 110).
4.   Acknowledging their own powerlessness to do anything about the chaos, Religious (especially their leaders) strive to be as open as possible to the new call from God in the context of urgent contemporary needs.
5.   Leaders release "prophetic" members (highly creative and visionary) to pursue the new possibilities.
6.   Some will be motivated enough to follow the new vision, and those who cannot will die with the old reality. In time, the new vision becomes the refounded Order or Congregation; this means effectively that it is founded again at a new starting point.

Initially, the notion of refounding inspired great enthusiasm, and workshops on the subject attracted large numbers, particularly in Australia, Europe, and the United States. It sounded like an idea that was right for its time, a lifeline that many Religious wanted to grasp. But

---

[1] In Arbuckle's words: "Religious Congregations can experience cultural trauma; failure to mourn the grief of this trauma results in dramatic loss of energy and innovation, leading eventually to extinction. . . . if people or cultures fail to process their grief—for example, in the closure of a valued school, parish, or hospital—through the tripartite stages of mourning rituals, the suppressed tensions will in the end prove more profoundly disruptive than the social conflicts which relieve them. If, however, appropriate rituals do occur, then within people's o'er-fraught hearts there is hope that many will begin to experience the joy of inner peace and embrace the future in hope" (Arbuckle 2013, 160, 200).

in a short while the idea lost its impetus, along with much of its initial energy and widespread appeal. Some reasons are clear; others, less so.

1. The initial vision was hyped with euphoria and false expectation. Some thought the refounding process could commence almost immediately and produce a new breakthrough in a matter of a few years.

2. Although Arbuckle contextualized the refounding process within the breakdown of an old system (the chaos), many did not grasp the crucial paschal dimension. Traditional groups hoped that new life could be activated while still resourcing their former commitments. *People were hoping for a resurrection without having to undergo a Calvary.*

3. More recently, Arbuckle highlights the grieving and mourning that a group must undergo before refounding can even be considered: "Integral to refounding is the gift of mourning" (Arbuckle 2015, 136). First, there is the informed need to enter into the grieving (and the accompanying letting go); and second, the more daunting challenge of ritualizing the painful letting go through a process of mourning, thus liberating the inner wisdom to let go of the old and embrace the new.[2]

4. Although many seemed to warm to the notion of the new being elsewhere, few seemed to grasp the transitional struggle of having to leave the old behind in order to move toward the new unencumbered by archaic baggage.

5. Although Arbuckle can evoke many historical precedents for his proposition for key refounding individuals, he underplays the critical role that discerning community plays in that process.

6. The theory of refounding often lacked appropriate historical contextualization. The fact that Religious Life in general is on a downward slope leads to an overwhelming conviction that refounding in any serious sense is unlikely for at least another sixty to seventy years.

7. An unquestioned assumption seemed to prevail that we, Religious, would refound ourselves. At every stage in the history of Religious Life founding and refounding have been the fruit of a divine,

---

[2] Walter Brueggemann offers several valuable insights on this grieving process and its urgent necessity for our entire contemporary culture imprisoned in several forms of denial: "Thus I propose that the prophetic community, right in the middle of a culture of denial, is a proper venue for grief work. Such a meeting will not, at the outset, be 'the happiest place in town'. It will only be the most honest place in town, where honesty is not an extreme concern in a culture of denial" (2014, 83; see 28–98).

graced prerogative and not the outcome of human initiative. Admittedly, it always takes place through people—not necessarily those ready and waiting, but often those, like the Old Testament prophets, unprepared and unwilling but nonetheless open to being surprised by our co-creative God.

Refounding is a notion for the twenty-first century that by accident or good fortune erupted in the twentieth century. While many Religious have explored the dynamics of the refounding process, relatively few seem to have converted to its underlying spirituality, which is what validates and authenticates its theory. *Refounding is firmly rooted in the paschal experience of death and resurrection*, vividly envisioned by Walter Brueggemann: "We may and do quibble about many matters in the church. But however we may parse those quibbles, we share this confession of newness, given in ways we know not how, at the bottomless pit of death. And we begin again!" (2014, 164).

There can be no new life without a dying, a letting go of all that we have loved and cherished. And there is no meaningful rationale—human or divine—to explain the chaos and confusion of Calvary. Even Jesus could not make rational sense of Calvary; in mystical abandonment and reckless trust, he chose to go through it. So must we, Religious, if we hope to encounter resurrection breakthrough.

How to Discern Our Way to the Future

How can we ready ourselves for refounding? Is it even possible for us to be favorably predisposed? The answer must be yes, since we have seen groups who have been refounded, some more than once. A radical sense of openness to the God who forever makes all things new is undoubtedly essential. Presumably, a readiness to experiment and explore new ways of being present to our God, to creation, and to one another in the context of the twenty-first century also is required. This translates into what feels like a reckless sense of trust in the unexpected breakthroughs of the creative Spirit.

In broader strokes the following six dispositions need to be integrated into our spirituality and sense of mission. I suggest it is not a case of converting substantial numbers within our ranks, but rather of aiming for that critical threshold that provides the leverage for the Holy Spirit to provide the refounding breakthrough. It certainly is not about a lot of feverish activity (sometimes visible at the dying stages), but rather about that contemplative waiting that sensitizes us to what the pregnant Spirit wants to bring to birth.

- *Fidelity to the new reign of God as a Companionship of Empowerment.* This concept is outlined in the opening chapters of this book, and I hope I have consistently and faithfully upheld the vision throughout each subsequent chapter. This has to be the starting point for all Christian discernment—seek *first* the kingdom and its justice! Despite the complexity of the concept in the Gospels and the diverse interpretations of scholars, and in spite of the superficial treatment often rendered by the institutional church, the call to serve God's new reign on earth remains the *primary foundation* upon which all discipleship grows and flourishes. The church's long ambivalence around the primacy of the kingdom must no longer hinder us from embarking upon daring new articulations focused on recreating the world in accordance with God's enduring love, transformative liberation, and empowering justice. In terms of our credibility and visibility, this, I suggest, is the single most formidable challenge facing Religious in the twenty-first century.

- *Embracing God's creation as our primary eschatological space.* All major religions exhibit an ambivalence toward God's creation and toward our own recreation as sacred earthlings. This anti-world stance is no longer tenable, spiritually or theologically. We need to transcend all the inherited dualisms that have bedeviled the evolution of our species for far too long. The promised eschatological breakthrough is modeled for us Christians in the Companionship of Empowerment (the kingdom). This new earth-centered spirituality resonates throughout Pope Francis's encyclical, *Laudato Si'*. He writes: "As Christians, we are also called to accept the world as a sacrament of communion, as a way of sharing with God and our neighbours on a global scale. It is our humble conviction that the divine and the human meet in the slightest detail in the seamless garment of God's creation, in the last speck of dust of our planet" (no. 14).

- *Dying to Rise Again.* Another central resource from our Christian scriptures is the vision popularly described as the paschal journey. Everything in God's creation undergoes the cycle of birth-death-rebirth. New life is not possible without the decline and death of what has gone before. Even the historical Jesus had to submit to this universal cosmic and personal process; he left us no rational explanation as to why creation operates in this way. Even scripture exhibits a resistance to, and ambivalence around, the process of death. According to St. Paul (Rom 5:12; 6:23), death is the consequence of sin and therefore an evil to get rid of. Perhaps St. Paul meant the meaninglessness of death rather than death itself, which is a God-given aspect of all life; without death, nothing would exist, nor could anything ever hope to be reborn and refounded.

- *Internalize a cyclic sense of history.* As indicated in earlier chapters, the history of Religious Life illustrates vividly the life cycle of the paschal journey. While we cannot provide a comprehensive explanation for the breakdown and breakthrough manifested in each cycle, we can discern a recurring pattern congruent with how life flourishes and is transformed right across the natural world. Clearly in our time, the twenty-first century, we, Religious, are on a downward slope, requiring a trustful letting go along with a willingness to grieve and enter the dark night of soul and spirit. From within that same fertile darkness we can expect to see the seedlings of resurrection, vague but enduring signals of the new life that the creative Spirit is already impregnating. This latter sense of rebirthing anticipation seems a rare gift, probably only available to the creative few who are prepared to risk everything.

- *The great foundresses are the historical models providing our primary wisdom and inspiration.* Infused with the radical vision of God's new reign on earth (the new companionship), boldly, creatively, and unambiguously the great foundresses read the signs of their times, identifying those marginalized and oppressed. And they responded courageously and unflinchingly. In an inspiring and challenging quotation, Sr. Joan Chittister expresses what was unique and distinctive in these outstanding women: "Hagiography, folklore, and the archives of religious congregations are full of stories of strong-minded women who challenged bishops and bested them, confronted popes and chastised them, contested the norms of society and corrected them. Feminism, the consciousness of the graced and gracing nature of women, despite the subordinating role definitions to which they were subject, is one of the gifts of religious life across time" (1995, 12).

- *Reading the signs of the times for the twenty-first century.* Ever since Vatican II, Religious have been striving to make sense of our world and have been striving to respond with fresh vigor and insight. In most cases our starting point has been the church rather than the world, culminating in religious perspectives that have been dualistic, narrowly moralistic, anthropocentric (only humans matter), imperialistic (prioritizing Western ways of being), and largely devoid of ecological and planetary discernment. Our reading has been too narrow; it has been at variance with the expanding and evolving worldview of the twenty-first century. That is not how the great foundresses did it. And it is not the reading of the signs of the times that will deliver the daring refounding that will characterize our next major cycle of the vowed life. In an earth community hungering for justice, nonviolent living, freedom for mutual flourishing, and healing, organic growth and enhancement for evolutionary breakthrough need to become the guidelines for twenty-first-century discernment. Along with *Laudato Si'*, the evolutionary and ecological vision of the Franciscan theologian Sister Ilia Delio is an inspiring source for this task (Delio 2013; 2014).

American psychotherapist Ted Dunn provides consultancy services for contemporary Religious Congregations, adopting Arbuckle's vision for refounding, which he summarizes in the following key points:

- *Transformation of consciousness:* see through new lenses
- *Transformative visioning:* create a prophetic vision and transforming life in community by the processes used in visioning
- *Reappropriation of your charism:* a reauthentication of your inner voice, the spirit gift and voice of community
- *Reconciliation and conversion:* the crucible of refounding, working through the brokenness in order to bring forth healing and redemption
- *Becoming a learning community:* being able to grow, learn, and experiment as a community in order to adapt to an evolving world (Dunn 2009).

Skilled for Mission

Throughout history, Religious exercised their liminal witness through various forms of presence. In all cases features such as prayer, community life, and service can be detected. While these are enduring features, they have been extensively adapted to suit different times and cultures. The service rendered to humanity, typically through the church, required certain skills, often related to the cultural and religious demands of the time. In general, one can detect two broad sets of skills that enabled Religious to bear liminal, prophetic witness. These are often expressed—in undesirable dualistic terms—as monastic skills (silence, contemplation, chant, study, seclusion) and apostolic skills (teaching, nursing, social work, parish ministry). Truthfully, both sets frequently overlap

The monastic strand can be viewed from the early Egyptian inculturation to the Cistercians in the High Middle Ages. The mystical tenor is strong, expressed through a life of interiority mediated by enclosure and monastic stability. Thus, the notion of the monastery became synonymous with the *fuga mundi*, the rejection of a problematic earthly existence, and the spirituality of escape from this vale of tears to the ultimate happiness of the heaven hereafter.

This is a kind of caricature that requires a more nuanced reading of the evidence. It was the Benedictine monks, from the seventh to the tenth centuries, who pioneered the cultural, economic, educational, and agricultural development of early Europe. The monastic and apostolic were integrally related. The distinction between the two expressions belongs more to the 1400s and 1500s, when women Religious began to transcend the restriction of enclosure, thus becoming apostolic rather than monastic. Meanwhile, the Benedictines, and later the Mendicants, witnessed to the more integrated expression of the two approaches.

Despite the imposition of enclosure, informally up till 1298, and canonically thereafter, Religious, male and female, retained a strong sense of mission to God's world—mainly through the church. For male Religious this took on a more explicit significance in the thirteenth century as the Mendicant groups—Franciscans, Dominicans, Servites, and others—moved out in various apostolic endeavors. Women began to pick up the same trail about three hundred years later, initially with a strong emphasis on social care for the sick and needy, moving gradually to education as a major focus, and later into healthcare in homes and hospitals. This three-pronged approach—social ministry, education, and healthcare—became the major focus of apostolic Religious Life from around 1500 to the present time. Additionally, in the case of priest Religious, the necessary training for parish administration and sacramentally based evangelization were put in place.

As Religious Life enters the twenty-first century, and as we anticipate a new wave of refounding, Religious will need to appropriate a whole new set of ministerial skills, largely unknown in previous epochs. The world and the church of the twenty-first century require a much broader set of abilities and skills if we are to be liminally credible for the globalized context in which we now find ourselves. Moreover, if Religious wish to embrace the justice threshold of the Companionship of Empowerment, and truly prioritize our commitment to the new reign of God (as the gospel requires us to do), then we must equip ourselves to be gospel heralds and ministers in the complex multicultural world of our time.

Among other things, this will require us to transcend our addiction to dualistic splitting, particularly the juxtaposition of the sacred and the secular. We will need to embrace a more integrated spirituality, including the wisdom of inherited religion but significantly transcending it as well.

While our contemporary colleagues in ministry—Religious and lay—tend to be trained for teaching, healthcare, social work, social development, parochial ministry, chaplaincies, counseling, and retreat work, Religious of the future will need new skills to engage the complex, evolving world of the twenty-first century. Even the 1996 church document *Vita Consecrata* envisaged a new departure in how we address the world of our time: "Consecrated persons must therefore keep themselves as intellectually open and adaptable as possible so that the apostolate will be envisaged and carried out according to the needs of their own time, making use of the means provided by cultural progress" (no. 71). Both cultural progress and the gospel imperative for the twenty-first century will require some or all of the following resources:

- *Cosmic consciousness.* With the wisdom of the new cosmology and quantum physics, we understand God's world beyond the mechanistic determinism that has prevailed in recent centuries and that has been adopted by the church in its dualistic stance over against the world. Religious of the future will need to be grounded in a more expansive, evolutionary understanding of God's creation.

- *Contemplation reclaimed.* Long associated with enclosure and monastic withdrawal, contemplation made a significant revival in the latter half of the twentieth century and is very much about a new depth of immersion in the sacredness of God's creation. The witness of Thomas Merton, inspiring models like Taizé, and the new monasticism, along with the emerging horizons of contemporary spirituality (Johnson and Ord 2012), together create a threshold for liminal witness unknown in previous times.

- *Earth literacy.* The exploitation of the earth and its resources throughout the twentieth century created enormous threats, not only for human well-being, but for the viability of the home planet itself. This may well be the primary "urgent need" of the twenty-first century, requiring of liminal people environmental and ecological resourcefulness largely unknown in previous times.

- *Community empowerment.* In the latter half of the twentieth century the power of networking took on new levels of breakthrough and transformation, mobilizing diverse gifts and resources to confront the global crises of our age (Hawken 2007). The art and discernment of networking to empower new possibilities for justice and liberation will require of future Religious skilled training in systems theory, group dynamics, and organizational wisdom in order to engage and challenge the destructive impact of mega-corporations on the modern world.
- *Economics.* Today, value tends to be dictated by capitalistic worth and consumerism, fueling fierce competition with many losers and few winners. Religious cannot hope to confront such large-scale economic injustice without being thoroughly versed in the science of economics and aware of creative alternatives to the pervasive capitalistic system, as proposed by contemporary thinkers such as Charles Eisenstein (2011).
- *Mass media.* The prevailing consumer values are delivered mainly through social networking and public media. Much of our advertising is slick and very aggressive. Again, if Religious are to provide an effective counterculture, we need to be versatile in media skills, and we need to have our members responsibly trained so that they can engage more actively in our information-saturated world.
- *Law.* We live in a climate of aggressive litigation, with millions deprived of any sense of responsible legal representation. To address this dilemma we will need members trained as lawyers or solicitors, people who will be competent and capable of handling the complexities of today's legal world.
- *Political networking.* In its glory days during the 1970s and 1980s, liberation theology seemed to be evolving in the direction of direct political involvement to rectify systemic injustice. Meanwhile, the underlying corruption of most major governments is more widely recognized, suggesting that for liminal people the art of networking probably holds greater potential than direct involvement in mainline politics. However, to wrestle with the challenges of our time, Religious will need training in, and increased awareness of, contemporary political science.
- *Multi-faith facilitation.* Catholic Religious tend to over-identify with Catholic concerns to the exclusion of pressing ecumenical and multi-faith challenges. This is particularly noticeable in the Asian subcontinent and in South America, where there is little

direct involvement in the burgeoning Pentecostal movement. Awareness of diverse religious traditions and facilitating skills to engage the culture of multiple religious belonging (Goosen 2011) will be pastorally and ministerially essential for Religious of the future.

- *Creative theology*. At one time known as the queen of the sciences, with several imperial connotations, theology today is emerging as the perennial catalyst for liberating multidisciplinary truth. This quality of theology is in short supply in seminaries and in most academic institutions. It is a theological consciousness from the ground up, developed by lay rather than priest theologians. Its primary focus is on the new companionship referenced many times in this book, and its strategy is one of orthopraxy rather than orthodoxy. It is the kind of theology liminal people will need for the missionary endeavors of the twenty-first century.

Undoubtedly, teaching, nursing, social work, and pastoral ministry will still be needed, particularly in areas of great social and spiritual need. And Religious working in several two-thirds-world contexts will need the financial and organizational support of the church to undertake and maintain their much-needed services. To that extent the focus will remain church centered. Increasingly, however, that paradigm will not be sustainable. Many church-based services from the past must no longer be reserved to the religious sphere. Humans have a right, in the name of divine justice, to adequate education, healthcare, and the resources to live meaningfully on the earth. Secular governments will need to be challenged and "evangelized" to provide the wherewithal for dignified living, and Religious as prophetic/liminal people will need to become the catalysts for this empowering and liberating breakthrough.

Religious cannot hope to play this prophetic role without the new skills outlined above. And our credibility and potential for transformation will be seriously undermined if we choose to prioritize more traditional ministries while rendering only token acknowledgment to the new skills. Indeed, the majority of our members will need to be versatile in the new approaches, with perhaps a minority serving in more traditional and church-approved ministries. This may well be one of the biggest challenges facing Religious in the refounding of the twenty-first century, an endeavor that will require the vision, audacity, and countercultural determination of the great foundresses.

Closure without Ending

I have concluded each of the first three parts of this book with some notes on its discerning challenges. I conclude this final part with an invitation to a quality of openness characteristic of our postmodern era but informed by the evolutionary wisdom that assures us that the radical wisdom of our age is imbued with a providential sense of direction, itself a phenomenon requiring profound and prolonged discernment.

This is a book without a proper conclusion, since the very purpose in its writing is to create a parable-type narrative defined by open-ended possibilities. It embraces a cyclic approach to the history of Religious Life in which each cycle yields pride of place to a new emergence. Nothing from the past is lost, but it takes a parable-type wisdom to see how the past is retained and fashioned anew in each recurring cycle. Like evolution itself, the unfolding process grows into deeper mystery and more engaging complexity. To one degree or another every religion acknowledges that this is how the creative Spirit works.

As a European, I write the book out of a context of decline, disintegration, and death. All around me I witness a model of Religious Life in terminal decline. I feel saddened by this fact but not frightened. Unlike many of my peers, I know this paschal journey has to happen, and the most authentic thing I or anybody else can do is to accept it and befriend its unfolding process. My faith in history—as I discern its meaning—reassures me that there is a future and that it has hope deeply inscribed in its possibilities.

As a student of the 1960s I recall the slogan "stop the world, I want to get off." A catchy statement but totally unreal. The only world we have is the one in which our co-creative God has placed us, and for weal or for woe, this is where we work out our "salvation." I have never had a desire to escape to another part of the planet where Religious Life fares much better than in the West. The crisis so deeply pronounced in the West that it will have an impact on Religious universally, and I suspect this will be abundantly clear by mid century. The old paradigm, no matter how numerically strong, is unlikely to survive anywhere. All over the planet it must yield pride of place to the creative wind of the Spirit.

And in time—in God's own time—new seedlings will sprout. For me, at least, history leaves us in no doubt about that fact. Sometime in the latter half of the twenty-first century, probably toward its end, we can expect a new breakthrough for the vowed life. We can do nothing to bring it about at an earlier date; it is a divine initiative and not of our making. However, we can anticipate it with eager faith, and by cultivating that discerning predisposition so characteristic of the great foundresses—and of the great founders too—prepare ourselves for the new horizons our God has waiting for us. Central to this discerning anticipation is the wisdom to read the signs of the times and identify urgent needs requiring a radical new gospel response.

In all probability that quality of response will need the new skills identified earlier in this chapter. However, we are unlikely to opt for those new strategies of gospel inculturation without first transcending the dualistic split between sacred and secular that has kept us deluded for too long. As servants to the Companionship of Empowerment (the new reign of God), we are missioned into God's world, earthlings serving the dream of a new heaven and a new earth, befriending all the sentient beings with whom we share the web of life.

We will continue to co-create these empowering horizons of love and justice primarily through communal processes. Consequently, whether the rebirthing of Religious Life happens within or outside the formal church, it will remain fundamentally *ecclesial* but not necessarily *ecclesiastical*. Who then discerns what is of the Spirit and what may be fraudulent? We will need new channels and structures to discern the Spirit's wisdom. Some of these channels are already emerging in the multidisciplinary culture of the twenty-first century, and others remain to be co-created.

As vowed liminars at these new daring and creative horizons we embrace our sisters and brothers in the shared enterprise of co-creating a world focused on liberating and empowering values. As lay colleagues we journey as equals before God, without special rank or exalted ecclesiastical status. We are united in our shared humanity, broken but also redeemed, seeking to reincarnate that fullness of humanity to which all people are called in the name of the gospel we cherish and proclaim.

In historical terms every new cycle casts the net farther out. Perhaps in the present work I have stretched the horizon to a degree that will seem impossible to some and frightening for others. Can our vision ever be big enough for the creative Spirit, who blows where she wills? It is better to err on the side of largess than to run the risk of minimalizing the surprises that await us at every new refounding horizon that the Spirit co-creates.

࿔

Study Guide

1. As you read this chapter, did you recognize dimensions of re-founding that have taken place in contemporary Religious Life? within your own Order/Congregation?

2. How do you relate to the notion of closure without ending?

3. How has this book encouraged and illuminated your experience of Religious Life today?

4. If you read this book with others, how are you ending the experience together? A ritual or ceremony might expand personal experience, if it feels appropriate to the group.

Works Cited

Alcoff, Linda, and Eduardo Mendieta. 2000. *Thinking from the Underside of History*. Lanham, MD: Rowman and Littlefield.

Alexander, Bobby C. 1991. *Victor Turner Revisited: Ritual as Social Change*. Atlanta: Scholars Press.

Arbuckle, Gerald A. 1988. *Out of Chaos: Refounding Religious Congregations*. New York: Paulist Press.

———. 1996. *From Chaos to Mission: Refounding Religious Life Formation*. London: Chapman.

———. 2013. *Catholic Identity or Identities: Refounding Ministries in Chaotic Times*. Collegeville, MN: Liturgical Press.

———. 2015. *The Francis Factor and the People of God*. Maryknoll, NY: Orbis Books.

Azevedo, Marcello. 1995. *The Consecrated Life: Crossroads and Directions*. Maryknoll, NY: Orbis Books.

Balducelli, Roger. 1975. "The Decision for Celibacy." *Theological Studies* 36: 219–42.

Bausch, William J. 1975. *Storytelling: Imagination and Faith*. Mystic, CT: Twenty-Third Publications.

Berger, Pamela. 1985. *The Goddess Obscured: Transformation of the Grain Protectress from Goddess to Saint*. Boston: Beacon Press.

Bianchi, Enzo. 2001. *Si tu Savais le don de Dieu*. Brussels: Lessius.

Boff, Leonardo. 1981. *God's Witnesses at the Heart of the World*. Maryknoll, NY: Orbis Books.

———. 2015. *Come Holy Spirit*. Maryknoll, NY: Orbis Books.

Boulding, Elise. 1976. *The Underside of History: A View of Women through Time*. New York: Halstead.

Brooks Hedstrom, Darlene L. 2013. "Models of Seeing and Reading Monastic Archaeology." *Cistercian Studies Quarterly* 48: 299–315.

Brown, Raymond. 1979. *The Community of the Beloved Disciple*. Mahwah, NJ: Paulist Press.

Brueggemann, Walter. 1978. *The Prophetic Imagination*. Minneapolis: Fortress Press.

———. 1979. "Trajectories in Old Testament Literature and the Sociology of Ancient Israel." *Journal of Biblical Literature* 98: 161–85.

———. 1986. *The Hopeful Imagination*. Minneapolis: Fortress Press.

———. 2014. *Reality, Grief, Hope: Three Urgent Prophetic Tasks.* Grand Rapids, MI: Eerdmans.

Bucko, Adam, and Rory McEntee. 2015. *The New Monasticism: An Interspiritual Manifesto for Contemplative Living.* Maryknoll, NY: Orbis Books.

Burkitt, F.C. 1904. *Early Eastern Christianity.* London: J. Murray.

Cada, Lawrence, Raymond Fitz, Gertrude Foley, and Thomas Giardino. 1979. *Shaping the Coming Age of Religious Life.* New York: Seabury Press.

Cameron, Averil et al. 1993. *Desert Mothers: Women Ascetics in Early Christian Egypt.* New York: Edwin Mellen Press.

Capra, Fritjof, and Pier Luigi Luisi. 2014. *The Systems View of Life.* Cambridge, UK: Cambridge University Press.

Carrette, Jeremy (and Richard King). 2005. *Selling Spirituality.* New York: Routledge.

Casey, Michael. 2005. *Strangers to the City.* Brewster, MA: Paraclete Press.

Castelli, Elizabeth. 1986. "Virginity and Its Meaning for Women's Sexuality in Early Christianity." *Journal of Feminist Studies in Religion* 2: 61–88.

Chittister, Joan. 1995. *The Fire in These Ashes.* Kansas City, MO: Sheed and Ward.

———. 1998. *Heart of Flesh.* Grand Rapids, MI: Eerdmans.

Chitty, Derwas J. 1966. *The Desert a City.* Oxford: Blackwell.

Choat, Malcolm. 2013. "The Epistolary Culture of Monasticism between Literature and Papyri." *Cistercian Studies Quarterly* 48: 227–37.

Christie, Douglas E. 2013. *The Blue Sapphire of the Mind: Notes for a Contemplative Ecology.* New York: Oxford University Press.

Cloke, Gillian. 1995. *This Female Man of God.* New York: Routledge.

Consedine, Sister M. Raphael. 1977. *One Pace Beyond: The Life of Nano Nagle.* Victoria, Australia: Congregation of the Presentation of the Blessed Virgin Mary.

Cozzens, Donald. 2006. *Freeing Celibacy.* Collegeville, MN: Liturgical Press.

———. 2008. *Confronting Power and Sex in the Catholic Church.* Collegeville, MN: Liturgical Press.

Crosby, Michael. 1996. *Celibacy: Means of Control or Mandate of the Heart?* Notre Dame, IN: Ave Maria Press.

———. 2004. *Can Religious Life Be Prophetic?* New York: Crossroad.

Cussianovich, Alejandro. 1979. *Religious Life and the Poor.* Dublin: Gill and Macmillan.

Davies, John D. 1983. *The Faith Abroad.* Oxford, UK: Blackwell.

De Dreuille, Mayeul. 1999. *From East to West: A History of Monasticism.* New York: Crossroad.

De Rossa, Peter. 1989. *Vicars of Christ.* London: Bantam Press.

Delio, Ilia. 2013. *The Unbearable Wholeness of Being.* Maryknoll, NY: Orbis Books.

———. 2014. *From Teilhard to Omega.* Maryknoll, NY: Orbis Books.

Driver, Steven. 2002. *John Cassian and the Reading of Egyptian Monastic Culture*. New York: Routledge.

Dunn, Ted. 2009. "Refounding Religious Life." *Human Development* 30/3: 5–13.

Durkin, Mary-Cabrini. 2005. *Angela Merici's Journey of the Heart*. Boulder, CO: Woven Word Press, 2005.

Earle, Mary C. 2007. *The Desert Mothers: Spiritual Practices from the Women of the Wilderness*. New York: Moorhouse Publishing.

Eigen, Michael. 1991. "Winnicott's Area of Freedom: The Unrecognizable." In *Liminality and Transitional Phenomena*, ed. Nathan Schwartz-Salant and Murray Stein, 67–88. Wilmette, IL: Chiron Publications.

Eisenstein, Charles. 2011. *Sacred Economics: Money, Gift, and Society in the Age of Transition*. Berkeley, CA: Evolver Editions.

Endress, Richard. 1975. "The Monastery as a Liminal Community." *American Benedictine Review* 26: 142–58.

Ezeani, Chinyeaka C. 2011. "Religious Formation and the Integral Psychosexual Development of Candidates." *Review for Religious* 70/3: 255–75.

Falkenham, John Mark. 2013. "Living Celibacy: A Proposed Model for Celibacy Formation Programs." *Human Development* 34/2: 23–29.

Farley, Margaret A. 2015. *Changing the Questions: Explorations in Christian Ethics*. Maryknoll, NY: Orbis Books.

Fedwick, Paul. 1979. *The Church and the Charisma of Leadership in Basil of Caesarea*. Toronto: Pontifical Institute of Mediaeval Studies.

Fiand, Barbara. 1996. *Wrestling with God: Religious Life in Search of Its Soul*. New York: Crossroad. 2001.

———. 2001. *Refocusing the Vision: Religious Life into the Future*. New York: Crossroad.

Fitz, Raymond, and Lawrence Cada. 1975. "The Recovery of Religious Life," *Review for Religious* 34: 690–718.

Flanagan, Bernadette. 2014. *Embracing Solitude: Women and New Monasticism*. Eugene, OR: Cascade Books.

Fox, Patricia. 2001. *God as Communion*. Collegeville, MN: Liturgical Press.

Futrell, John. 1970. *Making an Apostolic Community of Love: The Role of the Superior according to St. Ignatius of Loyola*. St. Louis: The Institute of Jesuit Sources.

Gardiner, Paul. 1993. *Mary McKillop: An Extraordinary Australian*. Melbourne: E. J. Dwyer.

Goehring, James E. 1996. "Withdrawing from the Desert: Pachomius and the Development of Village Monasticism in Upper Egypt." *Harvard Theological Review* 89/3: 267–85.

———. 1999. *Ascetics, Society and the Desert: Studies in Early Egyptian Monasticism*. Harrisburg, PA: Trinity Press International.

Goergen, Donald. 1994. *Letters to My Brothers and Sisters*. Dublin: Dominican Publications.

Goosen, Gideon. 2011. *Hyphenated Christians*. New York: Peter Lang.

Gould, Graham. 1993. *The Desert Fathers in Monastic Community*. Oxford: Clarendon Press.

Gribomont, Jean. 1965. "Le Monachisme un Sein de l'Eglise en Syrie et en Cappodoce." *Studia Monastica* 7: 7–24.

Gutiérrez, Gustavo. 1983. "Theology from the Underside of History." Chapter 7 in *The Power of the Poor in History*, 179–81. London: SCM Press.

Haughey, John C. 2015. *A Biography of the Spirit*. Maryknoll, NY: Orbis Books.

Haught, John F. 2010. *Making Sense of Evolution*. Louisville, KY: Westminster John Knox Press.

———. 2015. *Resting on the Future*. New York: Bloomsbury.

Hawken, Paul. 2007. *Blessed Unrest*. New York: Viking.

Heise, Ursula K. 2008. *Sense of Place, Sense of Planet*. New York: Oxford University Press.

Hereford, Amy. 2013. *Religious Life at the Crossroads*. Maryknoll, NY: Orbis Books.

Heschel, Abraham. 1969. *The Prophets*. New York: Harper and Row.

Horvath, Agnes, Bjorn Thomassen, and Harald Wydra, eds. 2015. *Breaking Boundaries: Varities of Liminality*. New York: Berghahn Books.

Hostie, Raymond. 1972. *Vie et Mort des Ordres Religieux*. Paris: Desclee de Brower.

Hubbard, Barbara Marx. 1998. *Conscious Evolution*. Novata, CA: New World Library.

Janzen, David. 2012. *The Intentional Christian Community Handbook*. Orleans, MA: Paraclete Press.

Joest, Christof. 2010. "Once Again: On the Origin of Christian Monasticism." *The American Benedictine Review* 61: 158–82.

Johnson, Elizabeth. 2007. *Quest for the Living God*. New York: Continuum.

———. 2013. *Ask the Beasts*. New York: Bloomsbury/Continuum.

Johnson, Mary. 2011. *The Unquenchable Thirst: Following Mother Teresa in Search of Love, Service, and Authentic Life*. New York: Spiegel and Grau.

Johnson, Kurt, and David Ord. 2012. *The Coming Inter-Spiritual Age*. Vancouver: Namaste Publishing.

Jordan, Mark. 2000. *The Silence of Sodom: Homosexuality in Modern Catholicism*. Chicago: University of Chicago Press.

Judge, Edwin A. 2020. "The Earliest Use of *Monachos* for 'Monk' and the Origins of Monasticism." In *Jerusalem and Athens: Cultural Transformation in Late Antiquity*, 156–77. Tubingen: Mohr Siebeck.

Keenan, Marie. 2011. *Child Sexual Abuse and the Catholic Church: Gender, Power, and Organizational Structure*. Oxford: Oxford University Press.

Kennedy, Eugene. 2001. *The Unhealed Wound*. New York: St. Martin's Press.

Knitter, Paul. 1985. *No Other Name? A Critical Survey of Christian Attitudes toward the World Religions*. Maryknoll, NY: Orbis Books.

——. 1995. *One Earth, Many Religions: Multifaith Dialogue and Global Responsibility*. Maryknoll, NY: Orbis Books.

Koch, Christof. 2004. *The Quest for Consciousness*. Greenwood Village, CO: Roberts and Co.

Kohn, Livia. 2003. *Monastic Life in Medieval China*. Honolulu: University of Hawaii Press.

Kübler-Ross, Elisabeth. 1969. *On Death and Dying*. New York: Methuen.

Küng, Hans. 1989. *Paradigm Change in Theology*. New York: Crossroad.

La Cugna, Catherine. 1991. *God for Us: The Trinity and Christian Life*. New York: HarperOne.

Langlois, Cyprian. 2002. *An Exploration of Monastic Life as Liminal Cultural Performance*. Master's thesis. Central Missouri State University.

Lanzetta, Beverley. 2005. *Radical Wisdom: A Feminist Mystical Theology*. Minneapolis: Augsburg Fortress Press.

——. 2014. "Contemporary Testimony to Embracing Solitude." In *Embracing Solitude: Women and New Monasticism*, edited by Bernadette Flanagan, 129–38. Eugene, OR: Cascade Books, 2014.

Launderville, Dale. 2010. *Celibacy in the Ancient World*. Collegeville, MN: Liturgical Press.

Leclercq, Jean. 1968. "Monastic Profession and the Sacraments." *Monastic Studies* 5: 59–85.

Lee, Bernard. J. 2008. "The Social Matrix of Religious Obedience." *Review for Religious* 67/3: 290–303.

Malone, Mary T. 2014. *The Elephant in the Church: A Woman's Tract for Our Times*. Dublin: The Columba Press.

Markham, Donna J. 1999. "Leadership for the Common Good. In *Journey in Faith and Fidelity*, ed. Nadine Foley, 156–69. New York: Continuum.

McFarland-Taylor, Sarah. 2009. *Green Sisters: A Spiritual Ecology*. Cambridge, MA: Harvard University Press.

McKenna, Megan. 2010. *This Will Be Remembered of Her: Stories of Women Reshaping the World*. Grand Rapids, MI: Eerdmans.

McNamara, Jo Ann Kay. 1996. *Sisters in Arms: Catholic Nuns through Two Millennia*. Cambridge, MA: Harvard University Press.

Merton, Thomas. 1992. *The Springs of Contemplation*. New York: Farrar Straus Giroux.

Mitchell, Penny Blaker. 2006. *Mother Theodore Guerin—Saint of God: A Woman for All Time*. Sisters of Providence.

Morrow, Diane Batts. 2002. *Persons of Color and Religious at the Same Time: The Oblate Sisters of Providence*. Chapel Hill: University of North Carolina Press.

Moss, Candida. 2013. *The Myth of Persecution*. New York: HarperCollins.

Nedungatt, George. 1973. "The Covenanters of the Early Syriac-Speaking Church." *Orientalia Christiana Periodica* 39 (1973): 191–215; 419–44.

Newman, Barbara. 1995. *From Virile Woman to WomanChrist*. Philadelphia: Pennsylvania University Press.

———. 2011. "A Tale of Two Scandals: Cornelia Connelly as Nouvelle Heloise." *Review for Religious* 70/4: 342–63.

Nussbaum, Martha. 2011. *Creating Capabilities: The Human Development Approach*. Cambridge, MA: Harvard University Press.

Olson, Carl, ed. 2008. *Celibacy and Religious Traditions*. Oxford: Oxford University Press.

O'Murchu, Diarmuid. 1991. *Religious Life: A Prophetic Vision*. Notre Dame, IN: Ave Maria Press.

———. 1999. *Poverty, Celibacy, and Obedience: A Preferential Option for Life*. New York: Crossroad.

———. 2002. *Evolutionary Faith: Rediscovering God in Our Great Story*. Maryknoll, NY: Orbis Books.

———. 2005. *Consecrated Religious Life: The Changing Paradigms*. Maryknoll, NY: Orbis Books.

———. 2007. *The Transformation of Desire*. London: Darton, Longman, and Todd.

———. 2008. *Ancestral Grace*. Maryknoll, NY: Orbis Books.

———. 2010. *Adult Faith*. Maryknoll, NY: Orbis Books.

———. 2011. *Christianity's Dangerous Memory*. New York: Crossroad.

———. 2012. *In the Beginning Was the Spirit*. Maryknoll, NY: Orbis Books.

———. 2014. *On Being a Postcolonial Christian*. North Charleston, SC: CreateSpace.

Panikkar, Raimundo. 1982. *Blessed Simplicity: The Monk as Universal Archetype*. New York: Seabury Press.

Peddigrew, Brenda. 2009. *Original Fire: The Hidden Heart of Religious Women*. North Charleston, SC: CreateSpace.

Peters, Ted. 1993. *God as Trinity*. Louisville, KY: Westminster John Knox Press.

Phipps, Carter. 2012. *Evolutionaries*. New York: Harper.

Piazza, Jo. 2014. *If Nuns Ruled the World: Ten Sisters on a Mission*. New York: Open Road Media.

Plumwood, Val. 2002. *Environmental Culture: The Ecological Crisis of Reason*. New York: Routledge.

Pohl, Christine. 2011. *Living into Community: Cultivating Practices that Sustain*. Grand Rapids, MI: Eerdmans.

Ponzetti, James. 2014. "Renewal in Catholic Community Life and the New Monasticism." *Journal for the Sociological Integration of Religion and Society* 4/2: 35–49.

Rapley, Elizabeth. 2011. *The Lord as Their Portion*. Grand Rapids, MI: Eerdmans.

Rousseau, P. 1985. *Pachomius: The Making of a Community in Fourth Century Egypt.* Berkeley and Los Angeles: University of California Press.

Rowson, Jonathan. 2014. *Spiritualize: Revitalizing Spirituality to Address Twenty-First Century Challenges.* London: RSA Publications.

Rubenson, Samuel. 1998. *Letters of St. Antony.* Harrisburg, PA: Trinity Press International.

Saffioti, Luisa. 2011. "Sexual Abuse and Systemic Dynamics in the Church." *Human Development* 32/1: 17–23.

Savary. Louis M. 2012. *New Spiritual Exercises, In the Spirit of Pierre Teilhard de Chardin.* Mahwah, NJ: Paulist Press.

Schneiders, Sandra. 1986. *New Wineskins: Re-imaging Religious Life Today.* Mahwah, NJ: Paulist Press.

———. 2000. *Finding the Treasure.* Mahwah, NJ: Paulist Press.

———. 2001. *Selling All.* Mahwah, NJ: Paulist Press.

———. 2013. *Buying the Field.* Mahwah, NJ: Paulist Press.

Schwartz-Salant, Nathan, and Murray Stein, eds. 1991. *Liminality and Transitional Phenomena.* Wilmette, IL: Chiron Publications.

Seasoltz, R. Kevin. 1997. "A Western Monastic Perspective on Ordained Ministry." In *A Concert of Charisms: Ordained Ministry in Religious Life,* ed. Paul K. Hennessy, 25–60. Mahwah, NJ: Paulist Press.

Sipe, A. W. Richard. 1995. *Sex, Priests and Power.* New York: Routledge.

Smith, Cyprian. 2004. *The Way of Paradox.* London: Darton, Longman, and Todd.

Spadaro, Antonio, SJ. 2014. "Wake Up the World! Conversation with Pope Francis about the Religious Life," trans. Donald Maldari, SJ. *La Civiltà Cattolica*: 3–17.

Stewart, Columba. 2015. "Another Cassian?" *Journal of Ecclesiastical History* 66: 372–76.

Stipl, Zdenek. 2013. "Christian Ashrams in India." Available online.

Szakolczai, Arpad. 2009. "Liminality and Experience: Structuring Transitory Situations and Transformative Events." *International Political Anthropology* 2/1: 141–72.

———. 2016. *Modern Permanent Liminality.* Farnham, Surrey, UK: Ashgate.

Turchin, Peter. 2003. *Historical Dynamics: Why States Rise and Fall.* Princeton, NJ: Princeton University Press.

Turner, Victor. 1969. *The Ritual Process: Structures and Anti-Structure.* Chicago: Aldine Publishing.

———. 1974. *Drama, Fields, and Metaphors: Symbolic Action in Human Society.* Ithaca, NY: Cornell University Press.

———, and Edith L. B. Turner. 1978. *Image and Pilgrimage in Christian Culture.* Oxford: Blackwell.

Vanier, Jean. 1989. *Community and Growth.* Mahwah, NJ: Paulist Press.

Van Kaam, Adrian. 1968. *The Vowed Life.* New York: Dimension Books.

Van Lommel, Pim. 2010. *Consciousness beyond Life.* New York: HarperOne.

Veilleux, Armand. 1971. "The Evolution of the Religious Life in Its Historical and Spiritual Context." *Cistercian Studies* 6: 8–34.

Voobus, Arthur. 1958. *History of Asceticism in the Syrian Orient.* 2 vols. Louvain (Belgium): Secrétariat du CorpuSCO.

———. 1961. "The Institution of the Benai Qeiama and Benat Qeiama in the Ancient Syrian Church." *Church History* 30 (1961): 19–27.

Walzer, Michael. 2012. *In God's Shadow: The Politics of the Hebrew Bible.* New Haven, CT: Yale University Press.

Wheatley, Margaret J. 1992. *Leadership and the New Science.* San Francisco: Berrett-Koehler.

Whitrow, G. J. 2004. *Time in History: Views of Time from Prehistory to the Present Day.* New York: Barnes and Noble Publishing.

Wilson, Jonathan. 1998. *Living Faithfully in a Fragmented World: Lessons for the Church from MacIntyre's* After Virtue. Harrisburg, PA: Trinity Press International.

Winter, Miriam Therese. 2009. *Paradoxology: Spirituality in a Quantum Universe.* Maryknoll, NY: Orbis Books.

Wittberg, Patricia. 1994. *The Rise and Fall of Catholic Religious Orders.* Albany: State University of New York Press.

———. 1996. *Pathways to Recreating Religious Communities.* Mahwah: Paulist Press.

———. 2006. *From Piety to Professionalism and Back? Transformations of Organized Religious Virtuosity.* Lanham, MD: Rowman and Littlefield.

Zizioulas, John. 2004. *Being as Communion.* London: Darton, Longman, and Todd.

Index

56
18
²16
94